Portraits of the Japanese Workplace

Social Change in Global Perspective
Mark Selden, Series Editor

Exploring the relationship between social change and social structures, this series considers the theory, praxis, promise, and pitfalls of movements in global and comparative perspective. The historical and contemporary social movements considered here challenge patterns of hierarchy and inequality of race, gender, nationality, ethnicity, class, and culture. The series will emphasize textbooks and broadly interpretive synthetic works.

Portraits of the Japanese Workplace
Kumazawa Makoto

Power Restructuring in China and Russia
Mark Lupher

The Transformation of Communist Systems: Economic Reform Since the 1950s
Bernard Chavance

The Challenge of Local Feminisms: Women's Movements in Global Perspective
edited by Amrita Basu, with the assistance of C. Elizabeth McGrory

Forthcoming

African Women: A Modern History
Catherine Coquery-Vidrovitch

Portraits of the Japanese Workplace

Labor Movements, Workers, and Managers

Kumazawa Makoto

Translated by Andrew Gordon and Mikiso Hane

WestviewPress

A Division of HarperCollinsPublishers

Social Change in Global Perspective

Copyright © 1996 by Westview Press, A Division of HarperCollins Publishers, Inc.

Published in 1996 in the United States of America by Westview Press, 5500 Central Avenue, Boulder, Colorado 80301-2877, and in the United Kingdom by Westview Press, 12 Hid's Copse Road, Cumnor Hill, Oxford OX2 9JJ

Library of Congress Cataloging-in-Publication Data
Kumazawa, Makoto, 1938–
   Portraits of the Japanese workplace : labor movements, workers,
and managers / by Kumazawa Makoto.
      p.   cm. — (Social change in global perspective)
   Translated from Japanese.
   Includes bibliographical references and index.
   ISBN 0-8133-1709-6 (hc). — ISBN 0-8133-1708-8 (pb)
      1. Industrial relations—Japan.   2. Industrial management—Japan.
3. Labor movement—Japan.   4. Trade-unions—Japan.   5. Women-
Employment—Japan.   6. Work environment—Japan.   I. Title.
II. Series: Social change in global perspective (Boulder, Colo.)
HD8726.5.K772   1996
331´.0952—dc20   96-15010
                                                                                CIP

The paper used in this publication meets the requirements of the American National Standard for Permanence of Paper for Printed Library Materials Z39.48-1984.

10   9   8   7   6   5   4   3   2   1

Contents

Tables and Figures

Tables

Figures

Translator's Foreword

"Feudal," "backward," "distorted." Readers aware of the recent worldwide enthusiasm to learn the secrets of labor and production management from Japan may find this surprising, but for much of the postwar era, Japanese economists, sociologists, journalists, and activists used these terms to describe wage laborers and labor-management relations in their country. And if Japan was backward, these critics argued, workers as well as managers in the West offered models to which Japanese people should aspire. When speaking of organized labor in particular, they posed British unionism and European social democracy as models of thought and behavior against which workers in Japan were measured and found wanting, and which they were exhorted to emulate.[1]

But beginning in the 1970s, a new body of writing emerged in Japan. It rejected the Eurocentric worship of Western models that had marked much of this earlier discussion of labor. This was largely the work of a younger generation impressed by the appearance of Japanese economic dynamism and Euro-American stagnation, although some scholars of the old school changed to this new tune as well.[2] Often enough, these advocates of Japanese-style management sang simple hymns of praise to the positive, advanced features of laboring practice in Japan, and some writings by such scholars are available in English.[3]

The importance of translating this work must first be understood in this context. Kumazawa Makoto* is a distinguished scholar whose intellectual roots are clearly in the critical tradition of commentary on Japanese labor, but he nonetheless takes account of the upbeat revisionism of the latter group. At the outset (see the first pages of Chapter 2), Kumazawa presents the British working class as an attractive alternative to prevailing practices in Japan. He sees in Britain a model in which coworkers maintain egalitarian relationships and restrain competition among themselves. To this extent, his work falls into what we might call the "British-model school" of labor studies, which judges Japanese labor as deficient in comparison to that of Britain and, more generally, the West. Yet his frequent use of images of "light and shadow" to describe Japanese practices reflects a considered

---

*All Japanese names are presented in the Japanese style, with the family name first, and given name second.

response to, and partial agreement with, the conclusions of the newer "Japanese-model" school as well.

Though a critical tone certainly dominates his analysis, the social landscape that he describes is not uniformly bleak. Kumazawa recognizes that the dynamism of the Japanese system of labor-management relations helped make possible the extraordinary performance of Japanese industry and economy from the 1950s through the 1980s. He describes the very important gains made by some workers as they participated in this system. But he ultimately returns to a belief that the social costs paid by Japanese working people over the past fifty years have been much too high. As the prolonged recession of the Japanese economy in the early 1990s has led many both in Japan and around the world to question celebratory renditions of the Japanese model (if for reasons of "economic performance" rather than human cost), Kumazawa's thoughtful skepticism makes a renewed claim on our attention.

Kumazawa's work demands attention for another related reason. He is a sociologist writing in a humanistic rather than a scientific tradition. That is, rather than constructing so-called testable hypotheses and seeking to tease out independent and dependent variables to explain "outcomes," he asks what meaning the experience of work held, or holds, for people in Japanese society. He begins the book with a relatively abstract theory of "worker society," but he sets himself apart from many labor scholars in Japan by moving quickly to join theory to the specifically rendered experience of particular individuals and groups of workers. What social values did people seek to realize at the workplace? What were the central features of their past experiences at work, and how, if at all, have these changed more recently? How does workplace experience relate to social life outside the company, to family and community life, to politics and public policy?

As Kumazawa responds to such questions he is always looking for a strategy by which workers themselves might act to improve their conditions or achieve greater control over their lives on the job. This sets him apart from the majority of commentators on the Japanese economy and management who are writing in English, who almost always adopt the perspective of management or the state; they assume that efficiency, productivity, and profit are sacred values and ends in themselves. Kumazawa's perspective is obviously different. He challenges the sacred values of the corporate society, and he asks how working women and men might change workplace society. The result of his critical appraisal is a compelling portrait of working life in contemporary Japan, comparative in perspective and firmly grounded both in an interpretation of the prewar and postwar history of twentieth-century Japan and in a close reading of experience in particular work sites.

Kumazawa's work holds particular importance for readers in the English-speaking world for two further reasons. It challenges the widespread stereotypes that hold that the cultural essence of the Japanese is an inherent docility and a deeply ingrained tendency to put group harmony and the interests of the collectivity ahead of individualistic strivings. Kumazawa neatly stands these images on their heads when he contrasts the fierce man-to-man competition of Japan's worker society (I use the male reference advisedly) with British or American worker cultures in which the interests of the group predominate and in which individuals are socialized to restrict competition for the collective good. The Japanese workers introduced in these pages are, if anything, individualistic to a fault, as they struggle to maintain secure livelihoods and a sense of personal dignity in a competitive workplace environment.

The value of making this critical yet sympathetic portrait available in English translation at the present moment can be cast in another light as well. In the 1990s, criticism of Japan is often dismissed, by so-called Japan-apologists, as the work of malevolent or ignorant outsiders. For roughly ten years now, a number of American and European scholars, journalists, and policymakers, dubbed revisionists by their critics, have been articulating a critical view of the Japanese political and social system with vigor and an angry edge in their voices.[4] They are by no means the only non-Japanese writing critically on contemporary Japanese society,[5] but they have commanded the widest audience. Politically minded defenders of the status quo in Japan have dismissed these critics as prejudiced Westerners, pinning the label "Japan-basher" on them to great effect. To be sure, the righteous ethnocentrism of the "revisionists" can be grating; the holier-than-thou stance of the messenger makes the message easy to ignore.

Against this background, a voice such as that of Kumazawa is important. It shows the English-speaking world that critical perspectives on Japanese labor and other issues are not solely or even mainly produced by cranky foreigners. Instead, distinguished Japanese people, beginning early in the postwar era with the intellectual historian Maruyama Masao and numerous others, have made many of the same points as the revisionists, and they have commanded wide audiences. These critics have included scholars working in the Marxist tradition, and others—such as Maruyama—whom we might call liberal modernists. They also include incisive feminist analysts, and the advocates of what in Japan is called "people's history" (*minshūshi*).[6] Over the past twenty years, Kumazawa Makoto has been the author of the most widely read books on organized labor and workplace life in contemporary Japan, and he is but one important cosmopolitan voice presenting a critique of the present state of affairs in Japan and an alternative vision of the desirable workplace and social order.

The notion of a cosmopolitan critique is worth dwelling on briefly. Some might, and some indeed do, dismiss the Kumazawas and Maruyamas of the Japanese intellectual world as self-hating Europhiles tainted by their study of foreign models. Under the sway of European intellectual traditions, as this argument sometimes goes, these people are hardly "authentic" Japanese voices. However persuasive this criticism might first appear, it cannot bear scrutiny. Since at least the mid-nineteenth century, to posit the existence of some authentic Japanese voice uncontaminated by Western ideas has been a gesture of a romantic Japanese nationalism that itself was inspired in part by Western thought. The work of scholars such as Kumazawa has been deeply embedded in a transnational flow of ideas between Japan and the West for 150 years, and before that, a trans-Asian flow.

Although it would be foolish to question the "authenticity" of a Western-oriented Japanese intellectual, readers familiar with recent trends in labor history in Europe and the United States may nonetheless question aspects of Kumazawa's rendition of British and American experience. In particular, he presents what we might call a pre-Thompsonian appreciation of the making of the British (and other) working classes. That is, Kumazawa sees industrial capitalism as an extraordinary force that "atomized" preindustrial societies to such an extent that older forms of community became largely irrelevant.

Beginning with the work of E. P. Thompson for Britain and Herbert Gutman for the United States, this view has been called into serious question. Numerous scholars have studied ways in which preindustrial habits of mind and behavior informed the responses of working people in the industrial age, and they no longer characterize worker communities of the early industrial (or any other) era as "atomized." Few parallel endeavors to question the "atomized worker" paradigm can be found in Japanese scholarship.[7] To understand why would require an extended inquiry into the history of the social sciences in twentieth-century Japan. Without presenting such a discussion here, I would simply note that Japanese social scientists have been powerfully committed to a structural analysis, derived mainly but not solely from Marxism, in which the revolutionary impact of capitalism dissolved past institutions and communities. Kumazawa's understanding of early industrial society reflects this intellectual context.

But to put it bluntly, I do not think this matters very much. Kumazawa's basic thesis is not affected by the fact that his historical perspective on the early days of the industrial era has been challenged by recent Euro-American analyses. What does matter is that his comparison of subsequent British, American, and Japanese labor history usefully directs our attention to important features of the Japanese experience.

The comparative claim at the heart of Kumazawa's analysis concerns the present and the more recent past, and it remains compelling. He argues that in the workplace cultures of Britain and North America a concern with the invidious impact of competition among coworkers, seen for example in the pejorative connotation of the term "rate-buster," is deeply rooted, although such concerns are weak in Japan. Thus, one finds no colloquial

Japanese expression comparable in meaning and nuance to rate-buster, despite the widespread use of various systems of payment-by-result in Japan's past.[8] This comparison leads Kumazawa to insist that working men and women ought to seek a greater voice in workplace affairs to restrict zero-sum competition, thus enhancing security in the workplace and the quality of coworker relations.

By way of introduction to some of the specific individuals or groups of workers described in this book, two final observations are in order. First, Kumazawa goes beyond many leading Japanese scholars of labor-management relations in ranging broadly across society. He studies the experiences of women workers as well as men, of white-collar office workers as well as blue-collar manufacturing operatives. Of great interest, Kumazawa's attention to working women is not limited to a separate chapter on the subject, although one is included. In several other chapters as well, he draws out contrasts and similarities in the situations of male and female workers when he looks at prewar mines and factories, at the experiences of men and women in Quality Control circles, and at the fate of union activism among young women and men in a bank office.

Second, of the several individuals introduced in the book, I expect readers will find the subject of the penultimate chapter, Kawabe Tomomi, to be the most fascinating and puzzling. Indeed, one way to approach this book is to read the Kawabe chapter first and then turn to the first few chapters for Kumazawa's analysis of the historical and social context for this banker's story.

Kawabe was a living oxymoron: a Marxist banker and a loan officer in one of the nation's largest financial institutions, who sought the revolutionary transformation of consciousness and society. Even though Japanese readers of Kumazawa's original (Japanese) version of this work who were adults in the 1950s and 1960s can easily recognize this as an authentic tale, younger Japanese readers may find Kawabe an improbable man. Readers of this translation may also see Kawabe as an impossible, even unimaginable, figure and are likely to ask: Given his beliefs, why didn't he quit? Why didn't the bank fire him? True, managers penalized him with low pay raises and delayed his promotions, but why did they ever promote him at all? Kawabe's case is fascinating precisely because it raises these questions and thus tells us something important about the distinctive features of Japanese society of Kawabe's time, the high-growth era of the 1950s through the mid-1970s. Kawabe's life story not only relates how powerful the hold of Marxism and New Left ideas was on university students and graduates of the 1950s and 1960s but also reveals that men like Kawabe nonetheless felt a responsibility to marry, raise families, and earn livings, even as they sustained their political commitments through many years in mainstream careers.

His story further shows us that even before the second wave of Western-inspired feminism hit Japan in the 1960s, and decades before debate and passage of the Equal Employment Opportunity Law (EEOL) in 1986, a significant minority of office women were vigorously committed to union activism. In addition to such subjective insights, readers learn an important structural lesson: The occupation legal reforms and the early postwar labor offensive had created a relatively safe space for such people. Kawabe's bank did not fire him because its managers felt they could not do so without stirring up more trouble than it was worth. As a result, white-collar workplaces, such as the Fuji Bank in the 1950s and 1960s, remained sites of diverse but ultimately well-contained challenge to managerial and union authority. Kumazawa offers us an intimate, painful glimpse of the torment suffered by one particular challenger.

This translation began with a simple question from my colleague Mark Selden: "If you could have one book on labor in Japan translated, what would it be?" As the passive-causitive of this question turned to an active role for me in translating the book, Mark has been an encouraging editor and persistently constructive critic throughout an unexpectedly long process. His sharp queries have greatly improved the translation. Mikiso Hane completed the first draft of the translation in record time, and I have dawdled considerably in revising it subsequently. Jeff Bayliss translated drafts of Kumazawa's emendations, and Margot Chamberlain offered able assistance in working these into the text.

Kumazawa Makoto went over both the first draft and the revised version of the translation with great care, saving readers from numerous errors of interpretation. He also responded to my queries by adding material in dozens of places to help make the analysis familiar or at least accessible to non-Japanese or nonexpert readers. He has added to several of the chapters substantial discussion of the decade since he wrote the Japanese version. I have also added a number of notes pointing readers to English-language sources that will allow them to find out about particular issues in more detail. In these ways, this translation differs from the original Japanese version. We have generally not distinguished my additions from emendations or additions inserted by the author, but in all cases Kumazawa has agreed to the changes. As editor and cotranslator, however, I remain responsible for any mistranslations or misinterpretations.

Andrew Gordon

Notes

1. For a representative and influential set of examples, consult the work of Ōkōchi Kazuo from the 1940s and 1950s concerning peculiarly "Japanese" and so-called feudal aspects of wage structures, unions, and labor-management relations. These are collected in *Ōkōchi Kazuo zenshū* [Collected works of Ōkōchi Kazuo], especially vols. 3, 4, and 5. For an early critique of such studies, see Totsuka Hideo,

"Chinrō dō ni okeru 'hokensei' ron" [The "feudal" paradigm of wage labor], in *Keizai seminaa* (May 1960).

2. For work of a prominent convert, see the theory of Japanese-style management advanced since the 1970s by Tsuda Masumi, especially *Nihon-teki keiei no yōgo* [A defense of Japanese-style management] (Tokyo: Tōyō Keizai Shinpōsha, 1976).

3. Among the many works that offer a positive view of Japanese labor-management relations, the most insightful scholarly studies include Koike Kazuo, *Shokuba no rōdō kumiai to sanka* [Unions and participation in the workplace] (Tokyo: Tōyō Keizai Shinpōsha, 1977) and *Shigoto no keizai gaku* [The economics of work] (Tokyo: Tōyō Keizai Shinpō sha, 1991); Nitta Michio, *Nihon no rōdōsha sanka* [Participation of Japanese workers] (Tokyo: Tokyo University Press, 1988); and Ishida Mitsuo, *Chingin no shakai gaku* [The sociology of wages] (Tokyo: Chūō Keizaisha, 1990). In English, see Koike Kazuo, *"The Economics of Work in Japan"* (Tokyo: LTCB Library Foundation, 1995).

4. For example, Karel van Wolferen, *The Enigma of Japanese Power* (New York: Random House, Vintage, 1990); James Fallows, "Containing Japan," *Atlantic Monthly* (May 1989); Chalmers Johnson, *Japan: Who Governs?* (New York: W. W. Norton, 1995).

5. A number of the essays in Andrew Gordon, ed., *Postwar Japan as History* (Berkeley: University of California Press, 1993) might fall into this category, as would the work of Gavan McCormick and Yoshio Sugimoto, *Democracy in Contemporary Japan* (Armonk, N.Y.: M. E. Sharpe, 1986) and Tessa Morris-Suzuki, *Beyond Computopia: Information, Automation, and Democracy in Japan* (London and New York: Kegan Paul International, 1988).

6. The classic interpretations of Maruyama Masao are available in English, in *Thought and Behavior in Japanese Politics* (London: Oxford University Press, 1963). Several Marxist perspectives are available in English, in T. Morris-Suzuki and T. Seiyama, eds., *Japanese Capitalism Since 1945: Critical Perspectives* (Armonk, N.Y.: M. E. Sharpe, 1989). The work of Japanese feminists can be found in translation in the English Supplement to the *U.S.-Japan Women's Journal*, published since 1991. One leading "people's historian" is Irokawa Daikichi, whose work is available in English as *The Culture of the Meiji Period* (Princeton: Princeton University Press, 1985).

7. One exceptional work that presents a sharp critique of the "atomized worker" theory is Nimura Kazuo, *Ashio bōdō no shiteki kenkyū: Kōzan rōdōsha no shakai shi* [A historical analysis of the Ashio mine riot: a social history of mine workers] (Tokyo: Tokyo University Press, 1988). Translation forthcoming from Duke University Press.

8. Kumazawa's comparative assessment is reinforced by works such as Ronald Dore's study, *British Factory–Japanese Factory* (Berkeley: University of California Press, 1973). In particular, see pp. 93–94.

1

Introduction

The Spread of Japanese-Style Management

Japanese-style management has been a topic of intense interest throughout the world for some time. In the 1980s in particular, business managers seeking to revitalize market economies—whether from the Western European welfare states, Asia's newly industrializing economies, or former socialist states—decided Japanese industry possessed unusual competitive strengths in cost and in quality control. They concluded that these strengths were not simply the result of technological advances, but were based on underlying features of Japanese enterprises: systems of production management and personnel management, and strategies of industrial relations. As a result, they began attempting to introduce these practices in their own countries.

The United States has been no exception. In this era of chronic trade friction, the American political and business communities criticize the closed Japanese market, but economic specialists are in fact concerned that American business in general has fallen behind Japanese business in producing superior products cheaply. Consequently, progressive American business leaders are endeavoring to learn management theory from their formerly "backward" students, studying, for example, the practices of Japanese corporations located in America.

Managers worldwide have sought to emulate a number of internal features seen to account for the vigor of Japanese corporations. Even if one confines oneself to the realms of production, personnel management, and industrial relations, one can easily compile a long list of Japanese management practices being studied or adopted in other nations.

A minimal list of the practices that workers in Japanese companies in America are coming to experience includes the following: First, in employment policy, Japanese-style management does not set out to "buy" workers with specific skills to perform specific tasks. Generally speaking, a company designs a complex selection process to carefully select long-term "team members" who are versatile and adaptable. The employees thus chosen are required to work in flexible fashion when it comes to job definition, job assignments, production norms, and working hours, including

1

overtime. The rule of such a workplace is "no demarcation" of job boundaries. Moreover, the workers are constantly pushed to strive on their own initiative to improve the general performance of the workplace by eliminating waste and excess in personnel, in working hours, in use of space, and more. Further, the pay system under Japanese-style management reflects the strict demand for such a posture at work. That is, the wages of workers assigned to the same jobs are not necessarily the same, for an individual's pay, and rate of pay increase, depends heavily on merit ratings that assess a worker's efforts to develop his or her work skills and exhibit appropriate behavior.[1]

In the realm of production management, narrowly defined, Japanese business made several rational innovations that were dubbed "just-in-time" management. One is a U-shaped production line in which a small number of workers can operate a large number of machines efficiently. Another closely related innovation is the training of multifunction workers, whose presence allows streamlined staffing. Further innovations include the automation of machines equipped with foolproof devices to prevent absentminded behavior by human operators and the implementation of alarm-light systems to make certain that the workers concentrate on constantly operating the facilities correctly.[2]

In addition, an essential strategy of Japanese-style management is to restrict union functions to make sure the union will not constrain these techniques of production and personnel management. Needless to say, labor unions are expected to keep wage demands below the productivity gains of the firm, but in addition they are not allowed to restrain the managerial free hand to make the most flexible use of its production facilities and manpower. To this end, a nonunion workplace is ideal, especially in a foreign country whose unionism is unfamiliar to Japanese managers. However, if recognizing unions is unavoidable, those who use Japanese-style management seek to induce horizontal industrial unions to abandon or ease traditional work rules (for example, restrictions on the range of work assignments or on strict seniority systems). They also communicate intensively with the workers in the firm without the interference of their unions. Japanese-style managers seek to convince them of the advantages of dedicating themselves to a competition among workers, which is inevitably stimulated by systems of flexibility in the workplace and individually based pay.

When such aspects of Japanese-style management are introduced in America, workers not surprisingly resist by drawing on the logic and behavior of traditional labor unionism. The strength of such grassroots labor movement resistance could potentially force Japanese managers to *adapt* to local worker practice rather than *adopt* Japanese-style management practices. For example, blue-collar wage scales incorporating performance evaluations, an essential element in Japanese-style management in Japan, have not yet been adopted in Japanese companies located in the United States. It appears, however, that America's national industrial unions have generally accepted the "Japanization" of the workplace. One example is the general shift in contracts concluded since 1982 by the United Automobile Workers (UAW). In negotiating with General Motors (GM) and Ford, the UAW has come to accept the practice of linking wages to the company's productivity rather than to macroeconomic indicators, in return for the agreement not to lay off workers in specified categories. Also, as part of a policy of cooperating with automakers' rationalization measures, the UAW has begun to cede to local unions the authority to recognize work rule changes that consolidate jobs, transfer workers, reallocate overtime, or revise standard workload or work-cycle times.[3]

Such shifts in American industrial relations have been subject to at least two interpretations. Some see these concessions as only temporary strategic moves by an organized labor movement that endured a "wintery season" of frequent bankruptcies, unemployment, and the Republican party's antiunion policies of the 1980s. This school of thought holds that industrial relations will soon return to their traditional "confrontational style." But from another perspective, the Japanese style of production and labor-management relations is supremely suited to the flexible specialization and flexible manufacturing of the "post-Fordist" era. Adherents of this view argue that the work rules of traditional American labor unions are behind the times and that changes in industrial relations are inevitable.[4]

I suspect the latter is a more accurate prediction of future changes. But this does not by any means imply that working people should applaud the Japanization of production and personnel management practices and industrial relations. Recently, many Japanese scholars have not only expounded on the rationality of Japanese-style management in product quality and productivity; they have also begun to praise the logic of Japanese management for an inherent quality of "human respect."[5] To be sure, in outward form Japanese-style management is certainly not an authoritarian system. It promises much to the workers, not only job security but also a "single-status" egalitarianism among different levels of workers, employee participation in decisionmaking at the workplace, and wider opportunities for individuals to develop their ability in numerous ways. But how faithfully are these promises kept? There are grounds for real skepticism.

For example, two studies based on interviews with employees and research on them at Japanese automobile factories in America describe in vivid detail the daily stress and frustration experienced by workers under Japanese-style management.[6] In these plants, flexibility apparently means that the supervisor has a free hand, unconstrained by the union, to decide on the assignments of individual workers and to order them at any time to put in whatever overtime is necessary. The content and procedures of the assigned work are fixed much more rigidly than in Big Three auto plants.

Moreover, the pace of work is intense, as all "wasted time and motion" is eliminated, with no consideration for that essential margin of rest that allows workers to survive at their jobs. The much vaunted "multiskilled worker" in such a system in fact stands at the opposite pole to the artisan who engages in varied work using his or her own ideas and judgment. To say that the multiskilled worker can think independently usually means that he or she is expected to figure out how to eliminate waste. In addition, employees are subject to the direct or indirect control of the workplace supervisor concerning attendance, time-recording, attire, and even activities outside working hours. In other words, to borrow Mike Parker and Jane Slaughter's apt expression, Japanese-style management is "management by stress." Its underlying principles are Taylorism plus nonunionism (or the maximum prerogative of management).

One must not dismiss such a perspective as the biased view of a minority of nonconformist workers. These criticisms of Japanese-style management reflect the situation at the workplace more accurately and concretely than accounts provided by management publicists. In particular, the study by Joseph and Suzy Fucini is extremely persuasive. They tell of the actual workplace experiences of men and women who initially placed high hopes in the promises of Japanese-style management, and they reveal the process whereby these promises were betrayed. The authors report that the company does not usually coerce workers with formal institutions or outright commands. It practices a more subtle, de facto coercion by convincing workers that they have no choice but to comply voluntarily. The Fucinis argue that such "mandatorily voluntary" behavior is a distinctive characteristic of Japanese management.[7] Their understanding is at one with my own. In Japan's company society the concept of mandatorily voluntary conduct is central to any apprehension of the behavior of workers.

Those who support the Japanization of the workplace might reply: We should discount these negative views; they simply reflect the imperfections of a transitional stage in which Japanese management strategy in America is not fully implemented. The strongest evidence in their favor is that workers in the homeland of Japanese-style management have accepted it peacefully for approximately thirty years. Indeed, this evidence bears close examination. Americans have good reason to ask both supporters and critics of Japanization a deceptively simple question: Why are contemporary Japanese industrial relations so apparently harmonious? At international symposia in Japan, even after the foreign guests have been provided various explanations of the "success" of Japanese industrial relations, this question is rarely answered fully.

My goal is to answer this question by exploring in depth the state of being and consciousness of Japanese workers, especially organized workers. I seek to clarify an image of the people who sustain the Japanese mode of management. In the following chapters I shall retrace the history of Japanese workers in the twentieth century, in recent decades in particular. I will attempt to apprehend the human image of Japan's organized workers by examining postwar workplace history and the current state of quality control circle activities, perhaps the most "typically Japanese" workplace activity.

In Search of Images of Japanese Workers

First, let me present one interpretation of international labor statistics as a device to apprehend the particular features of the thought and behavior of organized workers in Japan. Table 1.1 compares the number of workdays lost to labor disputes in the major industrial nations during three periods, the years 1967–1976, 1978–1987 and 1988–1991. The definitions of "labor dispute" that were used to compile these statistics differed from nation to nation,[8] but the figures do indicate national differences in the degree to which labor unions relied on that most traditional of means to defend their livelihood, the strike.

I have not analyzed rigorously the extent to which labor unions in each nation took government policies into account when they decided to strike, but I can say unions in seven of the ten nations exhibited a sort of commonsense behavior, in relation to the politics of their particular nation. Those under conservative governments rather frequently engaged in strikes, and those under progressive governments went on strike less often.

TABLE 1.1

Working Days Lost Per Worker Due to Labor Disputes in Each Nation

1967–1976		1978–1987		1988–1991	
Italy	14.5	Italy	21.87	Italy	–
Canada	7.4	Canada	5.21	Canada	1.31
Australia	5.7	Great Britain	4.73	Australia	0.89
United States	4.8	Australia	3.92	Sweden	0.50
Great Britain	4.3	Sweden	1.53	Great Britain	0.45
France	2.1	United States	1.27	France	0.15
Japan	1.3	France	0.83	United States	0.14
Sweden	0.4	West Germany	0.46	Holland	0.07
W. Germany	0.3	Holland	0.18	Germany	0.02
Holland	0.3	Japan	0.14	Japan	0.01

Note: The figures above were arrived at by taking the total number of working days lost to labor disputes in each of the periods concerned and dividing each of these totals by the total number of laborers employed in the final year of that period.

Source: International Labor Organization, *ILO Yearbook of Labor Statistics* (Geneva: ILO, 1977, 1988, and 1992 editions).

But three of the ten defy this expectation. Over the first ten-year period, labor parties held sole power in Great Britain and Australia for six and three years, respectively, yet strikes were rather frequent. And at the other extreme is Japan, where few strikes took place in the first period, and even fewer in the second and third, despite the fact that the Liberal Democratic party was in power throughout.

How can one explain Japan's unique pattern? Perhaps the extraordinary economic growth of the first period, and the relatively steady growth of the second period compared to other nations, allowed wage increases without labor disputes and led unions to conclude that strikes were not necessary. But I do not believe this is a sufficient explanation. Starting with the premise that the value systems of capital and labor are in conflict, the general proposition that labor disputes will decline in times of economic growth and prosperity does not follow. Looking beyond the impact of wages upon disputes to consider how rationalization affects the worker's immediate job, economic growth as an explanation for fewer strikes becomes even less plausible. In addition, in the period after 1975, Japan's economic growth rate fell sharply; if expansion reduces cause for conflict, the workers' need to engage in strikes should have increased in these years. Instead, the number of strikes dropped decisively.

Perhaps, then, Japan's legal system restricts industrial actions? To be sure, Japan's prohibition on strikes by government workers and employees in public corporations is unique among the advanced industrial nations (except for the United States). But this restriction does not amount to a persuasive explanation, for unions in the private sector, legally free to strike as they pleased, took the lead in abandoning the strike as a weapon.

Can one then attribute infrequent strikes to the predominance of "enterprise-based" union organizations? Given this mode of organization, workers are likely to conclude that if they engage in strikes, their company will fall behind in interfirm competition, and they will ultimately cut their own throats. This institutional explanation has much to recommend it. Unions in Japan are definitely enterprise-based. Japan's organized workers are predominantly the regular employees of large corporations, and the value systems of management and union are extremely similar. These are the principal characteristics in the dominant mode of industrial relations in Japan.

Nonetheless, I am not fully persuaded by an institutional approach that explains the propensity of unions to cooperate with managers solely in terms of organizational patterns. The human subjects who form the system of enterprise-based unions are Japan's workers. Their character, their particular consciousness and behavior, must be explained; therefore, in this study I first ask how the Japanese common people, in the course of their modern and contemporary history, chose or were forced to choose to become organized workers possessing a certain being and consciousness. In this approach, the pattern of enterprise-based unions is an institutional form that reflects the type of unionist who emerged over Japan's modern history. That is, although the institutional form of the union, to some extent, surely regulated consciousness in the postwar era, I give primacy to the being and consciousness of organized workers as independent variables that regulated the distinctive institution of enterprise-based unions.

This said, I must hasten to add that I am not a believer in some mystical "theory of the unique Japanese mind," which seeks to locate the origin of Japanese characteristics in the distant past, in the ancient or middle ages. I fundamentally reject any sort of "theory of the Japanese" that contends the Japanese in all ages and of all classes have maintained lives of harmony and community spirit that eliminated any "Western" type of class conflict. Such theories have no concern for the trials of members of the working class in the modern era, and no understanding that the deeply felt needs of such people are fundamentally international in character. Stubbornly adhering to the belief that, given certain changes in their circumstances, Japan's organized workers would gradually take on the attributes of their Western comrades and that Western workers would likewise gradually take on attributes of Japan's "regular employees" if they were to labor for long years under Japanese-style management, I seek to grasp the "Japanese type." Only such a methodological internationalism will make it possible to analyze critically a specific nation's labor movement.

Themes and Perspective

Let me begin this inquiry by clarifying my perspective and some basic assumptions about Japanese-style industrial relations. The first point begins with two questions. First, when organized workers defend their livelihoods, does the logic that informs their activity contain certain features different from that of members of other classes, including unorganized workers? The second question essentially rephrases the first: What are the links, and what are the discontinuities, between the culture—the norms and values—of organized workers and the "people" in general?

Informing these questions is a model of the autonomous society of "organized workers." These are people who have separated themselves culturally from members of society's middle class, as well as from unorganized workers, in that the culture of the latter two groups has been forged in the crucible of the individualistic competition demanded by capitalist society. Whether a segment of society in general—the organized workers—separates itself from the others depends on whether this group can build for itself what I call a "worker society." This is a society marked off by a common understanding of certain autonomous norms of working people, derived above all from the character of their work itself, the activity that relates workers to the rest of society.

In this book I will use the term "take-off" to describe this self-generated process of separation: the creation of a worker society by a portion of the working class. The history of the formation of labor unions is in a sense the history of this take-off; and the specific pattern of the take-off in a given nation is intimately related to that nation's economic, political, and social history. This history determines the answer to the two questions just posed.

I do not believe any country possesses a fixed social or cultural essence that transcends history. Nonetheless, in a nation that does experience a take-off of worker society, these historically constructed norms of organized workers—their sense of "what is necessary?" and "what is important?"—become quite different from those of workers in other countries who were unable or unwilling to take off. Examples of these distinctive norms include customary practices of collective self-government over procedures at work, guarantees of mutual support and equality among fellow workers, going beyond the promise of equality of opportunity, restrictions on competition to outperform fellow workers, and the willingness to strike when necessary. The logic that supports such behavior is completely different from the spirit of free, individualistic competition that characterizes the common sense of the nation at large, the publicly sanctioned philosophy of bourgeois society. When a worker society made up of people who have "taken off" nurtures its own autonomous culture, labor unions become "a state within a state."[9] In this situation, a state of "separation" of the norms of organized workers from the common sense of the people at large, including unorganized workers, prevails.

However, there are places where a variety of factors prevent such a separation of the thinking of organized workers from that of other members of society. I call this a state of "fusion." In such countries, the common sense of the nation at large permeates the thinking of organized workers. A struggle for cultural hegemony between working-class values and middle-class or bourgeois values is simply absent here. In such a nation, workers understand "equality" to mean fair access to a place at the starting line in a race for higher wages and promotions. Such a society condemns efforts typical of the workers in a separate society (to restrict the competition over choice job assignments, workloads, or wages) as excessive, even evil, forms of egalitarianism.

Japan, of course, is a nation marked by a high degree of fusion. Certainly today, and in the recent past as well, one is hard-pressed to identify a mode of living and working among organized workers that contrasts sharply to the patterns of the unorganized workers who exist above (as supervisers and managers) and below (as nonregular workers). For example, regular employees of large enterprises, who constitute the core of Japan's organized workforce, are party to a larger societal consensus that accepts competition to outperform fellow workers as quite natural. Of course, just as a condition of separation will not remain unchanged in the face of changing circumstances, a state of fusion is subject to change over time. Total fusion probably can exist only under fascism or as part of a rigid socialist dogma. In later chapters, readers will see that in some times and places, Japanese workers have actively sought to curtail competition among themselves. In any case, assessing the extent of separation and fusion that prevails in a given country offers one powerful perspective on the human face of organized workers.

Thus, my analysis is concerned first with the *extent* of take-off. My second interest lies in then clarifying its *form*. One model of this take-off is as follows: With the advent of capitalism, workers lose their place in existing communities and means of production. They are thrown into the labor market as atoms. From this position, they eventually find a place in a reconstructed worker society. As participants in such a society, workers discover comrades with whom they share a need for and a possiblity of defending a certain way of life. Based on a shared understanding of this need, they nurture a tacit agreement to mutually assist each other. They strive to limit competition over work assignments, wages, and job opportunities.[10]

In the history of labor around the world, some representative types of a worker's society in this sense include: (1) a trade society formed by artisans; (2) a workplace society emerging out of the harsh experience of the diverse nonskilled workers in mass production industries; and (3) a society created by mobile laborers in a given region who work in a shifting array of jobs. Relatively stable labor union organizations are built on the foundation of such worker societies. That is, at the risk of presenting a mechanistic schema, craft unions are created by an artisanal trade society, and industrial unions are the product of a workplace society of the second type. One dramatic example of the latter would be the unions built in America's mass production factories in the 1930s.[11] General unions emerge out of a regional worker society of mobile laborers.

To investigate the form of the take-off in a given nation, one must ask how the social and economic conditions of that country's workers shaped the particular worker society that emerged. At the outset of the following chapter I offer a sketch of this take-off in Britain and the United States. Key characteristics of the American case were identified early on in the writing of Selig Perlman and more recently in the work of Herbert Gutman.[12] They show that the historical character of the American working class—the persistence of the American dream, the high rate of social mobility, the gradual formation of the labor market, and the varied racial and ethnic identities of the workers—made for a less stable worker society in America than in Britain. One of the themes of this study is that, in contrast to both of these nations, in Japan, since roughly the mid-1920s, a peculiar sort of workplace society of the second type has emerged, although neither a trade society (type 1) nor a general workers society (type 3) has been created. This can be called the *company society*, or a pseudo-workers society. A major concern of this book is to analyze this society. It has been the foundation of a distinctive Japanese unionism in which the boundary of the worker's own society is coterminous with that of a specific enterprise.

The third major problem that is of concern is to discover what ideological potential there may be, even in a nation characterized by the fusion of workers and the general society, for labor unions to generate their own autonomous demands. That is, in a land of fusion, are autonomous worker demands not likely to erupt in the following way? First, workers observe a wide disparity between their actual conditions and the beautiful ideals proclaimed by the governing class to unify the people and by the managerial class to unify employees. Next, these workers argue that if these ideals are not simply lies, the reality of their working life should be made to conform with the ideals. This would seem to be a natural line of thinking among people in a land of fusion where workers either do not possess dissenting ideals or where such an alternative value system is weak. Workers in such a nation are likely to appropriate and reinterpret the publicly validated concepts of the general society.

In the first chapters of this book I focus attention on how workers in postwar Japan reinterpreted the prevailing ideas of the prewar and wartime years. From the late nineteenth century through 1945, the Japanese state waved a conceptual banner emblazoned with the slogan "all people are equal under the emperor (*tennō*)." During the same period, the public stance of managers in big business was that "all employees in the seniority (*nenkō*) system are respected." One can say that the demands raised in the postwar labor movement sought above all to bring the reality of working life in line with these slogans.

The thesis of Andrew Gordon's fine study of the history of Japanese labor relations is that the core issues of concern to Japanese workers have been "fair and just treatment" and "membership" or citizenship in the enterprise.[13] In a similar vein, Saguchi Kazurō has recently identified the "desire to eliminate the qualitative differences between labor and management" as a shared objective of all the actors working to realize "industrial democracy" in Japan.[14] I share their perception of the issues. As government and business management from about the latter half of the 1960s made some concessions that recognized these demands, Japanese labor unions had no more grounds to challenge the logic of the enterprise, and industrial relations became stable.

As I assess this worker reinterpretation of public slogans and rhetoric, my position is ambivalent. Some attribute the current unparalleled stability of Japan's industrial relations to the success of the labor offensive of 1945 through roughly 1965 in gaining most of the workers' demands. This intepretation has validity in that it recognizes that the subjective initiatives of Japanese workers helped constitute contemporary industrial relations. However, what if the postwar labor unions had persisted in the demands raised by workers such as the Mitsui Miike coal miners in the 1950s, demands still being insisted on by many British unionists—that is, efforts to curtail competition among workers by exercising control over labor organizations or personnel management? What if these unions had sustained their strong beliefs and actions that opposed commonly accepted practices of Japanese-style management? The current amicable industrial relationship would not then have come about.

In fact, the mainstream labor unions were not oppositional in this sense; instead, they struggled to realize ideals that were acceptable to the government, political parties, and managers. Precisely for this reason, after Japanese ruling groups had suppressed the dissenting opinions and activities of Miike-style unions and consolidated their power on the basis of economic growth, they were willing to make concessions. In a sense this outcome was inevitable, and today Japanese workers, and their unions struggling to justify their existence, are upholding a Japanese style of management premised on near-complete managerial authority over the working lives of employees.

Overview

I wrote the Japanese versions of the chapters of this book between the late 1970s and 1985, seeking to explore the themes and develop the perspectives laid out in this volume's Introduction. In Japan, these chapters were published in two separate volumes, *Portraits of Japanese Workers* (1981) and *Surviving the Turbulent Workplace* (1986).[15] The current translation includes slightly updated versions of the four chapters from each volume that received the most favorable reactions.

Chapter 2 describes the take-off of prewar Japanese workers from roughly the turn of this century to about 1940. In a particular historical context of political, industrial, and social developments, Japanese workers moved from a state of atomization, through an abortive attempt at a Euro-American mode of take-off, into the sphere of the enterprise-based seniority system elaborated by management. Chapter 3 then follows the course of postwar workers who were allowed to organize unions and who continued efforts to realize objectives first articulated before the war: equality as employees, equality as members of the nation, and minimal livelihood guarantees. Organized workers, raising numerous specific demands that addressed these three general goals, by the mid-1960s had followed a halting course to achieve many of their objectives, at least in part.[16] My analysis highlights the contrast to demands raised and won by American or European workers. I ask why postwar unions sought seniority-based, automatic annual pay raises, rather than Western-style "equal pay for equal work." I also seek to explain why the principle of person-based pay was more acceptable than that of job-based pay for both management and labor. Why did both sides prefer pay based on the latent ability of the employee who performed a job over a pay system based on the rating of that person's job?

Chapter 4 also examines postwar labor in general. Here, I focus on the limits and the costs of organized workers' "achievements." Despite the fact that a portion of Japan's organized workers in the 1940s and 1950s had gained some voice concerning the character of work itself and had begun to restrict competition among fellow workers, postwar organized labor on the whole could not persist in articulating and defending such a logic of organized labor, one comparable to that of European or American workers in those years. Rather, the thought and behavior of most enterprise-based unions in a society devoted to serving the needs of the enterprise essentially reinterpreted concepts such as "seniority and merit-based management" in terms favoring workers as much as possible. Management, for its part, was able to prohibit unions from interfering with numerous Japanese-style measures to reward employees on the basis of latent or demonstrated merit, beginning in the 1960s, in return for granting wage increases and employment guarantees sought by unions. As a result, a Japanese style of management emerged that faced virtually no formal restrictions on policies of work assignment or treatment of personnel. The corporation became a peculiarly Japanese place where so-called salary-men—who from about the mid-1960s were also blue-collar workers in large enterprises and who achieved a status such that this term is appropriate for them—competed with each other on the basis of their ability as perceived by management.[17] Chapters 2, 3, and 4 thus constitute an extended historical sketch.

In Chapter 5, I turn to an essential feature of Japanese-style management that emerged in the middle of the 1960s, the movement to improve business performance by creating Quality Control (QC) circles. I introduce sixteen specific examples of QC circle activity, describing the actual "improvements" (often termed *kaizen*) introduced and looking at their impact on the quality of workplace life. I view QC circle activity as a prototype of the "mandatory volunteering" that characterizes so much social behavior in Japan. By placing the emergence of widespread QC circle activity in the context of a simultaneous decline of what militant unions called "workplace struggles," I seek to understand what Japanese workers of this era were hoping to achieve through QC circle activities. I ask whether or not these aspirations have been futile.

In chapters 6, 7, and 8, I examine the experiences of particular groups of workers. Chapter 6 builds upon a number of thorough surveys of the iron and steel industries through about 1975 to offer an interpretation of that industry's workplace history. I detail the labor-management policies that systematized a Japanese-style emphasis on merit and ability, and I discuss the relationship of such meritocratic programs to the failure of enterprise-based unions to transcend those "limits" described in Chapter 4.

Women workers are the main characters in Chapter 7. I trace the post-war history of the work, workplace, livelihoods, and consciousness of blue-collar women and "office ladies" (the "OL"), devoting particular attention to the changing manifestations of an enduring gender-based division of labor. In so doing, I also take up the debate among feminists over the relative importance of seeking protection for women's special needs versus demanding equality with men. The discussion ends by considering the impact of the 1986 Equal Employment Opportunity Law. In the face of a stubbornly persistent gender-based division of labor in Japan, where women are typically made solely responsible for household management and labor, this law has in fact encouraged an increased workplace role for women, not as regular, full-time employees but as part-time workers. I argue that, even a decade after the passage of this law, Japanese-style management remains powerfully supported by a mutually dependent relationship between men and women. The former are typically regular employees assured of lifetime employment and required in exchange to offer a total and "functionally flexible" commitment to the enterprise. What makes this possible is that millions of women factory workers and the OL maintain their households while offering "numerical flexibility" to the firm by working on a part-time basis with no job security.

In the final chapter I discuss changes in management policy and the nature of work at a major bank during the years of high-speed growth by using a single bank worker's extensive diaries. I examine the twenty-three-year career of the late Kawabe Tomomi and try to recreate the anguish of his mental world as well as his exhausting daily routine as a loan officer who was simultaneously a conscientious employee, a committed activist in his union's "antimainstream" group, a voracious reader in the social sciences, and a devoted family man. He is precisely that white-collar worker who is so often seen as the prototypical "Japanese worker."

The book concludes with a brief essay that lays out a paradigm for apprehending the stressful plight of Japanese workers today. To put it in abstract terms, I suggest that in postwar Japan there is a mutually defining relationship between standardizing and differentiating processes that operate in people's lives and work. Concretely, this relationship involves the achievement of one goal of postwar democracy, a "standardized" middle-class lifestyle, simultaneous with the increased prominence since the mid-1970s of managerial policies that differentiate workers based on individual merit and ability.[18]

Through this study I have sought to identify why the industrial relations of the Japanese workplace and the lives of Japanese workers have taken their particular course to the present. Nevertheless, I remain critical of the current state of affairs. When compared to those of other nations, Japanese corporations have probably provided greater opportunities for success to the individual male employee who finds meaning and personal fulfillment in cultivating his ability and showing his determination to help his company achieve its objectives. Many ordinary workers, however, do not find life's primary value in testing themselves to the utmost by performing the company's work. These men and women cannot escape the stress that results from the many demands the company places on them. Moreover, they have lost the power to control their situations by means of labor unions. It is precisely this power that Japanese workers should seek to recapture. For similar reasons, as workers around the globe increasingly find themselves working under Japanese-style management, they must retain the power to limit corporate demands, even if managers resist such limits in the name of productivity. This should apply to American workers as well as those elsewhere.

In terms of an analysis of the extent of fusion and take-off, a far greater separation between organized labor and other members of society exists in the United States than in Japan, although the separation is less than that found in Britain. Between the 1930s and 1960s American labor unions resorted to strikes as well as collective bargaining and won for their members a very high standard of living compared to that of other nations. They also were able to enforce work rules that made their lives tolerable even under the "Fordist" regime of mass production. But as America's international industrial competitiveness then declined relative to places like Japan, and as the economic structure and composition of the workforce changed in ways that hampered efforts to organize workers, the power of the American labor union movement declined sharply.

Moreover, the neoliberal policies of the 1980s reduced the U.S. government's commitment to full employment and expanded social security measures, policies that had indirectly contributed to union strength in the postwar era. Neoliberalism in the United States also struck at a fundamental value of organized workers, the desire to restrict competition among workers. In these ways, U.S. neoliberal policies fostered a profound shift in the relationship between the worker society and the general society, a change from a state of separation toward one of fusion. In such circumstances, the American labor movement in the 1990s is struggling through a wintery time of declining organization rates and loss of vitality.[19]

Clearly there exists a mutually reinforcing relationship between this decline of organized labor and the introduction of Japanese business and Japanese-style management to America, because the principles underlying Japan's powerful economic performance are essentially those of neoliberalism. The ultimate source of the competitive strength of Japan's economy lies in the fusion of worker society and the nation as a whole, as well as the fusion of labor and management at the site of production.

In contrast to this Japanese performance, one can see in the case of the British economy in the period after 1960 the impact on the national economy of a profound state of separation between organized labor and the rest of society.[20] Union leaders are aware of these diverse situations, and as a sense of economic crisis intensifies in a society, the forces of realpolitiks in the labor movement inevitably compel unions toward a stance of fusion. Thus, American labor unions proclaim that in order to revive themselves they must strengthen the morale of workers by humanizing work, and they are reexamining old work rules. Perhaps such a new strategy is necessary. And perhaps American workers will do better than their Japanese counterparts in reinterpreting in their favor the showcase commitment of Japanese-style management to equality, worker participation, and respect for the individual.

Nonetheless, too much emphasis on fusion can erode the concept of "democracy by the worker," the idea that workers must collectively maintain a measure of decisionmaking control over matters of vital concern to their lives at work. If American workers fully accept what one might call "actually existing Japanese-style management," such erosion will surely result. For this reason, the following study of what Japanese workers have gained and what they have lost as they have labored under Japanese-style management should be of profound interest to American workers who must make decisions about resisting or accepting the "Japanization" of their working life.

Notes to Chapter 1

1. Although the following are comparisons with Europe, not the United States, they elaborate on the general comparison made here. Kumazawa Makoto, *Nihon teki keiei no meian* [Light and darkness of Japanese Management] (Tokyo: Chikuma Shobō, 1989) and "Industrial Relations and Management in Japanese Companies in Europe," in Tokunaga Shigeyoshi et al., eds., *New Impacts on Industrial Relations: Internationalization and Changing Production Strategies* (Munich: Indicium Verlag, 1992).

2. See Benjamin Coriat, *Penser a L'envers—Travail et Organization dans l'enterprise Japonaise* (Paris: Christian Bourgois Editeur, 1991).

3. See Harry C. Katz, *Shifting Gears—Changing Labor Relations in the U.S. Automobile Industry* (Cambridge, Mass.: MIT Press, 1985); Hagiwara Susumu, "1987 Jidōsha sangyō no kyōyaku kōkai kōshō" [1987 Automobile industry contract renewal negotiations], *Nihon Rōdō Kyōkai Zasshi* [Japan Institute of Labor journal], No. 343.

4. On the literature on Japanization of industrial relations see Paul Thompson, *The Nature of Work* (New York: Macmillan, 1989), chap. 2.

5. The representative work is Shimada Haruo, *Hyuman Ueaa no Keizaigaku* [Economics of human-ware] (Tokyo: Iwanami Shoten, 1988).

6. Mike Parker and Jane Slaughter, eds., *Choosing Sides—Unions and the Team Concept* (Boston: South End Press, 1988); Joseph J. Fucini and Suzy Fucini, *Working for the Japanese—Inside Mazda's American Auto Plant* (New York: Free Press, 1990).

7. *Ibid.*, pp. 104–106.

8. The figures are based on the number of employed workers at the end of each year in each country.

9. From the preface of the 1894 version of Sidney and Beatrice Webb, *The History of Trade Unionism* (London: Longmans, Green and Co., 1920).

10. My understanding of this situation is, in a sense, based on Frank Tannenbaum, *The Labor Movement: Its Conservative Functions and Social Consequences* (New York: Knickerbocker Press, 1921).

11. My picture of this process was obtained mainly from Sidney Fine, *Sit-down: The General Motors Strike of 1936–1937* (Ann Arbor: The University of Michigan Press, 1969).

12. Selig Perlman, *A History of Trade Unionism in the United States* (New York: Augustus M. Kelley, 1928); Herbert Gutman, *Work, Culture, and Society in Industrializing America* (New York: Knopf, 1976).

13. Andrew Gordon, *The Evolution of Labor Relations in Japan: Heavy Industry, 1853–1955* (Cambridge: Harvard Council on East Asian Studies, 1985).

14. Saguchi Kazurō, *Nihon ni okeru sangyō minshushugi no zentei* [Premises for industrial democracy in Japan] (Tokyo: Tokyo University Press, 1991).

15. Both were published by Chikuma Shobō. The Japanese titles were *Nihon no rōdōsha zō* and *Shokuba no shuran o ikite: Sairon, Nihon no rōdōsha zō*.

16. For an illuminating discussion of this point, see Andrew Gordon, "Japanese Labor Relations During the Twentieth Century," *Journal of Labor Research* (Department of Economics, George Mason University, Summer 1990).

17. A word on the history of the term *sararii-man* (salary-man) may be in order here. Until the mid-1960s in Japan, blue-collar operatives usually received daily wages and white-collar staff were paid monthly salaries. At this time, many Japanese enterprises did away with the status differentiation between blue-collar and white-collar workers and integrated both groups as employees who were paid a monthly salary. Such employees came to be called "salary-men."

18. For another general rendition of this paradigm, see William Kelly, "Finding a Place in Metropolitan Japan: Transpositions of Everyday Life," in Andrew Gordon, ed., *Postwar Japan as History* (Berkeley: University of California Press, 1993).

19. On the decline of the American labor movement in the 1980s, see Richard B. Freeman and James L. Medoff, *What Do Unions Do?* (New York: Basic Books, 1984) and Michael Goldfield, *The Decline of Organized Labor in the United States* (Chicago: University of Chicago Press, 1987).

20. For a study of this problem, see Kumazawa Makoto, *Kokka no naka no kokka: Rōdōtō seikenka no rōdō kumiai, 1964–1970* [A state within the state: Trade unions under the Labor government, 1964–1970] (Tokyo: Nihon hyōronsha, 1976).

2

The "Take-Off" of Japanese Workers

British and American Models

I use the expression *take-off* to refer to the process in which a segment of the working class separates itself from both the poor and the general citizenry of a capitalist society. This segment "takes off" to become a body of organized workers with its own distinct modes of existence and thought. To present an image of the organized workers of Japan, I trace the course of the Japanese take-off beginning in the early twentieth century. But to bring some key features of the Japanese case into sharper relief, I first take a detour through the British and American take-offs. The conditions of the British take-off and the choices made by British workers contrast sharply to those of Japanese working people, but the American course is relatively similar to the Japanese take-off.

As the Industrial Revolution progressed, the men and women who crowded into Britain's urban slums lived in a state of profound atomization. They had lost their traditional means of production and had become vendors of their labor power; their communal agrarian organizations had been destroyed, and the traditional organizations of artisans were on the verge of dissolution. What philosophy of living remained for people thus cast into an insecure labor market? If one excludes those who survived as pickpockets, people had only two alternatives. First, they could throw themselves on the mercy of the early poor laws and live as paupers. Second, they could individually commit themselves to backbreaking work and extreme frugality in a struggle to escape from proletarian status. In the infancy of industrial capitalism, few men or women yet had the pride and confidence to believe they could survive by remaining as workers.

But working people soon came to question both these attitudes. The attempt to survive by relying on the early poor laws denied workers their dignity and self-respect, the very qualities necessary to escape their dependent condition. Karl Polanyi spoke to this problem in writing of the famous

17

Speenhamland Act, designed to guarantee the poor a minimum income by pegging their welfare dole to the price of bread.

> As long as a man had a status to hold on to, a pattern set by his kin or fellows, he could fight for it [the human shape of life], and regain his soul. But in the case of the laborer this could happen only in one way: by his constituting himself the member of a new class. Unless he was able to make a living by his own labor, he was not a worker but a pauper. To reduce him artificially to such a condition was the supreme abomination of Speenhamland. This act of an ambiguous humanitarianism prevented laborers from constituting themselves an economic class and thus deprived them of the only means of staving off the fate to which they were doomed in the economic mill.[1]

After pressure from numerous sources led to the repeal of the poor laws, the only apparent avenue open to workers was to strive on their own in a competitive world; and indeed, the moral code of the new era sanctioned precisely this path. The philosophy of self-help exhorted each individual to work to make his own way through his own effort. One premise embodied in the bourgeois concept of freedom was that any worker with ability and the will to work could become an entrepreneur himself. In fact, the early era of industrial capitalism offered just enough promise of social mobility to keep people from dismissing this premise as a hoax. But ultimately, an individualistic faith in the chance for social mobility failed to draw masses of working people into an enduring competitive struggle for success.

The competition of the poor against the poor created two extremes: a tiny minority of the successful and a mass of those who failed. Moreover, the proportion of the latter steadily increased as the minimum start-up costs of a business venture rose. It soon became obvious to ordinary workers that without special financial resources, or business talent and education, individualism as defined here was not a viable route. At the same time, aware of the destructive and humiliating impact of the Speenhamland system, those I have called "failures"—the reserve army of unemployed—did not demand public assistance. Again, to quote Polyani: "The hatred of public relief, the distrust of state action, the insistence on respectability and self-reliance, remained for generations characteristics of the British worker."[2]

Among workers who thus hated public relief and had abandoned faith in competitive individualism, a philosophy of unionism slowly matured. Through this unionism, workers sought an independent livelihood by maintaining a class identity and building self-governing collective organizations. Seen here is a workers' reinterpretation of the prevailing morality of nineteenth-century Britain. The self-help of individualism was transformed into the self-help of the collectivity. The specific objectives of the emerging unionism were to implement mutual insurance, standardize conditions of labor, equalize work assignments and job opportunities, maintain favorable workplace customs, reject not only arbitrary discrimination among workers but also evaluations based on merit, and eliminate competition among fellow workers. This British logic of labor is summed up in the notion that "when 'we' compete, 'they' exploit us." Without here detailing the union policies by which such attitudes and objectives were realized in practice, I simply note that the unionism outlined here represented the take-off of British workers. It was a unionism based not on individualism but on collective solidarity, one achieved less through national politics and more via industrial self-government.

This take-off occurred in two stages. The first involved skilled workers who retained considerable pride and insisted their work could not be undertaken easily by just anyone. By reorganizing the apprentice system and setting standards for the skill required of those entering their trade, they established a framework of craft union policies. Theirs was a conscious effort to shore up craft societies that would otherwise be destroyed by the entry of machines. Thus, early trade unionists formed institutions based on a society that protected them from the logic of a capitalism that set workers against each other. Within their society, craft workers became citizens who enjoyed a true equality, at first among themselves, and then in bourgeois society. Perhaps nineteenth-century British workers built their trade unions directly out of the surviving institutions of a traditional craft-based society, or perhaps they established new unions that then reconstructed a craft-based society. Whatever the case, these unions certainly enabled a society of artisans to distinguish itself from the lower strata of the proletarian world. In some combination, this unionism got its start by inheriting and reconstituting a still-viable world of artisanal trade society.

After the skilled workers had thus taken off, a proletariat that probably numbered over two-thirds of Britain's wage workers was left behind in lower-class society. The take-off of the latter as a collective entity came only half-a-century later, impeded by such characteristics of unskilled workers as their ready replaceability, their low wages, and their lack of employment security or occupational stability. Even in Britain in the late nineteenth-century, unskilled factory workers remained part of the impoverished lower class.

As British peasants became unskilled factory laborers, entire families often left the village. Accompanied by their families, unskilled workers congregated in the urban slums. Working-class neighborhoods developed from clusters of families who were driven from their village communities in similar fashion. The children of these workers were born in these neighborhoods, commuted to school from them, made friends there, and eventually found jobs and commuted from there. The customs and norms of a working-class society, whether habits of solidarity or self-destructive behavior, were reproduced in the form of family and community tradition.

Of course, some aspired to escape this environment. The desire to escape was strongest in working-class neighborhoods of great urban centers like the East End of London, where immigrants of many races lived together. It appears that an individualism that lacked any sense of social obligation or humaneness slowly eroded the spirit of community, and the primary social ties of the workers gradually shifted from the residential district to the workplace. Still, according to Arnold Weskar's play, *Chicken Soup with Barley*, what the East End lacked in privacy it made up for in the intimacy of a neighborhood like "a big mother."[3] Even this heterogeneous district retained a working-class community spirit, through which residents scorned the philosophy of individualism.

The men and women in such communities initially held insecure jobs outside the core manufacturing industries, and their community solidarity did not provide a sufficient foundation for building labor unions. But when new production technologies allowed unskilled workers to move into basic manufacturing industries, these communities provided the base for the second stage in the take-off of British workers. To switch metaphors, they were the soil in which a newly emerged working-class society sunk its roots, and they endowed this take-off with two distinctively British characteristics: first, the organizational pattern of the general union, which drew members from various industries; and second, the independence of these unions from the corporation. These general unions also shared one organizational feature with craft unions, in that membership was not limited to employees at a specific workplace. They drew members from throughout the working-class neighborhoods where the workers, their family members, and their friends resided.

Only with this second stage in the take-off did Britain's union movement make gains among semiskilled blue-collar workers. These men were employed primarily in large plants using new manufacturing methods, and the character of their work, as well as their treatment, tended to stamp them as workers of a particular company. But in Britain, both the general unions, with unskilled workers as their core, and the craft unions, which were gradually opening up their gates to a broader constituency, competed to win these workers as members.

These competing endeavors to draw in the semiskilled workers had two results that contrast significantly to the Japanese case. First, workers never became "company employees." When joining general or craft unions, semiskilled men did not separate themselves from their fellow workers by focusing their activities within the walls of a single factory. Second, the initially quite divergent policies of craft unions and general unions began to influence and converge with each other. To be sure, important differences remain to this day in the policies of the Amalgamated Engineering Union, which traces its origin to craft unions, and the Transport and General Workers Union, a product of the second stage of take-off. But today both unions have as their operating philosophy the principle of "security through equality," implemented via collective self-rule. Union members seeking to impose this principle within a bourgeois society relied primarily on industrial actions—collective bargaining and strikes—and secondarily on political action. As Britain's workers consolidated these unions, they carved out a realm of existence where they could avoid the two forbidding alternatives of welfare dependence and individual struggle.

Because the British union movement persisted as a powerful force, Britain's capitalist system quickly adopted conciliatory policies aimed to integrate workers into the nation, and from an early point it was even able to endure the political rule of the Labor party. Nonetheless, Britain's organized workers, especially the unionists on the shop floor, still stubbornly maintained their separate world, resistant to the demands of the enterprise or the state.

In the United States, faith in the possibility of making it alone prevailed more broadly and endured for longer than it did in Britain. Wage laborers in industry believed they could eventually ascend the social ladder to become independent farmers or businessmen. Needless to say, the youthful vitality of American capitalism undergirded this "American dream." Moreover, the impoverished immigrants who flowed into the country until the 1920s had fled rigid social systems in their native countries. They hoped to realize their dreams in the paradise of a "land of the free."

Against this background, the founding of the American Federation of Labor (AFL) in the 1880s marks the moment at which an organization of skilled workers first recognized that the frontier was vanishing, the start of the take off of worker society. The logic of these men was essentially that of their counterparts in British craft unions. Toward the end of the 1920s Selig Perlman identified the core of this logic as the equal distribution of job opportunity based on the "consciousness of scarcity" of job opportunity, that is, "a communism of opportunity."[4] Here, as in Britain, free competition was regarded as a crime against fellow workers. Perlman juxtaposed organized workers who lived by this logic against entrepreneurs who believed opportunities were abundant. Thorstein Veblen echoed Perlman's view with a critical twist when he argued that true businessmen were progressive even though the AFL was conservative.

In the 1910s, in order to protect their powers to regulate the labor of their skilled members, craft unions opposed Frederick W. Taylor's scientific management system, which sought to impose wages paid not to "workers as part of the masses" but to the individual who works to the best of his ability. The following words, delivered at a meeting of the Wisconsin Federation of Labor by a member of congress linked to the AFL are of special interest. He said, "We don't want to work as fast as we are able to. We want to work as fast as we think it's comfortable for us to work. We haven't come into existence for the purpose of seeing how great a task we can perform throughout a lifetime. We are trying to regulate our work so as to make it an auxiliary to our lives and be benefited thereby."[5] Here we see workers in the first stage of their take-off, repudiating faith in an American dream of competing, thus demonstrating ability, thereby leading to success and progress.

Despite the take-off of a worker's society among skilled artisans, in America's mines and docks and in its steel mills and auto factories, workers from Eastern Europe, southern Europe, and from the farmlands of the South continued their arduous tasks unprotected by any rights of labor. In addition, at least in the 1920s, it was possible for some to enjoy "American lives" of mass consumption and popular entertainment by virtue of individual hard work. The ruling ideas of the age were those of capitalist philosophers who denied the need for socialism, for labor unions, or for social security programs in America. Those who challenged this philosophy too vociferously faced violent repression. The spirit of unionism shrivelled, intimidated by violence and overwhelmed by a civic faith in America, the land of opportunity. Needless to say, for unskilled workers the real America was no dream. But the ripening of their grapes of wrath did not come until the Depression slashed their wages and eliminated their jobs. At this point, masses of working men and women lost faith in the ruling ideas of American opportunity.

American workers thus began a second take-off in the New Deal era, as they began to resist the continuing violence directed at them. By the end of the 1930s they had succeeded in establishing industrial unions in basic industries. But the long years of autocratic managerial control of the production process in basic manufacturing industries, the heterogeneity of work processes and working conditions among semiskilled workers, and the ethnic and racial diversity and division of working-class communities all had an impact. American workers had trouble nurturing a new, shared working-class culture. Compared to those of Britain, America's industrial unions tended to retain some characteristics of in-house unions.

The thought and behavior of workers invariably manifests itself as a reinterpretation of the existing system and philosophy of industrial relations. Semiskilled American workers, rather than building upon class and community ties that transcended the framework of the enterprise, built upon a solidarity born of bitter shared experiences at the production site. They demanded the right to a voice, to seniority-based priority of employment at that factory. What ultimately broke the back of antiunion sentiments in the business world and among some workers was their realization of solidarity in the course of sit-down strikes. A centerpiece of union strategy was the demand that seniority—length of service at a given factory—serve as a basic principle to restrict competition among workers. It is said that the activists who succeeded in organizing these workers pinned both the union's tiepin and the company's badge to their chests. This fact symbolically reveals that the workers who participated in this second take-off of worker society were raising their demands as residents in a given factory.

Certainly, the industrial unions founded in this way possessed some characteristics of in-house unions, and this diminished the potential for organized workers to build a movement in tandem with their unorganized comrades. To this extent, the American and Japanese cases have something in common. Even today organized workers are surrounded by huge numbers of nonunion workers who stake their futures on the possibility of realizing the American dream, and unionized workers in the United States remain more isolated from their fellow workers than their British counterparts. But when compared to Japanese workers, their situations also retain important features in common with those in Britain: The boundary for membership in a union goes beyond the "regular workers" in a company to include workers who have been laid off; and above all, the manner in which union members in America defend their livelihoods differs clearly from that of nonunion citizens. The unionist position reflects the defiant attitude of common people who do not aspire to rise up the social hierarchy through individualistic struggle.

In the Anglo-American mode of take-off, then, organized workers came to distinguish themselves from unorganized employees of high status, such as higher grade white-collar workers, foremen, and those with special ambitions and objectives. In the world of such high-level nonunion employees, a stout faith in individualism and the possiblity of rising up the ladder of success induces people to compete to advance in their careers. Such people recognize effort and merit as defining elements of the hierarchical order. However, as C. Wright Mills noted in his classic work, *White Collar*, such people must also subordinate themselves to the enterprise and management.[6] Further, their pursuit of higher status also means insecurity, a price for advancement that organized workers have refused to pay.

Union workers also came to distinguish themselves from unorganized workers of low status, that is, the lumpen proletariat of workers in small shops, immigrant workers, and workers on the margins of the labor market. In contrast to the self-motivated behavior of those in the upper strata of nonunion workers, these men and women labor in silence, with no choice but to accede to a competitive ethos. At the same time, they tend to become dependent upon, even addicted to, the social welfare benefits provided by an affluent nation. Riding the crest of this dependent wave is the so-called street corner society of those American youths with no lasting ties to job or a work group, who brag to their street corner buddies about money earned past the edge of the law.

Organized workers are in contrast to both of these groups in their mode of living. They generally value cooperative endeavor over competition, security over progress, and collective self-help and self-sufficiency over dependence and submission. Such unionists will neither loaf nor overwork. Although their work is not usually exhilarating or gratifying, it is something they find security in, something that puts food on their table, and something they therefore seek to control and make as bearable as possible. Such attitudes are expressed in the customary behavior of workers, behavior that determines the rules of what American labor economists call the two forms of "internal labor markets," the restricted market of skilled craft workers and the enterprise-based market of semiskilled workers.[7] The logic of such customary behavior, when consciously adopted as union policy, seeks to acquire an equal level of security through a thoroughgoing principle of collectivism.

This returns us to a central theme of this book. Given the importance of collectivist logic among British and American organized workers, one cannot describe them, in an assumed sharp contrast to Japanese workers, as individualistic. One cannot assume that they join unions voluntarily, on the basis of a rational, individual calculation. That is, if one overemphasizes the individualism of Anglo-American workers and the groupism of the Japanese, one misunderstands workers in all three places. One thus fails to perceive that organized workers in Britain and America for a long time rejected the individualistic "common sense" of the people, as defined by bourgeois society. In addition, one will not recognize that competitive, individualistic values are at the very heart of the system of industrial cooperation accepted by Japanese unions. As one examines the take-off for workers in Japan, one must thus abandon the deeply rooted and ubiquitous notion that in their basic mode of thinking Western workers are individualistic and Japanese are group-oriented.

Approaches to Japan

Workers in Japan built a stable social world of unions for the first time after World War II. They constructed these within the confines of a corporate-dominated society that had first emerged in the 1920s and 1930s. These two important facts suggest that the process of take-off for workers in Japan was an effort to win a place as employees of large corporations as much as or more than an endeavor to organize their own labor unions. Why did the Japanese take-off follow such a course? What imprint has this history left on the character of organized workers?

The Japanese take-off proceeded through four stages, as follows:

1. the turn of the century through World War I (late Meiji–early Taishō),[8]
2. the interwar era (late Taishō and early Shōwa);
3. the early post–World War II years; and
4. the era of high-speed economic growth.

In the remainder of this chapter I discuss the general features of the formative period of the Japanese take-off, the two stages of the pre–World War II era, with particular attention to several questions.

First, state-society relations must be considered. To what extent did the state encourage social mobility to enable workers to rise up a social ladder? To what extent did this actually happen? What kind of social security or public relief was offered those at the bottom of the social hierarchy? Did the state sanction institutions of industrial democracy to enable workers to defend their livelihoods?

Second, one must look into the changing demand for industrial labor, both in quality and quantity, and the formal policies of labor management. For example, at what pace were older artisanal skills eliminated from the basic manufacturing processes of big businesses? What organizing principles were adopted to rank and classify the workers?

A third key issue, the one of greatest interest to me, is the ethos of Japanese workers. What did they feel were the conditions necessary to sustain their livelihood? How did they view the possibility of achieving these conditions? A basic question as I develop a notion of the workers' ethos is the following: To what extent did Japanese workers possess or create communities imbued with a "logic of labor" opposed to, or simply distinct from, the logic of the state or of capital? In any nation the state or big business takes the initiative to transform traditional culture in the face of an emerging body of modern workers. Nonetheless, this process is interactive. The character of a bourgeois society formed in this manner is in turn shaped by surviving community groups and self-governing bodies among common people, even as the latter are being transformed by this bourgeois society. In the emergence of "the modern," common people manifest their subjectivity as they articulate possibilities for change.

With the above stages as the warp and areas of inquiry as the weft, I shall weave an understanding of the Japanese take-off.

Early Conditions

The first generation of Japanese workers at the turn of the century could not reasonably hope to escape up the social ladder or to defend themselves in their status as workers. They did not possess an instrumentalism that could have allowed them to endure wage labor as a transitional phase in their lives. Nor did they have a class-conscious determination to defend themselves as lifelong factory workers. This was as true of former skilled artisans working in shipyards or arsenals as it was of unskilled men and women who migrated from farm villages to work in textile mills, mines, or construction projects.

The village homes of the latter, a foundation of extended families and farm communities, was constricted economically by powerful landlords and by the extraordinary deflationary policies of the 1880s. In contrast to Japan's homemakers of recent decades who live in urban apartments and hold part-time jobs, these young workers of one century ago did not seek work for the sake of discretionary income; they were pushed from the villages to earn money for their families, even at the cost of sacrificing labor needed at home to work the farm or aid in household work and child care.

The young women in textile mills were the prototype and the majority of workers at this time. They endured arduous conditions to help their families in the villages meet their financial needs. They sent back to the villages approximately 90 percent of their wages. When the tenure of their contracts expired or when they lost their jobs because of ill health, they returned to their villages.

In the conventional view of Japanese scholars and popular understanding, such young women (and some men as well) failed to form the core of a new working class because they had left the village only temporarily to earn wages, and they retained the ethos of the farm villages. But this view is problematic. It must not be forgotten that women left villages for "push" rather than "pull" factors. To be sure, approximately 15 percent of these young women—dubbed "superior factory girls" or "hundred yen factory girls"—went to the factory to help their parents buy back their rice fields, and they could happily return to the village.[9] But the economic condition of most of the farm families did not allow them to rejoice when their daughters eventually returned home. Were young women who told themselves it was "for my own good and for my parents' sake" and who girded their spirits to cross the snow-covered Nomugi Pass en route to the silk filatures in Okaya or who borrowed money for train fare to come from the northeast to the cotton-spinning plants around Tokyo really welcomed back to their villages after enduring painful experiences in the factories? Strangely enough, the classic accounts provide no data on how many of these girls returned to their villages and remained there. After shifting from job to job, a fairly high percentage probably married men who worked in urban factories, and many others likely continued to work in the lower levels of the urban job market, including the sex trades.

One can be sure that male, as well as female workers found it hard to go home again. For instance, many miners came from the lowest levels of their rural communities, and they had no prospect of returning to farm life. They were destined to live precariously for their whole lives as wage workers.

In sum, the unskilled workers of this era did not follow the so-called *dekasegi* pattern of "leaving home temporarily to work." They could not fall back on the material and spiritual support of a stable village community or extended family. Although still psychologically connected to their home village, these people had, in fact, lost their homes. Often sent out reluctantly from their families, they were cast upon the "devil's millstone," where the logic of capitalism reigned supreme.

It is very important to recognize that material deprivation was by no means the cruelest aspect of this logic.[10] The testimony of women who were formerly silk filature workers, recorded in Yamamoto Shigemi's *Aah,*

Nomugi Pass, makes this quite clear. These young girls reported that work in their home village was just as strenuous as silk reeling. Further, their living standards, especially the quality of food, were better in the factory than back home. Their most painful memories are not those one might expect, such as long hours, low wages, or poor diet. Instead, they complained most bitterly of the humiliation and the wage reductions they received in front of fellow workers when quality inspections exposed their work as defective. They "cried in anguish" over such practices that inevitably forced them to compete with their fellow workers and over the cold, inhumane treatment of the employer when their health broke down.[11] In their home communities they suffered from grueling farm work and poverty, but they did not face performance ratings leading to competition and ostracism. In addition, an important government survey published in 1903, *Conditions of Factory Workers*, correctly noted that "all-night shifts were a nightmare beyond their imagination back in their home villages," and that this practice caused the extremely high turnover in personnel among the spinning workers.[12]

These workers had to adjust themselves to an unfamiliar culture of free competition. They did this while cut off from home communities whose cultural traditions might have provided grounds to resist this threatening new ethos. Further, they had often not even completed elementary school. Is it any surprise that they had difficulty either adapting to the newly dominant culture through autonomous initiatives or creating their own culture of resistance? These young women and men lacked the assurance of a stable attachment to their workplace, they developed no pride in themselves as wage workers, and they were deeply fearful of asserting themselves.

The 1920s were years of relatively democratic politics in Japan and a period of a significant unionizing drive among textile workers. Hosoi Wakizō's classic work of social reportage, *The Sad History of Women Factory Workers*, noted that these factory employees had gone so far as to invent a slang variation of the word democracy (*demokura*) to mean "complain" or "make a fuss." And yet, Hosoi describes these textile workers in 1925 as "intimidated and afraid of the products of civilization." In his view, the female textile workers "tend to dislike bright places, and prefer shadowy places." They avoid colorful department stores and do their shopping "usually at small, out-of-the-way dry-goods shops." "They fear people excessively." "In their dress and appearance, they are extremely plain." "When they go out, they rarely seem carefree"; their facial expressions are "always somber."[13] This evidence of stunted development and the painful loss of self-expression undoubtedly resulted from (and enabled) the restrictions on their personal freedom imposed by the prevailing system of labor management. But these characteristics also reflect the cultural maladjustment or dissolution experienced by these early unskilled factory hands. This is the original image of Japanese women workers.

In contrast to these migrants, workers who commuted from home or the home of a relative were able to escape (though barely) from being ground to bits by the devil's millstone. Although their impoverished families were not self-sufficient economically, each one formed a microcommunity of mutual support whose members possessed cultural values that remained outside the logic of capitalist enterprises. And to the extent that collections of commuters' poor families constituted neighborhood communities, they enlarged the space in which people could maintain independence. Thus, I firmly deny that Japan's corporate paternalism (or familyism) was created directly out of a unique, traditional family system. Instead, corporate society and the state were able to extend control over workers to the very extent that the latter were separated from their families and forced to survive in a culture of free competition.

One sees evidence of the relative autonomy *and* stability of workers who were still connected to their families in various behaviors that were cited in the 1903 report *Conditions of Factory Workers*. For example, during harvest time or festivals "absenteeism rose sharply" among men who came from nearby farm villages who were engaged in heavy labor in cement factories. Yet their commitment to the local community did not mean that these workers were transient employees. In fact, their average seniority exceeded that of machinists in engineering works, whose working conditions were far better. Similarly, average seniority was greater among "the motley collection" of women or children from impoverished families in large urban centers like Imamiya in Osaka, who commuted to part-time work in match factories—sometimes caring for their children while working in the factory—than it was among workers in spinning mills that had introduced a whole array of relief and aid measures.[14] Of course, seniority by itself is not a sufficient index of the workers' social stability, but it does indicate a degree of commitment that may be a necessary precondition for workers to maintain their own cultural life.

These examples show that in the early years of the emergence of a Japanese proletariat, workers who were not separated from their families had the ability to incorporate capitalistic culture as a limited and instrumental part of their lives. But workers plagued with homesickness, who had lost their ties to their home community, could not do this. The women who worked in the spinning mills were certainly willing to endure hardship. If they believed they could go home whenever they wished, they might have stuck it out at one factory instead of moving aimlessly from job to job and sacrifing their accumulated "forced savings" each time they moved. But they lacked this certainty. Many of the unskilled workers lived in isolation from their homes, and they saw their entire way of life smashed by the onslaught of liberal culture. Handicapped by their lack of high-grade skills, they drifted in the margins of a competitive society.

What, then, of the conditions facing the artisans and skilled workers at this initial stage of industrialization? Here, too, the communal groups of the urban artisan, built upon the paternal labor-boss system and the master-apprentice relation, were collapsing rapidly. The famous social reporter, Yokoyama Gen'nosuke, wrote in 1899 that carpenters, masons, stone cutters, and shipwrights, "unlike the spinning and textile plant workers who have so recently emerged, possess rich work experience and have created a certain society among themselves." But Yokoyama claimed that "recently," in the face of "competition upon competition," even these traditional craftsmen have experienced erosion of their age old "moral principles," which involve such practices as setting standard fees to abstain from poaching each others' regular customers.[15] Moreover, it was customary for a young man in one of these crafts to live in the home provided by his boss, serve a fixed period of apprenticeship in accord with guild regulations, and then join the guild after acquiring the skills of a full-fledged artisan. Yokoyama observed that master artisans had come to ignore "the craft training that is the lifeblood of the artisan" and that they had begun to compete for customers, paying no heed to the deteriorating quality of work in their trade. "There are no longer such things as human feeling (*ninjō*) or obligation (*giri*)," lamented Yokoyama.[16] Apparently, the world of the craftsman was not able to survive the storm of competition that swept across modern Japan.

If artisans in traditional workplaces were unable to cope with competition, this was even truer of skilled workers who managed to gain employment in large factories, either practicing trades with indigenous roots—as blacksmiths, boilermakers, or metal casters—or trades such as lathe-worker, assembler, or fitter, which involved new technologies. None of these workers had any ties to a worker society outside their own enterprise. According to *Conditions of Factory Workers,* these men acquired their skills in one of two ways: (1) Some were nominally the direct employees of a large company, but were in fact apprenticed to a particular master worker and followed him into a large factory, working under his direction and receiving training from him; (2) others were in name and reality the direct employees of a factory, which designated them as "trainees" and offered some formal training program.[17] Over time, the former declined in number as the latter increased. Both patterns are versions of an apprentice system; but because few indigenous artisanal skills were relevant to the technologies of Japan's new heavy industries and because no trade unions existed that might have standardized the vocational education offered the young trainees, the latter had no secure prospect of advancing to the level of a well-rounded skilled worker. Instead, companies tended to take advantage of their trainees as a convenient form of cheap labor.

In this context, the "skilled worker" with credentials from a defined experience as an apprentice or trainee did not emerge as a socially normative category. This is a distinctive feature of Japanese labor history. The uncertain prospects offered a worker trainee in a large factory led these young men to "leave a particular factory and find employment elsewhere as soon as they had acquired enough skill to earn a slightly decent wage."[18] As they repeatedly changed jobs, these men were dubbed the "travelling workers."

Of course, one could take a positive view of the emergence of travelers and see in them a confidence rooted in the common currency of their skills as machinists. Still, I would distinguish their job switching from that undertaken by socially credentialed skilled workers in the West, who were also union members. The Japanese travelers appear to me as itinerant workers who had not developed a strong moral economy. Several aspects of working life among the traveling machinists support this view. They had no customary conception of a "standard workday." They accepted overtime as a matter of course. They welcomed "contract" or "piece rate" wages that stirred up competition among fellow workers. They accepted arbitrary labor management practices that encouraged sycophancy. All these practices led Yokoyama Gen'nosuke to castigate the skilled workers, asking, "Are factory workers opportunists who would do anything for the sake of money?"[19]

Moreover, in contrast to Western workers who had completed the first stage of their take-off, Japan's early industrial workers often lacked a fixed commitment to an occupation. Though perhaps an extreme case, the meandering work history of "An Rui" illustrates this tendency dramatically.[20] This worker had changed jobs fifty-seven times in twenty years. He described himself as a victim who had suffered "darkness and tears" (the literal meaning of his pen name). On job number six, at "a Naval Shipyard," he was invited to become a "regular worker." Among other benefits, this status would grant him a 300- to 400-yen bonus after working ten years, plus the right after that span to take a special four-month paid leave in addition to his normal holidays. But An Rui "turned this down without a second thought. After all, I was young and vigorous. I thought, 'why in the world would I want to grow old in a place like this?'" For this man, "a place like this" probably meant a specific factory. But it could also have meant a particular job, that of a lathe operator.

Conditions of Factory Workers had earlier stated of machinists that "from the outset very few of those who begin work in this trade make it a lifelong career. Most quit after getting bored with the work or after saving some of their wages."[21] These men usually hoped to become owners of small machine shops or retail stores after quitting jobs in large factories. At this early stage in Japan's industrial growth, factory workers *as yet* had no faith that a lifetime of wage labor could offer them security, and they were *no longer* able to rely on a community from which they might launch a new collective endeavor to achieve this security. Japan's new class of skilled workers included "former samurai, former students and many with considerable education."²² With an ambivalent mix of self-confidence and self-hatred, these men hewed to the ideals of "getting ahead and succeeding in the world," (*risshin shusse*), seen then as "the guiding spirit of modern Japan."²³

Experiments with Independence and Self-Help

What was the relationship between the lives of these workers and the rest of the inhabitants of Japan's lower-class society in the early twentieth century? Briefly stated, even skilled wage workers were part of the *saimin* ("thin people"), as impoverished slum dwellers were called at the time. The modern working class was enveloped in the world of the urban lower class, a motley army of rickshaw pullers, day laborers, artisans, itinerant peddlers, home workers, and providers of all sorts of petty services. Mixed into older communities of the "traditional poor" engaged in a variety of undesirable trades were households whose members had left their home villages for the cities en masse, as well as factory workers' households in which both spouses held jobs.

Tsuda Masumi makes a detailed comparison of the living standards of the factory workers and the lower-class urban dwellers. He concludes that around the turn of the twentieth century, factory workers in modern sites such as the Ishikawajima shipyard or the huge army arsenal at Koishikawa "had an identical living standard" with that of the typical lower-class city dwellers such as rickshaw pullers. He also maintains that a decade later, on the eve of World War I, "at least the lower half [of factory workers]. . . were situated at the same level as the slum dwellers."²⁴ Surveying the various constituents of the labor market, one finds that unskilled workers who migrated from farm villages lived in the slums and that the young apprentices of skilled workers were children in slum dwellers' households. The slums were home to failed male factory workers whose wives and children worked at odd jobs to support the family.

To appreciate the distinctive features of this period, one only has to consider for a moment the enormous difference between the lifestyles of blue-collar workers in large companies in Japan today and their slum dwelling counterparts who worked in major factories eighty years ago. Although the former are still burdened with overtime assignments they cannot refuse, most of them are able in their own lifetime to purchase a home, grant their wives the option of leaving the labor force, and send their children to college. The workers of eighty years ago had no social security whatsoever, and could not hope to advance in this fashion. Moreover, under a hierarchical regime of labor management lacking even a nominal commitment to equality or fairness, they could not claim any pride in being a factory worker. It was not only the miners (who "felt as if they were condemned criminals") and the morose female textile mill workers but also the "high-spirited" factory workers with an artisanal spirit who felt that they were essentially paupers. "Workers" and "paupers" may have been differentiated conceptually in Japan by the start of this century, but in the reality of lived experience the two terms were then synonymous. The social world of the urban lower class embraced so many different elements that one cannot call it simply a worker society. For its inhabitants to construct a collectivity resistant to bourgeois society on the basis of trade solidarity or to establish groups for "community mutual aid" was an almost hopeless undertaking.

And yet, some very significant appeals to organize labor unions were directed at these workers. Yokoyama may have lamented that "even though the forces of capitalism are rising day by day, Japanese workers compete with each other, and each year their status is declining. Yet they pay no heed to this. Oh, what foolish fellows," but this same man issued a dramatic call to arms the very next year.[25] He began with a meditation on the desperate state of the factory worker: "Dear factory workers who are engaged in sacred labor: Those who lack the means to earn a living are paupers. Paupers are burdens on the society. Nothing could be more shameful to a human being. How then do you feel about the fact that 60 to 70 percent of your fellow workers live just like paupers?" Yokoyama went on to exhort workers to stop complaining behind the backs of labor managers who encourage toadyism, stop taking out their anger on their wives or getting drunk in despair, and instead to "join hands with large numbers of workers, make plans with unions, and confront the factory owners with a list of your complaints."

Yokoyama's anguish and his call to action were echoed by Katayama Sen, a pioneer union organizer in the late 1890s. Katayama called for workers to awaken to their plight, asserting, "laborers working for wages are proletarians; they are not recipients of charity. They are not being supported by the society. On the contrary, they are the ones who are sustaining society with their labor."[26] His goal was to help workers to organize trade unions.

> Today when a factory worker experiences some disaster he has to rely on the help of others. This results in considerable loss of face. Sometimes he has nobody to turn to for help, and he falls into deep trouble. On the other hand, to get help from a union is not to take charity; it is to take money that he is entitled to receive through prior arrangement. This does not entail any loss of face at all. Also, because [unions] take measures to help members cope when disaster strikes, one need not demean oneself out of worry over difficult times. Thus the spirit of self-help and self-confidence are strengthened, and consequently the dignity of the factory workers is greatly enhanced.[27]

Katayama elsewhere continued this argument:

> When the spirit of independence is weak, work cannot be performed effectively. When a worker does not realize the significance of his place in society, he is likely to leave his job or lose his self-respect. How can we prevent a worker from falling into such a negative state of mind? How to arouse his spirit of independence and make him realize the importance of his position? The way to accomplish this is to have the workers organize unions. This will enable them to help each other in good times and bad, augment their strengths and overcome their weaknesses. . . . The value of unions is evident from examining history. Unions have enabled workers to build their spirit of independence and self-esteem, helping them to improve their skills on their own without relying on capitalists, to support each other in times of disaster and sickness, to enhance their dignity, and to uplift their moral principles.[28]

With hindsight it is not difficult to see that one premise of these appeals to Japanese workers is a discriminatory attitude toward "paupers," presented as a parasitic class who have only themselves to blame. But one must still recognize the profound significance of this appeal to the workers' sense of independence, self-reliance, autonomy, and mutual assistance. Katayama and others were arguing that only by organizing their own "society" could wage laborers be able to survive as workers.

Several organizations were created in response to such appeals for workers to follow, in essence, an Anglo-American path to the take-off of a worker society; these included the Metalworkers Union, the Japanese Railroad Reform Society, and the Printers Union. But the very modes of thought and behavior criticized by Katayama and others prevented these groups from fulfilling the expectations of their founders. The Metalworkers Union tried to help members find employment, but in the face of the ethos of skilled workers described above, it was unable to impose the basic rules of a craft union to regulate master-apprentice relations and entry to a trade. Further, the union could not build a system of unemployment insurance on its own, and its mutual aid system for sickness and death quickly ran into financial problems.[29] When designing the system, union leaders based their projections on the aid system used by the American Federation of Labor, but the much higher rates of sickness and death in Japan led to a revenue shortfall, and the benefits were soon cut sharply. Finally, after an initial surge of entrants, membership stagnated among workers with steady jobs, whose dues or contributions might have stabilized union finances. Although the Police and Public Order Law enacted in 1900 virtually wiped out the unions of the late 1890s, these groups were declining before this final blow.

Following the collapse of this first cluster of unions, the early history of labor organizing in Japan can be summed up as follows: Katayama became a political socialist. It was almost as if he had adopted the ideal of a commoners' restoration, earlier expounded by Tokutomi Sohō, a pioneering journalist who asserted that all Japanese people were equal under the emperor. Katayama declared that under "Our Constitution" it was possible to enact reformist laws in the Diet, and thus "it [would] be simple to practice socialism in Japan." His most important opponent among the early socialists, Kōtoku Shōsui (executed in 1911 for "high treason") sharply criticized Katayama and his colleagues. Kōtoku maintained the Diet was useless; workers needed bread, not political power, food and clothing, not laws.

This critique was telling, but Kōtoku and his faction were nonetheless insensitive to the need to formulate a logic of labor that might help working people sustain themselves and construct a worker society. When miners and factory laborers around the nation engaged in unprecedented riots and strikes following the Russo-Japanese War (1904–1905), activists such as Katayama and Kōtoku published accounts of these acts and built some ties to the workers themselves. This incipient alliance raised public awareness (and fear) of the socialists, but the actions of the strikers and rioters were not related to the theoretical struggles among the intellectual "advocates of isms." Further, the bloody suppression of these protests forced union organizers and socialists on the defensive. Thus, when the Factory Act was finally ratified by the Diet in 1911, the bureaucrat most responsible for writing and promoting the law, Oka Minoru, proudly proclaimed that Japan was "devoid of labor problems of the kind that prevails in the West." This law, he said, was enacted *not as a cure but as a preventive measure* against the "labor disease"—in today's terms "the British disease"—and he added, "the laws were enacted without the workers asking for them."[30] Even though Katayama persisted in arguing that the government should not "protect" workers by means of labor laws, insurance, or public aid, but rather should grant "freedom to organize and to strike," Japanese workers in the age of early industrial capitalism did not achieve a first stage of take-off similar to that of Euro-American workers.

After a so-called wintry era of repression between the Russo-Japanese War and 1911, a second round of labor movement activities commenced at the start of the Taishō era (1912–1926). The Yūaikai (Friendly Society) was organized in 1912 in a spirit of nonconfrontation and self-help similar to that of worker organizations of the 1890s. After several years of growth and an influx of both assertive young workers and university graduates, the Yūaikai moved in the direction of a more aggressive unionism. With perhaps 30,000 members, it took on a new name in 1919, the Nihon Rōdō Sōdōmei, or Sōdōmei (Japan Federation of Labor), and adopted a platform reflecting influences of Leninism, syndicalism, and British trade unionism. The spirit of this body had clearly become one favoring labor-capital confrontation. Also in the immediate years after World War I, these union ideologues joined hands with a segment of the old guard of skilled workers—

who were being driven out of the mainstream production processes of big business—and carried out a number of major strikes. In these acts, workers challenged the state and capitalists who firmly rejected any move toward industrial democracy.

Nonetheless, I am not convinced that ordinary workers of this era maintained a widespread or deep commitment to ideas of collective self-help independent of reliance on business or the state. According to contemporary observations by Yanagida Kunio, Japan's pioneer in the field of folklore studies and ethnography, workers lacked a secure social foothold, and labor unions were unable to replace or restore institutions of autonomous community mutual aid that in the past had helped ameliorate poverty.[31] Specifically, unions did not adequately compensate for the declining function of "the labor boss system." What Yanagida describes as the "poverty of isolation" persisted in the lives of the workers. Of course, this poverty of isolation, in the absence of a clear plan of action, on occasion helped energize the famous rice riots *(kome-sōdō)* and labor disputes, but through the 1920s and into the 1930s, as Japan moved to a system of fascism under the emperor, many Japanese workers focused on securing a stable position in a large corporation, rather than seeking to build independent organizations.

The Route to a Japanese-Style Take-Off

The term *nenkō* is often, and incorrectly, translated as seniority. In fact, it is a compound made up of two words, *nen* and *ko*, which, respectively, refer to seniority and merit. The meaning of merit can be further defined as consisting of two components, demonstrated performance and latent ability. A system of wages based on *nenkō*, correctly understood as seniority *and* merit-based pay, has been a defining feature of Japan's labor-management relationship from pre–World War II through the postwar years. Other key features have been a system of long-term employment, lump-sum retirement payouts, company-based welfare provisions, and occasional mobilization of temporary workers. To briefly summarize, I simply note that the following conditions brought this seniority and merit system into existence in the 1920s and 1930s. First, a two-tier structure of monopolistic big businesses and small companies emerged. Second, a process of rationalization took place in which artisanal skilled workers were replaced by skilled and semiskilled workers trained by the company and promoted from within. Third, a profound and lengthy depression choked off employment opportunities and threatened the economic foundations of farming villages. Fourth, the national institutional framework provided neither adequate social insurance nor a legal system of labor unions. Under these four conditions, the seniority and merit system of labor management allowed corporations to retain a segment of the second generation of the Japanese working class as "homebred workers."

Japanese workers basically accepted this system and worked for reform only within its confines. In so doing, they followed a course of take-off in which a Western style of unionism had little impact on their thought or behavior. Why did they accept and work within such a system? Three reasons come to mind.

First, by accepting the initiatives of prewar managers, workers were able to confirm that their labor held social value. When a worker endured a job with pride, that labor gained a public as well as a private significance. In private terms, the job provided a living to the worker; in public terms, it brought recognition from fellow workers.

The isolated workers of the early industrial era, before this system emerged, received ambiguous public recognition at best. On one hand, the huge Tōyō Spinning Company's "guiding principles for training" spinners offered only private recognition, as they told the trainers that "you should remember that the factory girls have come to work here in order to make money. You should strive to ready them for the most coveted status of piece-rate workers as quickly as possible."[32] On the other hand, a spinning song referred to a sort of public recognition in the refrain that "factory girls are the only ones who earn foreign exchange." But this claim is too abstract to be credible as the true sentiments of the spinners. Is it plausible that women spinners of that era, or male workers, for that matter, labored assiduously to earn foreign exchange to profit the Great Japanese Empire which offered only meager reward for their efforts?

But the labor-management policy of large corporations of the 1920s and 1930s began to offer a sort of public recognition. As production processes became increasingly integrated, these companies taught their workers not only that individual achievement determined the well-being of fellow workers but also that their combined labor determined the success or failure of the enterprise upon which all depended. Japanese workers took this preaching to heart not because they inhabited a groupish culture incompatible with individualism; instead, common people who sought a community that offered some public recognition could hardly avoid taking such claims seriously.

Second, by accepting management initiatives, workers gained some long-term social security. The explanation here is simple. Not only the unskilled but even those with considerable ability can be stranded. As Yūaikai founder Suzuki Bunji wrote, "For some unforeseen circumstances they lose their job, and lose their workplace. They are like men who have fallen into an old well in the middle of the meadow. They may yell and scream for help, but no help will come."[33] But if one found a job in a large company, one could hope to avoid such a predicament. The impoverished character of government-funded social insurance, the lack of unemployment insurance, and the existence of some company-based welfare combined to make such jobs attractive.

Moreover, technological innovations were making it increasingly difficult for the aging "traveler" type of worker with artisanal skills to make ends meet. But as long as such a man abandoned his former determination never "to rot into old age in a place like this," he could sustain himself as he aged by clinging to a job at a single large firm that offered wages reflecting seniority and merit, plus a lump-sum retirement payment. The wage and employment practices of the *nenkō* system in effect substituted for the functions of a labor union—increasing wages, guaranteeing employment, and providing mutual aid—and thus hammered home to workers the idea that unions were unnecessary. Can one not then say that Japanese corporations devised a system that prevented worker society from taking off along a Euro-American path? In 1921 the workers at the huge Kawasaki and Mitsubishi shipyards in Kobe went on strike together. They demanded recognition of collective bargaining and a union cutting across enterprise boundaries. In retrospect, this great dispute, involving over 20,000 shipbuilders, was the decisive labor-capital confrontation that set the course of the Japanese workers' take-off. The strike ended with the dismissal of 1,300 workers and the arrest and jailing of 100 men. The Kobe Federated Yūaikai (Friendly Society) was driven out of big business in the region. With this outcome, an alternative route of take-off was closed off.

The third factor behind the workers' acceptance of the *nenkō* system, and a distinctive feature of modernity in Japan, was the participation of workers in a social system that allowed some interclass mobility. By the 1920s, the 1880s and 1890s ethos of the freewheeling pursuit (if not always the achievement) of social advancement and success had long since evaporated. In its place had emerged a spirit of, and the institutional mechanisms for, the supremely well-ordered pursuit of success. Ambitious young men now aspired to advance by rising up the steps of major organizations, and one's point of entry and destination were both determined by one's education.[34] According to the late Fujita Wakao, an eminent labor sociologist in the early postwar years, employees first were clearly differentiated on the basis of education into a clerical and managerial staff with a middle school or high school education, and factory workers who had completed elementary school. They were then further ranged along a hierarchical ladder within each of these two categories. But finally, a narrow path for advancement was created through which a temporary factory worker could become a regular worker, and a regular factory worker could become a staff employee.[35] Looking back from the present, this system seems rigidly hierarchical and status-bound.

Nonetheless, this social world probably offered Japanese workers more opportunity to rise vertically across class boundaries than did Euro-American workplaces divided into horizontal classes of unskilled, skilled, and white-collar workers. For under the *nenkō* system, Japanese workers could at least advance within their level, and might even rise into the next level. Also, intergenerational mobility was possible, because workers could possibly use their wages that rose to reflect increased seniority and assessments of merit to provide their sons with an education greater than their own. "Success" for a male worker in prewar Japan could mean several things: rising himself to the level of staff worker, starting a small business after retirement, or enabling a child to enter the ranks of the white-collar "salaryman." The percentage of workers who actually succeeded in any of these endeavors is less important than the fact that many workers certainly expended great energy in trying. Moreover, the *nenkō* system offered some degree of security even to those who failed to win promotion, so long as they continued to serve the company faithfully. Considering that only the student sons of wealthy farmers had any realistic hopes of success in the heady late-nineteenth-century heyday of the ethos of the self-made man, the workers' hopes of rising in society were not particularly diminished when they accepted the *nenkō* system.

By their acceptance of this basic framework, some of those in Japan's second generation of male factory workers escaped from a life in which basic survival required that their wives take in piecework at home and their children scrounge for odd jobs and forego even compulsory elementary education. Such men were no longer faced with a daily anxiety that some chance occurrence might throw them into the depths of poverty; their living standards were no longer those of slum dwellers. In essence, they were able to put distance between themselves and those remaining in lower-class society.

By the mid-1920s (the end of the Taishō period), the number of factory workers living in the slums began to decrease.[36] The workers employed in large factories no longer quit or switched jobs frequently, driven by feelings of inferiority and helplessness mixed with wounded pride. They began to settle down and identify themselves as workers (regular employees) in a specific company. Japan's company society, which even today is the site of an internally contained "workers society," was created in this fashion. In later years, as external conditions changed, the enterprise-specific union came to be a constituent element of this society.

Even though this take-off into an enterprise-focused workers' society did not follow Western models, it was an *individualistic* choice of Japanese workers. Many theorists of "the Japanese" at home and abroad will object to this claim. The conventional view of such observers is that Japan's workers, in contrast to those of the West, were originally group-oriented people, as seen for example in the ethos of their family system. Given this value orientation, the argument goes, Japanese workers easily accepted managerial paternalism or "family-ism" and the concept of the company as "one big family." Even today, such people argue, Japan's workers have not been able to develop a sense of independence as individuals or citizens within the company.[37]

I object to such a view. If individualism is a concept that embraces competition on the basis of equal opportunity, either to demonstrate one's abilities or to enhance one's private life, then the philosophy of organized workers in the West was not individualistic. These workers did not take off by forming unions as a means to achieve individualistic goals. They formed unions as institutions of collective self-governance and self-help, out of a belief that average workers could not survive by competing as individuals in bourgeois society. That is to say, they defended a mode of living qualitatively different from the competitive lifestyles of those people outside their organization. I do not believe that this sort of collective ethos, in which workers sustained a tacit understanding with each other and strove to achieve independence from the state and the corporation, was fundamentally alien to workers in Japan. But I do believe that in the early history of Japanese factory labor, rapid political and economic "progress" posed a profound threat to the traditional community, its mutual aid organizations, and the extended family system rooted in this community. As a result, workers were cast out as isolated individuals into an urban "mass society" where the culture of free competition reigned unchecked.[38]

If the tempo of modernization in a given society is slow enough to allow workers to remain part of artisanal or agricultural communities as they enter the wage labor market, these new producers might build a culture of collective self-help out of still-viable, prior customs of mutual aid. Such a situation prevailed, if barely, in the West, but in Japan it did not. The combined force of a new, competitive organizational principle of using so-called men of talent selected through the school system and a political framework that completely rooted out independent movements of resistance, ruled out a Western form of take-off. And in an ironic reversal, this created a situation in which people who were at a disadvantage in individualistic competition had no choice but to appropriate the philosophy of individual competition to defend their place in state and society.

Japanese capitalists then articulated programs of managerial paternalism, literally "managerial family-ism," to induce these workers to join the pseudo-community of the firm. Now, the extended family system of Japanese commoners at the time may have been a basically classless structure in that all its members shared the hardships of daily life; but the corporation was a fundamentally hierarchical system. For this very reason, just as the emperor-centered state denied in shrill tones that class conflict existed in Japan, the corporation presented itself as a community, as one big family; so one must take care not to misread the relationship between this pseudo-community of the company and older communities among commoners. Japanese workers did not accept the appeal to join the company community because they maintained strong, ongoing links to an older, organic community; they did so because they had been forced out of traditional communities and lived in a state of isolation.

I find support for this claim, ironically enough, in the work of an eminent scholar of Japanese management history, Hazama Hiroshi, who generally adheres to the view that management built paternalism directly upon older forms of communal life. Hazama carefully examined managerial ideology and practice industry-by-industry, and he in fact discovered an *inverse* relationship between paternalism and traditional community. When family or community exerted a strong pull on workers, they were relatively less dependent upon managerial paternalism; where community had broken down, paternalism flourished.[39]

The contradiction between my claims that in the Japanese take-off workers were forced to choose individualistic competition and that workers sought to recover a lost community in the workplaces of big business is more apparent than real. To depict Japanese workers as people unwilling to undertake collective endeavors under any circumstances would be as foolish as to embrace without qualification the common wisdom concerning their groupishness. In fact, as workers began to identify as members of the corporate community, they sought security through equality of treatment with their fellow employees. They did so by appropriating and reinterpreting the principle of compensation for seniority and merit. In the most dramatic moments of the early postwar labor movement, organized workers openly demanded a working-class version of the *nenkō* system. But this is a topic for the following chapters. In the prewar and wartime era, the climate of the enterprise-dominated society was too harsh to allow these demands to succeed.

A corporation in which reward is based on assessments of merit and ability, plus length of service, forms a fundamentally hierarchical society saturated with the culture of free competition. A basic premise of the corporation is the need to control total wage cost and the total number of workers, and competition among fellow workers is therefore promoted not only to determine one's rank in the company but one's wage level and job security as well. When one worker wins in this competition, a fellow worker loses. And because the workforce is not separated into impermeable, horizontal class divisions, one is competing from the time of hiring to the day of retirement. In contrast to American business organizations, which generally evaluate worker performance in objective terms of manifest performance on clearly defined jobs, workers in Japan are required to prove their worth in terms of potential ability over the long haul and in terms of their total quality as a person. In the world after the take-off of a worker society in Japan, the course of competition and rivalry was more clearly visible than before.

In this world, the few who succeeded in winning high ratings for their ability and loyalty over long years of service inevitably came to scorn the large number who did not succeed. Because the *nenkō* system in theory offered equal opportunity to workers to compete to demonstrate their ability, it ruled out any fundamental critique of the system as unjust. For the same reason, it produced in those on the lower rungs of the hierarchy an acute awareness of low status and the desire to escape it. Such workers came to attribute their status not to bad luck, but to their lack of ability or their failure to work hard enough. For this reason, Japanese workers in the post-take-off world could take no pride in their status as workers. Inhabitants of the company society might differentiate themselves from the general run of workers because they had a certain guarantee of a livelihood, but their lives at work were no less demanding than those of the outsiders, for they were constantly reminded of the need to work hard and repay management for granting them the status of an insider.

Features of the Japanese-Style Take-Off

The lives and thoughts of men and women who participated in the take-off of a worker society in Japan contrasted sharply to the experience of Euro-American workers in their take-off. The participants in the Japanese take-off covered a wide social range. At the upper levels, a middling group of white-collar office employees spilled over ambiguously into the sphere of the managers, whereas the lower bounds of participation were demarcated with no ambiguity by the wall erected around the great factories of Japan's modern capitalist sector. The workers who groped toward a take-off within these bounds found themselves manipulated from above by the labor management policies of elite company personnel and threatened from below by workers in small plants and by nonregular part-time workers who endured even more arduous labor than they did. Pressed from both sides, these participants in the take-off of Japanese workers imbibed and were driven by a spirit of competition and a desire to rise in the company's hierarchy; they displayed very little of the self-imposed separation from a culture of free competition that marked the take-off among organized workers in Europe and North America. Putting this point in more positive terms, one can say that in their take-off Japanese workers strove to emulate the culture of the middle class of an economically expanding nation, a culture dominated by an ethos of social advance, of "competition enabling demonstration of ability, leading to success." The site of this take-off was the corporation.

However appealing the ultimate destination, committing oneself to such a take-off forced an individual worker into a desperate struggle for survival. Even workers who possess the right to vote or a system of social security will find it impossible to create an independent culture if they must venture out into the bourgeois world as isolated individuals or members of isolated nuclear families. If Japan's workers lost their autonomy of thought and behavior, was this not the direct result of the absence of a homegrown working-class society—be it an extension or a reconstruction of a preexisting society—that could have helped them develop values sustaining a position independent of, or opposed to, the culture of free competition? An independent workers' ideology and an autonomous worker society are mutually dependent; one cannot exist without the other.

In 1977 I had an opportunity to speak with the widow of a worker employed for thirty years at Japan Chemical Company's Southern Komatsukawa factory. He had died at age fifty-three due to an occupational disease originating in the use of chrome in the factory. He had started working in the factory in 1931, after graduating elementary school. Breathing chrome dust and making contact with chrome liquid, he worked frequent overtime and double shifts of sixteen straight hours, often giving up his days off. Even before World War II had begun, his eyes had become chronically red and his nose ran continuously, his throat was hoarse and his skin was covered with bandages. But this worker rarely ever expressed any bitterness about his work. On rare days off, he spent his time fishing. Although he had absolutely no desire for his children to work in the same factory, he himself never considered changing jobs. In 1967 he achieved his lifetime ambition of becoming a foreman and finally gained relief from direct production work. Of course, this man had worked so hard all those years for the sake of his family. With the savings from a lifetime of labor, he built, by local standards, a fairly large house (thirty *tsubo*, or about 640 square feet) in Edogawa Ward in Tokyo. He sent his oldest son to a part-time high school, his second son to a barbers' school, and he died from lung cancer in 1971 when his third son (now a white-collar worker) entered college.

This worker provided his family the gift of a living standard of a man who has taken-off into the working society of the large corporation. But he could not endow them with the pride of being a worker. This lonely father's life as a worker exemplifies the prewar Japanese mode of take-off, which has bequeathed a difficult legacy to the organized workers of postwar Japan.

Notes to Chapter 2

1. Karl Polanyi, *The Great Transformation* (New York: Rinehart and Company, 1957), p. 99.

2. Ibid., p. 101.

3. Arnold Weskar, *Chicken Soup with Barley* (London: Wesker Trilogy, Penguin Plays, [1959] 1960), p. 63.

4. Selig Perlman, *A Theory of the Labor Movement* (New York: Augustus M. Kelley, [1928] 1970), p. 6.

5. Milton Nadworny, *Scientific Management and the Unions, 1900–1930: A Historical Analysis* (Cambridge: Harvard University Press, 1955), p. 70.

6. C. Wright Mills, *White Collar* (New York: Oxford University Press, 1951).

7. P. B. Doeringer, and M. J. Piore, *Internal Labor Markets and Manpower Analysis* (Boston: D. C. Heath and Company, 1971).

8. Meiji (1868–1912), Taishō (1912–1926), and Shōwa (1926–1989) are "reign names," marking the reigns of successive Japanese emperors. Years in Japan are counted in terms of these reigns (thus, 1945 is Shōwa 20), and the reign names are used to mark historical eras as well. We are presently in the Heisei era.

9. Yamamoto Shigemi, *Aa, Nomugi Tōge* [Aah, Nomugi Pass] (Tokyo: Asahi Shimbun, 1986).

10. A point completely ignored in the narrow economism of rational choice ideologues. See, for example, Mark Ramseyer, "Credibly Committing to Efficiency Wages: Cotton Spinning Cartels in Imperial Japan," *Roundtable* (University of Chicago Law School, 1993), pp. 176–179.

11. On the health of textile workers, see William Johnston, *The Modern Epidemic: A History of Tuberculosis in Japan* (Cambridge: Harvard Council on East Asian Studies, 1996).

12. Nōshōmushō, shōkō kyoku [Bureau of Commerce and Industry of the Ministry of Agriculture and Commerce], *Shokkō Jijō* [Conditions of factory workers] (Tokyo: Koseikan, [1903] 1971), pp. 62, 78. This work is a report on the state of factory labor in Japan, published in 1903 by the Ministry of Agriculture and Commerce. The government, moved to consider establishing a factory law by the outbreak of social problems that accompanied the development of capitalism, directed the ministry to study the actual conditions of factory workers and to prepare for the drafting of legislation. The ministry's study variously examines hours of labor, employment terms, wages, living environment, and the actual condition of workers in diverse industries such as cotton spinning, silk reeling and weaving, metal trades, and glass and match production. The report realistically records the working conditions of the day. It is an indispensable document for understanding the state of labor during the period when industrial capitalism took root in Japan.

13. Hosoi Wakizō, *Jokō Aishi* [The sad history of women factory workers] (Tokyo: Iwanami Shoten, Bunko ed., [1925] 1954), pp. 287–299.

14. Nōshōmushō, *Shokkō Jijō*, pp. 79, 303–309.

15. Yokoyama Gen'nosuke, *Nihon no kasō shakai* [Japanese lower-class society] (Tokyo: Iwanami Bunko, 1949), pp. 73, 80.

16. Yokoyama Gen'nosuke, *Naichi Zakkyo-go no Nihon* [Japan after foreigners were granted residency right] (Tokyo: Iwanami Bunko, [1900] 1954), pp. 19–21.

17. Nōshōmushō *Shokkō Jijō,* pp. 244–245.

18. Yokoyama, *Nihon no kasō shakai,* p. 237.

19. Yokoyama, *Naichi Zakkyo-go no Nihon,* p. 32. For a slightly different view of the travelers, see Gordon, *Evolution,* chap. 1.

20. Suzuki Bunji, *Rōdō Undō Nijyūnen* [Twenty years in the labor movement] (Tokyo: Koyosha, [1931] 1966), pp. 134–143.

21. Nōshōmushō, *Shokkō Jijō,* p. 231.

22. Ibid., p. 228.

23. Mita Sosuke, *Gendai Nihon no Shinjō to Ronri* [Contemporary Japanese psychology and logic] (Tokyo: Chikuma Shobō, 1971), p. 185.

24. Tsuda Masumi, *Nihon no toshi kasō shakai* [Japan's lower-class urban sociey] (Tokyo: Mineruba Shobō, 1972), pp. 119, 136–137, 143–144.

25. Yokoyama, *Nihon no kasō shakai* (p. 314) for the first quote and *Naichi Zakkyo-go no Nihon* (pp. 39–41) for the second.

26. Cited in Kishimoto Eitarō, ed., *Shiryō: Nihon shakai undō shisō shi* [Documents: History of the ideas of Japan's social movement], vol. 3 (Tokyo: Aoki Shoten, 1968).

27. Katayama Sen, "Shokkō shokun ni yōsu" [To the factory workers] (1897), in Kishimoto, ed., ibid.

28. Katayama Sen, "Rōdō kumiai Kiseikai: Setsuritsu Shushi" ["Inaugural Manifesto" of the Preparatory Association for the Establishment of Unions] 1897, cited in ibid.

29. Katayama Sen, *Nihon no Rōdō Undō* [Japanese labor movement] (Tokyo: Iwanami Bunko, [1901] 1952).

30. Oka Minoru, *Kōjō hō ron* [Discourse on factory laws] (Tokyo Yuhikaku-shobo, 1917), pp. 142–143.

31. Yanagida Kunio, *Meiji Taishō-shi, sesō-hen* [History of Meiji and Taishō social phenomena] (Tokyo: Chūōkoronsha, [1931] 1974), pp. 299, 310.

32. Hosoi, *Jokō Aishi*, p. 253.

33. Suzuki, *Rōdō Undō Nijyūnen*.

34. For a study in English of this shift, with particular focus on the earlier period, see Earl Kinmoth, *The Self-Made Man in Meiji Japanese Thought: From Samurai to Salary Man* (Berkeley: University of California Press, 1981).

35. Fujita Wakao, *Nihon rōdō kyōyaku-ron* [On Japanese labor contracts] (Tokyo: Tokyo University Press, 1961).

36. For an English study of the changing social composition of the poor in prewar Japan, see Chubachi Masayoshi and Taira Koji, "Poverty in Modern Japan: Perceptions and Realities," in Hugh Patrick, ed., *Japanese Industrialization and Its Social Consequences* (Berkeley: University of California Press, 1976).

37. According to Ezra F. Vogel, the working people of Japan place group interest before individual interest, are content to make their own personal goals one with those of the group, take to heart the consensus opinion of their group, and are thoroughly immersed in this tradition of collectivism. Ezra F. Vogel, *Japan's New Middle Class* (Berkeley: University of California Press, 1963).

Arguments put forward by Japanese researchers are admittedly more subtle than this, but not by that great a margin. Works such as Hazama Hiroshi, *Nihonteki keiei* [Japanese-style management] (Tokyo: Nikkei Shinsho, 1971), and Iwada Ryūshi, *Nihonteki keiei no hensei genri* [The Organizational principle of Japanese-style management] (Tokyo: Bunshindō, 1977) present the mentality of Japanese salary-men in essence as a collectivism at odds with individualism. One can fairly call this the dominant conventional wisdom in Japan today.

38. I use "mass society" (*gunka shakai*) as the term is articulated by Kamishima Jirō, *Gendai Nihon no seishin kōzō* [The spiritual structure of contemporary Japan] (Tokyo: Iwanami Shoten, 1961).

39. Hazama Hiroshi, *Nihon rōmu kanri shi kenkyū* [Studies in the history of Japanese labor management] (Tokyo: Daiyamondo-sha, 1964).

3 J51, N36 JAPAN
J30, J21

Features of Organized
Workers in Postwar Japan

Fukuda Tatsuo and a Woman Miner

Fukuda Tatsuo was an activist in the early Yūaikai. In May 1917 he reflected on his life in the union's magazine, *Labor and Industry*:

> When everyone else is happily going to middle school, why must I alone go to work in this sad factory? When my old friends see me on the streets, they just razz me, calling me a smith's "blackie." They've rejected me. Oh, what's to become of me? My friends have become important and moved ahead in the world. Will I be scoffed at and spend the rest of my life at backbreaking jobs, an impoverished worker? Oh, I wish I could quit my job in the factory. I want to go to school. What has happened? What has happened? I am overwhelmed by a forlorn, weary feeling. I wish I could quit the factory and find another job. I feel hopeless. . . . The distribution of wealth in the society is so unbalanced. Poor parents are overwhelmed by all they cannot do for their children.[1]

Among the many similar statements that survive from this era, Fukuda's is especially poignant. It so powerfully voices the frustration and despair of factory workers at the time. It expresses the impassioned sentiments of the inhabitants of "lower-class society" who lacked any hope of realizing the ideal of "success in the world" (*risshin shusse*), which had so permeated society since the Meiji Restoration. Inseparable from this desperation was a latent ambition to escape from lower-class society, an ambition that manifested itself as soon as conditions allowed. For example, even in 1940, twenty-three years after Fukuda's lament, a time when the wartime labor shortage meant that "for the most part, skilled workers had nothing to worry about," a panel discussion published in an influential social policy journal included the following statements by workers "A" and "F":

> **A:**   I certainly don't want my children to become factory workers.
> . . . If possible I would like them to become government officials
> or something like that. . . .
> **F:**   No matter what we say, status [of a factory worker] is status,
> and I want to send my child to school so he can enter a profession
> like that [technician].[2]

The melancholy tone of such comments helps one to understand what
the children of people like Fukuda Tatsuo expected in the postwar era.
These self-deprecating voices hint at the kind of society that prewar working-class children sought to create as adults after the war, when they joined
progressive political forces. They wanted a society that offered all workers
a fair and honest chance to use their talents to get ahead. Was it not to this
end that workers tried to create an "equal society" in the postwar years? I
would argue that the reformist surge of the immediate postwar years sought
a society whose institutions afforded equality of competitive opportunity,
and that such equality was realized to a significant degree in the period of
rapid economic growth that followed.

But one must not ignore the voices of other workers who testify to the
shadows cast by such achievements. About 1960, Morisaki Kazue recorded
the following view of Japan's postwar experience from an old woman who
had worked as a coal miner.

> In those days (about 1927) all the miners in the coal pits helped one other.
> . . . We never distinguished between "ourself" and "another." It was a com-
> munal life. Somebody else's pain became our own pain. Just see, if you
> got sick, people constantly came and went [taking care of you]. We all
> worried about the sick as if we ourselves were sick. . . . Nowadays, think-
> ing back to those days, things seem worse since the end of the war. Every
> family has a television set, electric washing machine, electric rice cooker,
> electric fans, and some can send their children to college. Yes, there are
> people like that. But we're worse off in spirit. Anyway, I think so. In the
> old days, people didn't go to school. Many had no family register. Many
> were bums. Just surviving was a struggle. But we lived and breathed
> together in our heart and spirit. Nobody thought of knocking down other
> people to get ahead alone.[3]

As the interviewer herself noted, memory can easily turn to nostalgia,
and one cannot assume that these old workers told all concerning "things
that were painful to speak of."[4] But this mine worker's powerful evocation
of a sharp contrast between prewar and postwar conditions probably
reflects a so-called postwar situation not limited to mining towns: the
ascendance of a philosophy of individualistic competition in the postwar
years, a process that extended so far that even ordinary workers could not

deny its force. In this situation, feelings of solidarity—the belief that workers must help each other to protect their livelihoods—eroded at an accelerated pace.

I have discussed these statements of prewar and postwar workers at length for a reason. One can discover and define "postwar democracy," its power and its flaws, at precisely the site where former mine worker Fukuda's liberation from despair, achieved by his children's entry into a middle-class meritocracy, overlaps with this woman miner's deep sense of loss. Furthermore, I believe that the meaning of postwar democracy as thus understood by Japanese workers defined the characteristics of the postwar labor union movement.

One further comment by the woman who worked in the prewar mines is especially intriguing, as one begins to assess this complex formation called postwar democracy. She concluded, "But now the coal miners have a labor union, so their problems are not as awful as the town workers'. They try to make it so they can live comfortably as a community."[5] For this woman the postwar union of coal miners was an organization to preserve a community that was being lost even as living standards improved. But her view was not necessarily shared by postwar labor unions in general. In fact, from the early 1960s it would seem that many unionists came to consider such concerns to defend the community as anachronistic. Her observation has only come to have relevance at the present moment, as I seek a critical perspective on the behavior of unions during the period of rapid economic growth.

A Japanese Mode of Worker Thought

The men and women who embraced postwar democracy, created postwar labor unions, and became organized workers were above all inhabitants of the company society. This postwar point of departure reflects the characteristics of the *prewar* take-off of the workers in Japan.

By take-off I mean the social and ideological process in which a portion of the working class creates a worker society, a secure space in which working men and women find a community of fellow workers and nurture a tacit understanding of their situation, which, in turn, enables resistance. This understanding opposes a philosophy of competition based on individualistic demonstration of ability, a philosophy that had inexorably been spreading among pre-take-off workers. Instead of competition, a worker society posits security through equality and denies the individualistic aspiration to escape the working class. A strong labor union is nothing so much as the conscious embodiment of a worker society in which this tacit understanding prevails. Britain can be seen as one place where this trajectory is clear: take-off creating a worker society, generating a tacit agreement concerning labor union functions. In such a place, an extremely distinctive logic that defends the livelihood of organized workers comes into existence, a logic that differs from a "national common sense" affirming free competition as the highest value.

In Japan, however, such a take-off was repeatedly undercut for several reasons: the particular pattern of working-class formation, the rapidity of industrial modernization, and a political structure to integrate people into the nation by validating interclass mobility while sternly suppressing class-based attempts at industrial democracy. The resulting isolation of Japanese workers from each other, and the insecurity of their livelihoods, led one strata of the working class to opt consciously to seek security inside the big corporations that instituted seniority-and-merit-based pay, company-based welfare, and long-term employment.

This choice for security *inside* the firm decisively shaped the Japanese form of take-off. The company society gave scarce encouragement to an independent worker society that might have opposed the philosophy of efficiency and competition. The people who defined the Japanese take-off were controlled from above by labor-management programs of the corporate elite, and they were pressured from below by the arduous labor of temporary workers and workers in small shops. They imbibed a spirit of competition and ambition to move up the social ladder. Organized workers who led the drive for postwar reforms accepted such ambitions. They possessed at best a clouded tradition of working-class thought and behavior.

Even so, one cannot deny or ignore the fact that some very militant unions emerged after World War II. How can this be? I believe that in certain circumstances even workers whose sense of cultural distinctness is blurred can make themselves into severe critics of the wielders of power. When such people, who lack a "heretical" value system, nonetheless mount a critique, they charge the managing class with betraying the beautiful promises originally propounded to pacify the managed class. They demand that managers live up to their ideals.

The scholarship of Yasumaru Yoshio, Ichii Saburō, and Nunogawa Seiji on social movements in early modern Japan offers instructive insight into this process of appropriating the ideas of the rulers.[6] According to their studies, farmers who staged peasant uprisings had constructed a proud subjectivity through practice of a "conventional morality" of diligence, frugality, humility, and filial piety. But when their livelihoods fell to unbearable levels despite adhering strictly to these ideals, they brandished the publicly acknowledged Confucian ideal of "benevolent rule" to attack the actual behavior of their lords. This ideological course of peasants of the Tokugawa era (1600–1868), who lacked a heretical religious faith, offers a valuable analogy to the postwar labor union movement. It leads to the question: What was the conventional morality that provided postwar workers with ideals to use to indict their employers? In brief, this was first the idea that all the company's employees should be guaranteed regular wage increases and job security, and second, that all the people of Japan should be provided equal opportunities to improve their standards of living.

Both of these notions have been important ideals in the history of modern Japanese society. The former is in effect a call for the *nenkō* system rewarding merit and seniority. The latter has roots in the ideal of the all-embracing emperor system in that "the myriad people are equal before the august personage [of the *tennō* (emperor)]." But fulfilling these ideals was hardly the primary objective of the people who ruled various organizations in prewar or postwar Japan. In the prewar years, the corporate world and society in general was marked by profound discrimination and class distinction. Factory workers were not allowed to be full-fledged "imperial subjects." The emperor system did not in fact allow workers to engage in struggles such as strikes to win rights for, or a standard of living appropriate to, "imperial subjects."[7] But then, amidst the unprecedented immediate postwar crisis of disarray in the old power structure, emasculation of stringent credos of "endurance," the institutionalization of democracy "granted from outside," and an economic crisis that impoverished almost all Japanese people, a newly empowered labor movement allowed workers who had experienced continual betrayal of their hopes to liberate themselves from their humiliating prewar circumstances.

The stance of appropriating and seeking to bring substance to the ideals of rulers and managers may lack a certain fullness, in comparison to worker ideologies in the West. For example, Japan's organized workers have consistently seen themselves as employees of a specific firm. Whereas they have been reluctant to take a hard-headed view positing a working-class "us" opposed to a managerial "them," Japanese workers have thoroughly internalized this stance and mode of thinking. The task here is to specify more precisely what such men and women sought. To this end, one may divide the objectives pursued by organized postwar workers into three clusters and examine efforts to achieve these goals over the course of postwar history, roughly divided into ten-year periods.

Equality as an Employee

The first goal that postwar workers sought with their new unions was "equality as an employee." This involved a related set of demands. Unions first sought to destroy status distinctions premised on discrimination between white- and blue-collar workers. Organized workers demanded that companies undertake several major reforms: replace the "status-based" labels of "staff person" and "production person" with a single classification, literally "company person";[8] end the system of day wages for production workers and monthly salaries for staff, and calculate pay for all employees as a monthly salary; and eliminate differential status-based access to company welfare facilities. Immediately after the war, workers raised these demands vehemently and passionately, out of bitter anger at long-standing, invidious divisions.

Perhaps surprising at first glance, the superintendents of Japanese-style management only briefly resisted these demands of enterprise-based unions. Managers themselves recognized the need to reconfigure the hierarchy of employees in the face of several changes: increased differentation of tasks *within* the old "staff" category, the emergence of an intermediate group of "gray-collar" workers, and a narrowed gap in the educational backgrounds of production and office workers. For instance, an increasing number of female high school graduates were taking on lower-level office work, and large numbers of male high school grads were being hired as factory workers for the first time. Old distinctions between office and factory workers had been largely premised on differences in education; when levels of schooling for the two groups became similar, these divisions no longer made sense. Thus, by the late 1960s, distinctions based on educational background and social standing had been largely replaced by new divisions among workers based on gradations of "qualification" and ability to perform their jobs. Figure 3.1 offers a schematic picture of the contrast.[9] I shall discuss the significance of this new classification system in the following chapters. For the moment, the key point is that those inhabitants of the despised world of factory workers in prewar times—who now filled the category of regular employee—had become citizens of the corporation on a plane with white-collar workers.

A second change that gave workers a new equality as employees, a form of citizenship in the corporation, was a transformation of the *nenkō* wage system. Namely, all employees were guaranteed virtually automatic pay raises based on seniority. In the prewar version of the *nenkō* wage system, one completely governed by the logic of capital, pay raises were based on a complex mix of factors: the employee's social status, educational record, length of service, gender, the nature of the work being performed, performance evaluation, and managerial favoritism. By setting pay raises with these various criteria, managers were able to divide and thus control the workers, as well as control the total wage budget in a regular, predictable fashion, whatever the age distribution of the workforce.

Postwar labor unions seeking to change this system began with the principle that all employees deserved a secure livelihood. They insisted that all employees deserved the security of regular pay raises that provided a wage reflecting increased needs with age. Previously, regular pay raises had been granted only to the minority of super-loyal, "home-bred" workers hired directly out of middle school into company training programs. In the particular conditions of early postwar Japan, the form of equality sought by unions was not the internationally prevalent "equal pay for equal work"; rather, it was "equal pay for equal age," to be achieved by eliminating so-called discriminatory pay raises.

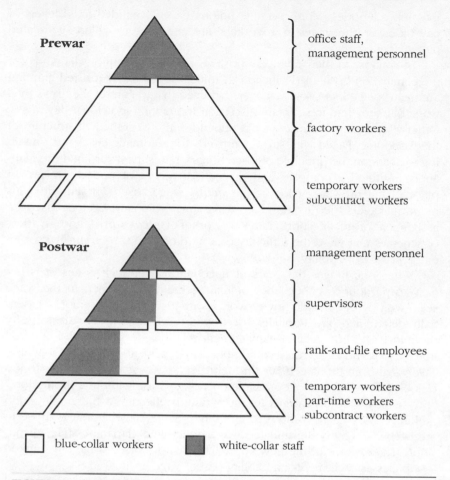

Prewar

} office staff,
   management personnel

} factory workers

} temporary workers
   subcontract workers

Postwar

} management personnel

} supervisors

} rank-and-file employees

} temporary workers
   part-time workers
   subcontract workers

☐ blue-collar workers   ▨ white-collar staff

FIGURE 3.1 Diagram of Corporate Personnel
Source: For the prewar situation see Tsuda Masaṁi, *Neñko teki roshi kankei ron*
[On seniority based industrial relations] (Tokyō: Mineruba shobo, 1968), p. 55.

The famous 1946 strike by the electric power workers' union (Densan) won a major concession: a pay structure in which wages primarily reflected age, seniority, and family size, with a small portion tied to a merit rating. Beginning with this drive for need-based pay, postwar labor unions have demanded some form or another of an automatic pay raise in virtually all their wage demands.[10] In the 1950s and 1960s, this entailed demanding an end to the practice of cutting back on wage increases when workers reached middle age (40 to 50 years old), seeking guarantees of an age-graded minimum wage scale and uniform pay increments, and opposing a "job-based" wage scale in which pay reflected company assessment of various job categories. More recently, unions have demanded fixed levels of pay based on the stages in a workers' life cycle, the so-called age-related pay guarantee.

In contrast to their relatively positive response to union demands for the elimination of status distinctions, capitalists stubbornly resisted granting automatic wage increases. Managers believed that to control the firm's total wage bill, they had to maintain discretion in granting individual pay raises. Otherwise, total wage costs would depend entirely on the age structure of the workforce. Faced with strong demands for automatic raises, yet unwilling to abandon the principle of discretionary raises, postwar Japanese managers instituted a complex and diversified system of periodic raises. In place of the prewar version of the *nenkō* wage based on seniority plus merit, managers tried to introduce wage and promotion ladders based on assignment of qualification grades to workers (*shikaku-kyū*), and a variety of schemes that rated the difficulty of a worker's job (*shokumu-kyū*) or an employee's work ability (*shokunō-kyū*).[11]

When one judges the years of negotiation over such issues, it is not easy to pronounce either labor or management the winner. In the wage scale won by the electric power workers in 1946, age and seniority essentially determined pay. Capitalists destroyed this system in its pure form by the mid-1950s, but as labor-management relations developed and matured in the 1960s and 1970s, they could not easily replace it with something else. Their goal from the late 1950s through the 1960s was to link wages to job classes, adhere strictly to a principle of "no pay raise without a promotion," and thereby structure wages into a pyramid reflecting a hierarchy of job rankings. They failed to do this, and when acute labor shortages arose in the late 1960s, they reformulated wage policy in a "Japanese-style" disposition. The essence of the new approach was to replace wage rates linked to job classes with merit- and ability-based wage evaluations.[12]

This effort to peg wages to the assessed qualifications or ability of employees fared better, for labor unions welcomed this shift. In "qualification" and "ability" pay systems, wages were at base understood to reflect the value added by a *person* rather than that added by a particular *job*. Depending on the interpretation of qualification and ability, these forms of wage-setting left room for pay to increase regularly, albeit with some individual variation, even without promotion up a ladder of jobs. Labor unions had for the most part already decided it was not realistic to defend a system of completely automatic seniority raises, and they saw these policies as appropriate to a reformed Japanese-style labor-management system. Thus, they did not respond with all-out opposition. As a result, pay scales taking account of qualifications and ability spread throughout big business in the late 1960s, together with the "new employee system," or *shain seido*. These reforms came to be regarded as the essence of capital-labor cooperation.[13]

Postwar labor unions, by discussing and bargaining with companies over these wage policies, did enable increased numbers of employees to receive pay raises regularly, and they reduced the incidence of highly arbitrary pay raises. But they were unable (perhaps unwilling) to resist when managers introduced multiple factors into the wage-setting process. This was not simply a matter of the union's strategic failure to defend the concept of fully automatic pay raises. Rather, organized workers accepted these various factors because the nature of work itself was not their major concern and because they felt a special affinity for principles of ability or merit.

The third dimension to the postwar achievement of "equality as an employee" was the effort to give substance to so-called lifetime employment. In the prewar period, no countervailing force constrained the logic of capital, which was concerned to preserve flexibility in the total size of the workforce. Any offers of "lifetime employment" remained rhetorical gestures. For the average worker, even the so-called regular worker, lifetime employment was no more than a possiblity. Managers maintained a pyramid-shaped distribution of workers in terms of both seniority and job; if they judged a regular worker to lack ability or dedication to the company, they could dismiss him freely. But postwar labor unions challenged this arrangement. At least until 1960, when companies announced dismissals of regular employees, enterprise-based unions were willing to engage in lengthy strikes.

Although most of these intense, sometimes violent, "antidismissal struggles" ended in defeat for the workers, corporate managers became acutely aware of the high cost of strikes. They came to believe it prudent to accept some limitations on their freedom to dismiss regular employees, even when cutbacks in temporary workers or the forced early retirement of women workers (steps that most unions did not contest) were not sufficient to reduce workforce size. To borrow Tsuda's nice turn of phrase, the essence of lifetime employment as a customary practice was a "tacit agreement to avoid labor disputes" between companies and their cooperatively inclined enterprise-based unions.[14] Because of this union stance, Japanese workers came to believe that "even if times are pretty tough, we have the right to work for this company until we retire."

Between the 1960s and the first oil crisis (1973–1974), conflicts between capital and labor over dismissals became less intense. In an era of labor shortage, managers were concerned more with finding workers than with firing them, and employees felt less need to rely on unions to preserve their jobs. But during this period of truce, a quiet trend continued in the dissolution of community-like work groups that had formed the basis for earlier struggles against dismissal. As a result, unions' interest in the day-to-day conditions of work decreased, and organized workers gradually concluded that job security depended upon economic growth rather than upon union resistance to corporate "rationalization" plans. This shift in thinking and the weakening of workplace community were mutually reinforcing. Employers *and workers* came to view economic performance as an external factor that "can not be helped." When the economy faltered in the decade after the first oil crisis (1975–1984), managers regained freedom to "streamline" excess personnel, including regular employees, without union opposition. Was this in any way different from the prewar situation? To answer this question, one must look outside the corporation.

Equality as a Member of the Nation

The second set of objectives for postwar unions was to raise the living standards of working people in general, both union and nonunion, to the level of an average "citizen of the nation."[15] To understand the significance of this goal, one must recall the prewar situation of industrial labor. Official ideology told all Japanese people they were equal under the emperor, but factory workers in fact constituted a lower social order than people in society at large.[16] In public perception, factory workers were losers or dropouts in the struggle for survival. Matsuzawa Hiroaki explains this well. On one hand, he argues, workers possessed a self-denigrating, despairing consciousness. Many were simply resigned to their plight. On the other hand, many workers displayed powerful ambitions to get ahead in the world and escape their class through self-realization and self-improvement.

These varied ambitions fostered several beliefs. First, that factory work was a natural vocation and the kind of work they were most suited to.[17] Second, that by fulfilling one's natural vocation one wins the right to full-fledged membership in the nation state. Third, that workers to some extent deserved their scornful treatment and, in order to join the general society, must remake their character—their overall conduct, their speech, dress, and leisure activities—into something acceptable to the mainstream.[18]

Prewar workers were unable to integrate the goals of realizing and improving themselves with that of establishing an independent, self-reliant existence as a distinct class, and many of the attitudes that impeded the linking of a drive for self-improvement to a consciousness of class survived into the postwar period. But the thinking of workers did change somewhat in the postwar years. As the prewar and wartime emperor system disintegrated, workers abandoned the concept of their natural or "suitable" vocation, which had posited service to the state as their primary responsibility. They also turned away from status-bound attitudes of self-denigration and resignation to a life of poverty. Assisted by labor unions, postwar workers pushed individual desires for an improved standard of living in two slightly different directions. One path was for blue-collar workers to raise their living standards to middle-class levels while retaining an identity as workers.

The other was to promote their children, the next generation of workers, to a higher social class. The regular pay raises discussed previously were viewed as a means to achieve a mainstream standard of living. That is, workers hoped over the course of a lifetime to own a modest home, accumulate adequate savings for old age, and provide their children a higher level of education than their own.

In part because Japan's prewar and wartime rulers had proudly proclaimed their society to be free from the divisive class conflicts and antagonistic class consciousness found in Western nations, in the early postwar era they did not seek to restrain the desire of workers for a mainstream life or bludgeon them into accepting a restricted status as worker. Moreover, postwar Japanese capitalism was compelled to recognize that Japanese consumers comprised their largest potential market. This recognition effectively reinforced the desires of postwar workers.

Thus, during the decades of rapid economic growth (1955–1975) the expanding economy led to labor shortages, large wage increases, and a high level of average wages. To some extent, of course, the simple fact of a labor shortage would have led to some wage increases even if organized workers had not demanded them. But in any case, the repeated large wage increases of these years dramatically improved the living standards of both organized and nonorganized workers, whose incomes increased due to the related pressures of a labor shortage and the annual wage offensives. Early signs of this change, in the first decade of high growth (1955–1965), included the standardization of clothing such that one could no longer distinguish factory workers from other people in public and the fact that working families shared in the mass accumulation of numerous consumer durables, including the "three precious jewels" (electric washing machine, electric refrigerator, and electric vacuum cleaner). And, of course, the television, the ultimate instrument of recreation and communication, spread more rapidly than any other product. It not only incorporated the workers culturally into the rest of the populace but also played a significant role in arousing their desire as consumers.

The consumer revolution reached a new level over the next decade (1965–1975). Spurred on by rapidly changing fashion trends, clothing became ever more colorful and glamorous. Workers now used their bonuses to purchase the "three new precious jewels" (color televison, air conditioner, and automobile).[19] A travel boom spread even among lower-middle-class households. During summer vacation, average urban working families combined trips to visit their ancestral homes in the countryside with auto excursions to national parks, where they avidly took photos with their new cameras. The albums full of pictures from these happy days no doubt boosted the spirits of workers during the many dreary days back on the job. In these same years, many organized workers purchased condominiums or small houses through corporate programs to encourage employee home ownership. Moreover, blue-collar union workers as well as white-collar workers now typically aspired to send their children to college. According to a 1977 survey, 72 percent of office workers and 49 percent of industrial workers planned to send their children to college.[20]

This improvement in the living standards of workers was in large measure enabled by an increase in the overall percentage of job holders in each household. This percentage can be calculated as the number of economically active household members divided by the total number of household members.[21] The proportion in 1955 was 31 percent, and this rose steadily to 41 percent in 1975. And according to a 1977 survey, in nuclear families 51.5 percent of wives and mothers in their forties in families with unmarried children held jobs. In families with only husband and wife, 55.6 percent of the women were economically active.[22]

Did this trend apply to families of workers in large corporations, where one important measure of a working man's success in the prewar *and* the postwar era had been whether his wife had to work? Consider the results of two surveys of households whose husbands worked in two big corporations (Table 3.1). Between 22 percent and 44 percent of the wives held jobs of some sort. A mutually reinforcing relationship surely existed between the emergence of these two-income households and the desire for a mainstream standard of living, between the rapid spread of part-time work among homemakers from the mid–1960s and the desire to possess consumer durables. A pithy poem by Shōzu Tsutomu, "The Sacred Family," offered an ironic criticism of this state of affairs: "Yes. Let's work hard, all together, for happy, happy days."[23]

Yet, to portray the increase in two-income families seeking to join the national mainstream solely in a negative light is an excessively dogmatic impulse. The second decade of rapid economic growth was arguably the time of the most stable material conditions for wage earners in Japanese history. Compare, for example, this portrait of postwar workers during the consumer revolution with images of prewar working people, whether miners perceived as "subhuman" or the female factory workers depicted by Hosoi Wakizō. Hosoi wrote of the dark expressions of young women who "feared the instruments of civilization," and who "dressed and adorned themselves with utter plain-ness."[24]

Men and women workers in the era of postwar growth, by contrast, asked, "What's wrong if a worker is sophisticated and affluent?" They wholeheartedly embraced the consumer culture and entered their children in the education race. To fulfill these desires they used the higher wages won by labor unions. And precisely because they satisfied their ambitions to a certain extent (granting that one cannot measure the exact contribution of labor unions in this process), many workers decided they had joined the middle-class mainsteam of society. In the case of workers in large com-

TABLE 3.1

Source of Income of Worker Households (%)

Age	Households of All Telephone and Telegram Workers Union Members[a]				Households of Yasukawa Electrical Workers[b]		
	30-34	35-39	45	55	30-34	35-39	Over 40
Income from household head only	54.7	58.8	50.3	49.9	67.8	66.5	53.6
Husband and wife working	28.6	22.6	24.1	14.7	13.8	18.8	21.4
Work at home, part-time and others	9.6	12.8	19.6	14.3	8.6	9.6	15.6

Sources: [a] Sōhyō Survey Monthly Report, no. 126 (February 1977), p. 28; [b] Federation of Electrical Workers' Unions, Survey Current Report (April 1977), p. 36.

panies, essentially synonymous with organized workers, the high proportion found in the middle-to-upper income categories clearly accounts for their mainstream consciousness (see Table 3.2). To be sure, following critics such as Kishimoto Shigenobu, one can question the certitude of this mainstream consciousness, but speaking simply in terms of the *relative level of consumption* of employees in big companies, one cannot deny its basis in material experience.[25]

In later chapters I shall ask what might be omitted or concealed by a discourse framed in terms of national equality. But here let me simply affirm that for postwar workers, who had seen their prewar and wartime rulers betray the publicly proclaimed concept of the equality of imperial subjects, the liberation of desire and the achievement of a certain degree of personal material security were the most authentic components of postwar democracy.

Minimum Livelihood Guarantees

The third set of objectives pursued by postwar labor unions aimed to establish systematic minimum livelihood guarantees for those who had the misfortune to fall by the wayside in competition with other workers. Endeavors to this end were indeed multifaceted. Within the company boundaries, union demands for job security and uniform raises were part of the effort to establish a stable minimum. In society at large, this drive included calls for welfare programs for the poor as well as for social insurance programs: unemployment insurance, injury compensation, health insurance, and pensions. Also in this category was the fight for a minimum wage extending to as many workers as possible.

The struggle for such forms of social security was particularly important to postwar Japanese workers because prewar institutions or customs, which had offered some social support in times of crisis, steadily declined in the postwar decades. (These included the support of an extended family, specifically the possibility of a man or woman returning to a family farm or fishing operation in an ancestral village.) The decline in primary sector population is so well known that I can dispense with statistical demonstrations. As for changes in family structure, the 1976 *White Paper on National Life* reveals that from 1955 to 1975 the percentage of nuclear households increased from 59.6 percent to over 64 percent, while the percentage of single-member households increased from 3.4 percent to 13.7 percent.[26] Though these growing numbers of urban workers living by themselves or in nuclear families were liberated from the demands of the old family system (the household [*ie*] system inscribed in prewar law and ideology), they could no longer count on a network of willing supporters in the case of old age or a misfortune such as unemployment or illness. Thus wage-earning workers in the decades of postwar economic growth felt increasing need

TABLE 3.2

Household Income Distribution Based on Employment Types—Households Divided into Four Levels by Income, in Order of the Top One-Quarter Down to the Bottom One-Quarter

| | Total | Lowest 25% | | | Top 25% | Average Annual Income Per Household | Percentage of Households in Different Employment Types |
		I	II	III	IV		
Total number	100.0	25.0	25.0	25.0	25.0	2,352,000	100.0
Households with employees in total	100.0	16.4	26.2	29.1	28.3	2,520,000	61.8
Households with regular employees	100.0	14.3	26.1	30.1	29.5	2,583,000	58.7
Directors of companies and organizations	100.0	5.1	9.6	23.2	62.1	4,729,000	2.6
Regular employees	100.0	14.8	26.9	30.4	28.0	2,483,000	56.1
Employees in companies with fewer than 30 employees	100.0	29.8	36.0	21.1	13.1	1,858,000	14.9
Thirty to 999 employees	100.0	12.9	29.0	34.0	24.0	2,404,000	23.3
One thousand-plus employees	100.0	4.6	16.6	33.4	45.4	3,107,000	17.9
Households with temporary employees	100.0	55.6	23.2	11.1	10.1	1,475,000	1.3
Households with day laborers	100.0	58.6	30.1	9.0	2.3	1,179,000	1.7
Households with self-employed	100.0	34.0	25.5	17.4	23.0	2,404,000	15.9

Note: Employers of over 1,000 employees include government offices and corporations. The figures do not include farm households.

Source: Kōsei-shō (Ministry of Welfare), Survey on the State of Peoples' Living Conditions (Tokyo: Ministry of Welfare, 1975 edition).

of social guarantees—whether from their employer or from the state—to insure their survival in the face of misfortune. The postwar labor union movement responded by fighting for systematic minimum levels of social support for workers.

But I must qualify these assertions in two ways. First, one cannot measure the precise effect of union activities upon the creation of such supports. Regardless of union pressures, when companies faced labor shortages, the managers were properly generous to those who had lagged in competition with other workers. In serious need of workers, companies had no choice but to depend upon and seek to elicit the best efforts of even mediocre employees, so managers voluntarily raised their wages and provided fringe benefits. To boost the morale of such people, personnel mangers used company newsletters to report that "Mr. B of division A is a skilled chess (*shōgi*) player with a rank of second class," or "Mr. C is an expert fisherman."[27]

In society at large, a parallel pressure was at work. To insure their ongoing electoral hegemony, successive Liberal Democratic Party (LDP) governments had to construct a postwar system of full employment, social security, and other programs of the welfare state. The LDP's pursuit of this course was somewhat lukewarm until the 1970s, but I see no fundamental contradiction between the trajectory toward the welfare state and the core LDP program of rapid economic growth. Many observers seeking to bring out the contrast between conservatives and progressives tend to pose this issue in terms of a choice between polices favoring "growth" or those favoring "welfare." But framing the issue in this way strikes me as meaningless. The LDP government itself insisted that economic growth was designed to further "social welfare," and this assertion is not unreasonable. In all capitalist nations the welfare state typically adopts an economic policy for growth. And, in fact, leaving aside for a moment the question of what form these social security measures took, I find that, in many ways, Japan's rapid economic growth brought a quantitative improvement in popular welfare.

Rather than simply clamoring that funding for social insurance was inadequate and falling back on a false dichotomy between growth and welfare, I believe that reformers should have staked out a distinctive position by questioning the basic form and ideological premise of the evolving social guarantees.

This claim brings me to the second qualification of the general point that postwar unions sought and won a set of minimum social guarantees. In its campaigns for such guarantees, the labor union movement failed to build or even press for any institutional links between national social security benefits on the one hand and guarantees provided by private companies on the other. Unions did not seek uniform standards for the guarantees due all workers, whether they were members of the "company society" or not.

Critics of this state of affairs have typically contended that enterprise-based unions were not forceful enough in fighting for social security benefits. As a result, these critics claim, such benefits in Japan were simply handed down "from above" by the government and its advisory councils even before the workers demanded them. I do not reject such criticism, but my point is a bit different. The more fundamental problem has not been a lack of fighting spirit, but the fact that unions have confined the circle of comrades entitled to these guarantees to the regular employees of a given company. The idea that those outside this circle should naturally receive a different level of compensation or social security sunk powerful roots among organized workers in the era of high growth.

Of course, for enterprise-based unions to concentrate primarily on winning benefits for their employees is hardly surprising. And on occasion these enterprise-based unions do, in fact, call to expand state welfare programs to help those left out of the enterprise circle. Further, under certain circumstances the standards established by the organized workers within the charmed circle of the large company can become standards for the society as a whole. This was the result of "spring-offensive" wage bargaining; the annual wage gains achieved by large-company unions during the period of rapid economic growth spilled over and were extended to workers in smaller firms and nonunion firms.

But putting aside such cases of *equalization as a by-product*, the inventory of cases in which mainstream unions have endeavored to broaden the circle of their fellow workers is scarce. If one examines the history of union demands concerning wage payments, job guarantees, unemployment or health insurance, injury compensation, or pension payments, one finds virtually no efforts to place both those on the inside of the company society and those on its outside within the same system, be it the system of industrial relations or the larger political system of social welfare. If such efforts had been made, the organized workers who were regular employees in large firms would have had to shoulder the burden of the insecurity of workers in general. Enterprise-based unions avoided this situation by favoring relatively generous in-company welfare for themselves and national welfare systems that applied only to the weak.

By choosing this course, organized workers in postwar Japan, with a few exceptions, never seriously addressed the unfinished business of transcending enterprise-based consciousness and action. One exception worth noting is the Dentsū Kyōtō [Joint Struggle Council of Telecommunication Workers.] This organization was formed in 1962 to regulate and standardize working conditions in the large number of subcontracting companies and companies with ties to the Japan Telephone and Telegraph Public Corporation (NTT at present) and the International Telegraph and Telephone Corporation (ITT). The Struggle Council took as its model the working conditions (minimum wages, pay raise practices, and injury compensation) found in the two parent companies and aggressively sought to extend these to all subsidiary and related firms by negotiating jointly with these subcontracting companies. In addition, in 1977 the enterprise-based unions of dozens of companies that were engaged in the construction of communication facilities consolidated themselves into ten single unions, six organized on a regional basis and four organized in the four largest enterprises.

In the years following, the Dentsū Kyōtō organization responded to changes in the structure of the information industry, such as the privatization of NTT, by twice changing its name, first to the Dentsū rōren (Federation of Telecommunication Workers) in 1980, and then to the Jōhō rōren (Federation of Information Industry Workers) in 1991. The organization today encompasses the information transmission and processing workers at firms attached to NTT. A standardized, systemized job security system has yet to be achieved, but since 1988 the minimum wage within the industry has been agreed upon every year through collective bargaining. Though this agreement only covers core workers at NTT subcontractors, excluding those employed for simple or supplementary work, the organization's endeavors and achievements are rare in the world of Japanese labor. It has won an arrangement that enables the union to set working conditions beyond the framework of a single enterprise.[28]

Such achievements have been few and far between in the past thirty years. As a result, organized workers have been unable to control access to the circle of fellow workers; labor unions have had no choice but to accept the boundaries set by the meritocratic policies of management. Thus any solidarity of those within and without the company society has fallen far short of the notion that all workers were in the same boat. The walls of the factory have blocked the call of organized workers to the unorganized.

I have examined the postwar labor movement in three realms of endeavor: pursuit of equality among employees in a firm, equality among the people as a whole, and guarantees of a basic social security for the weak. That postwar unions sought these goals was in a sense inevitable. These objectives were shaped by the conditions imposed upon workers in the prewar era and the ideas workers articulated in response. They were adopted enthusiastically by workers granted democratic institutions after World War II. The labor union movement that resulted was not able to challenge the fundamentals of the Japanese management system and company society, yet precisely by making use of these labor unions, Fukuda's children and grandchildren were able to escape the status of straggler and claim a place among the ordinary people of the nation. At the same time, as the testimony of the women miners interviewed by Morisaki suggests, we cannot ignore the shadows cast by this achievement. The concern of the following chapter will be to explore these shadows.

Notes to Chapter 3

1. *Rōdō oyobi sangyō* [Labor and industry] (May 1917) reprinted in Ohara Shakai Mondai Kenkyūjo, ed., *Nihon shakai undō shiryō* [Documents on the Japanese social movement] (Tokyo: Hōsei University Press, 1972), p. 303.

2. "Tekisei chingin o meguru mitsu no zadankai" [Three symposia on appropriate wages], *Shakai seisaku jihō* [Social policy bulletin] (November 1940), p. 180.

3. Morisaki Kazue, *Makkura* [Pitch dark] (Tokyo: San'ichi Shobō, 1977), pp. 183–185.

4. Ibid., p. 189.

5. Ibid., p. 186.

6. Yasumaru Yoshio, *Nihon no kindaika to minshū shisō* [The modernization of Japan and the thinking of the masses] (Tokyo: Aoki Shoten, 1974). Ichii Saburō and Nunogawa Seiji, *Dentōteki kakushin shisōron* [Traditional theory of renovation] (Tokyo: Heibonsha, 1972).

7. Saki Ryūzō, *Dai-higyō* [The great strike] (Tokyo: Tabata Shoten, 1961). This work is a literary reconstruction of the 1920 Yahata Iron Works strike, based on detailed interviews with participants in the event. It paints a vivid picture of the mentality of laborers who justified the strike in terms of their loyalty as subjects under the emperor system.

8. The Japanese for these three terms is *shokuin, kōin,* and *shain.* For discussion of the issue of status and membership in the firm, and the struggle between employers and employees over these labels, see Andrew Gordon, *The Evolution of Labor Relations in Japan: Heavy Industry, 1853–1955* (Cambridge: Harvard Council on East Asian Studies, 1985), pp. 347–348.

9. See Fujita Wakao, *Nihon rōdo kyōyaku ron* [On Japanese industrial contracts] (Tokyo: Tokyo University Press, 1961) and Tsuda Masumi, *Nenkō teki rōshi kankei ron* [On seniority-based labor-management relations] (Tokyo: Mineruba Shobō, 1968). Orii Hyūga, *Rōmu kanri nijū nen* [Twenty years as a labor manager] (Tokyo: Tōyō Keizai Shinpōsha, 1973) provides details about the history of postwar labor management at the Nippon Kōkan steel company. Orii describes the process in which various plans to control labor led to a new system to classify company employees by the late 1960s.

10. On the Densan wage structure, see Gordon, *Evolution,* pp. 351–356.

11. The term for qualification-grade wages is *shikaku-kyū,* for job wage *shokumu-kyū,* and for ability or work-ability wage *shokunō-kyū.*

12. For one analysis, see Ishida Mitsuo, *Chingin no shakaikagaku* [The sociology of wages] (Tokyo: Chūō Keizai Sha, 1990), chap. 2.

13. For detail on these reforms, see Kumazawa Makoto, *Rōdō no naka no fukken* [Restoration of rights in labor] (Tokyo: San'ichi Shobō, 1972), chaps. 1, 2, 6. Also, on postwar patterns in worker demands, consult Yoshimura Rei, *Shokumu-kyū to ōdan chinritsu* [Job-based wages and inter-firms wage rates] (Tokyo: Nihon Hyōronsha, 1965) and other works by this tireless researcher.

14. Tsuda Masumi, *Nihonteki keiei no yōgo* [The defense of Japanese-style business management] (Tokyo: Tōyō Keizai Shinpō sha, 1976), p. 73.

15. The term used in the Japanese text is *kokumin,* which literally means "the nation's people," rather than *shimin,* which is a literal translation of "citizen." In the prewar and wartime era, the center of gravity of the expression *kokumin* fell somewhere between the English terms "subject" and "citizen." Between the 1890s and

the 1920s, its sense shifted in the direction of citizen, but in the 1930s and during wartime, it moved sharply back toward subject. In postwar usage, the term can be considered to cover a range of meaning from the "people" to the "nation" to the "citizenry."

16. Some right-wing elements, especially the *Kōdōha* (Imperial Way Faction), strongly supported the principle of equality under the emperor, but by the mid-1930s the *Tōseiha* (Control Faction) had taken control of the army. Control Faction leaders at heart saw calls for "equality before the emperor" as foolish nonsense and crushed the Imperial Way group, but when the Control group in turn had to call upon the people to dedicate themselves totally to the nation, they too fell back on this principle. Perhaps one should call this an internal contradiction in Japanese-style fascism.

17. *Tenshoku* is here translated "natural vocation."

18. Matsuzawa Hiroaki, *Nihon shakai-shugi no shisō* [Japanese socialist thought] (Tokyo: Chikuma Shobō, 1973).

19. Here, I rely on the data on percentage of diffusion of consumer goods among employee families, presented in the annual *Shōhi dōkō yosoku chōsa* [Survey of consumption trend predictions] of the Economic Planning Agency.

20. *Asahi shimbun*, March 1, 1977.

21. Kōsei-shō (Ministry of Welfare), *Kakei chōsa nenpō* [Annual survey report on household economy], 1955, 1960, 1965, 1970, 1975 editions.

22. Kōsei-shō (Ministry of Welfare), *Kōsei gyōsei kiso chōsa* [Basic survey on welfare administration], 1977 edition.

23. Shōzu Tsutomu, *Seikazoku* [The sacred family] (Shōzu's collection of poems) (Tokyo: Shichōsha, 1982), p. 25.

24. Hosoi Wakizō, *Jokō Aishi* [The sad history of women factory workers] (Tokyo: Iwanami Shoten, Bunko ed., [1925] 1954), pp. 287, 290.

25. Kishimoto Shigenobu, *Chūryū no Gensō* [The "middle-class" fantasy] (Tokyo: Kōdansha, 1978).

26. Economic Planning Agency, ed., *Kokumin seikatsu hakusho* [White Paper on National Life] (Tokyo: Economic Planning Agency, 1976), p. 132.

27. See the interesting comments by Ono Tsutomu in Hazama Hiroshi, Tsuchiya Moriaki, et al., *Wareware ni totte kigyō to wa nani ka* [What do companies mean to us?] (Tokyo: Tōyō keizai Shinpōsha, 1976), vol. 1, p. 166.

28. For the Dentsū Kyōtō story, see Jōhō rōren, *Jōhō rōren sanjū-nen* [Thirty years of the Federation of Information Industry Workers] (Tokyo, 1992), pp. 27–28, 44–49, 94–95.

4

J51, M12
N36   JAPAN

Limits and Costs of the Postwar Labor Movement

Business Unionism

In postwar Japan, labor unions took direct action to end various forms of discriminatory treatment within corporations. They attacked differentials in employment status (such as labeling workers as staff or operatives) and differential criteria for pay raises or job security between blue- and white-collar employees. In essence, they purified the seniority system of its caprice and forced companies to recognize ordinary workers as citizens of the enterprise. Unions also acted indirectly to exert an impact on society as a whole. In wage struggles that had a ripple effect, they raised income and consumption levels to the extent that many workers escaped their lower-class status. Further, postwar unions supported new welfare systems that would preserve for employees and citizens a minimum protection against unexpected misfortune. The nation's rulers had formerly wielded the myth of homogeneity ("In Japan there is no class system") as a tool of social control, but in the changed postwar conditions unions appropriated this myth. They used it as a weapon to win concessions, and they forced the rulers to lend some substance to previously false claims of equality and unity.

But concessions can easily become an even stronger means of control. As postwar workers consolidated their gains between 1955 and the mid-1970s, the nation's rulers once more took control of these ideological weapons of the "classless society." Why could this not be prevented? The critical messages implied in the previous chapter are relevant here. The critiques all converge on the production site. The key questions are two. In the particular concept of equality embraced by postwar Japanese workers and unions, how was the workplace understood? What sorts of reforms were sought there?

To put the conclusion first, postwar union activists on the whole considered the content of work and the relationships among coworkers to fall outside the purview of union functions.

One can find some exceptions. When management was in a general state of shock and bewilderment immediately after the war, unions exercised strong authority over production and personnel matters. In addition, from about 1952 to 1957 organized workers in several industries built a vigorous movement that engaged in a "Japanese-style" struggle at the workplace by taking advantage of some contradictions in that era's *nenkō* system of seniority and merit. These unions focused on the poor fit between the numerical distribution of workers by seniority (with a large bulge in the middle) and the pyramid-shaped structure of job assignments.

Examples of successful movements of the 1950s include the following: Unranked employees at the National Railroad Machine Shop gained the self-confidence to perform their work without the supervision of foremen and grasped the initiative at their workplace. Private railway company workers successfully fought for authority to set limits over such matters as maximum hours per shift actually driving the train, maximum distance traveled, and the scope of job definitions. Coal miners demanded rotation of job assignments at the coal face and egalitarian distribution of production-quota premiums. They forced the mines to abolish pay differentials between pit miners and support crews. They fought against the authority of staff who made arbitrary job assignments. And they forged an agreement among themselves to prevent output competition. Organized miners further sought "three rights" for the union's workplace units: the right to negotiate directly with supervisors at the production site, to conclude agreements based on these negotiations, and to engage in local strikes without authorization from headquarters. They also pressed an "equalization movement," analogous to the "most-favored-nation" clause in trade treaties, in which the union demanded that gains won by a single local unit be extended to all locals.[1] These organization-building movements reflected worker expectations that the labor unions as a collectivity formulate and impose egalitarian rules to regulate the work.

But in large factories at the cutting edge of the economy, sites employing many newly hired workers and boasting mechanized and automated facilities, such grass-roots organizing movements began to decline rapidly in the 1960s. In 1960 the Miike Labor Union at the Mitsui Mines, the mecca of these organizing movements, suffered a total defeat in a battle to prevent the dismissal of workers. This failure contributed much to the ensuing retreat from workplace activism in many industries, although unions of public employees continued the tradition of struggle at the workplace for another fifteen years or more. The efforts of public sector unions to enhance the workers' voice concerning labor conditions compares favorably to those of their private sector counterparts in such industries as petrochemicals or automobiles. Unionized public sector employees, including those at such ultramodern workplaces as the Shinkansen (bullet) trains, the Data Communications Bureau in the Public Corporation of Telecommunications, or the Central Parcels Bureau of the Postal Ministry, continued to act even at the production site in what we may call the manner of true organized workers. In sharp contrast, those in private firms largely abandoned activism at the point of production after 1960, and in the labor movement in general the concern of union activities with the quality of work at the production site steadily weakened from this point forward. As the economy expanded dramatically, labor unions became primarily organs to fight for higher wages. In other words, most union members came to view themselves as "workers" in those moments when they demanded higher wages through their unions, but in their daily life, they identified and acted as company employees.

The turn away from activism at the workplace was in part, no doubt, the responsibility of the union movement's leaders. Beginning around 1960, they took considered steps toward a narrow mode of business unionism, steps best exemplified in two decisions. First, in 1958 the Sōhyō (General Council of Trade Unions of Japan) national convention refused to adopt the "Organization Platform (draft)" authored by Shimizu Shinzō, which called on unions to struggle in their local units by confronting supervisors at the workplace. Second, at its 1962 convention Sōhyō adopted an "Organizational Policy" that emphasized the "unifying function" of unions and limited workplace activism.[2] Yet one cannot lay the matter to rest by simply criticizing these leadership decisions. Quite possibily, these men had good reason to believe their change of direction accurately reflected the attitude of the rank and file.

I advance the following interpretation in this chapter: The core function of unions originally and necessarily is to limit competition among workers. But by the mid 1960s a mode of thinking took hold among Japanese workers that placed greatest value on giving individuals a fair opportunity to compete to demonstrate their ability to the fullest. This attitude is the very essence of Japan's postwar democracy, and its ascendance accounts for both the failure of postwar unionism focused primarily on work roles and relationships among coworkers and the much-noted "flexible deployment" of labor in Japan. Contrary to conventional wisdom on this topic, flexible deployment not only resulted from a managerial triumph over a rigid seniority (*nenkō*) system but also was intrinsic to the *nenkō* system from the start.

Life at the Production Site

"Flexible deployment" refers to fluidity in the nature of the work to be performed and the assignment of workers to given tasks.[3] In Japan's big business workplaces, such matters as job definitions, staffing norms, work speed, or performance targets are quite loosely or vaguely defined. Decades of ceaseless rationalization demanded constant change in production and work processes, which served constantly to erode the stability of procedures based on customary practices or explicit work rules. Assignments of workers to specific tasks tended to be fluid. Of course, the extent of such flexibility varies from place to place; white-collar salespeople or employees in a trading company work more flexibly than blue-collar machine operators or assembly workers on a conveyor line. But as many observers have noted, flexible deployment characterizes many Japanese workplaces, even as technological innovations lead to "deskilling" and reduced scope for workers to make decisions on the job.

The flexibility of Japanese workplaces offers some benefit for workers: It leaves them space in which to demonstrate and use their talents. But it has a cost as well. The inner logic of a system of flexible deployment relentlessly drives workers to broaden the scope of their jobs, raise performance targets, and work at a faster pace. In careers at a flexible workplace, the more senior the employees become the more they must hustle to prove themselves. Why do they compete so strenuously? Some hope to escape repetitive, boring work and rise to any position of slight supervisory or managerial authority. Others anxiously seek recognition of their ability so they will not be "encouraged" to retire early when business slows and the workforce is streamlined. Still others want to fulfill their responsibilities as fathers by winning sufficient pay raises. Whether employees achieve these goals depends entirely on the successive managerial appraisals of their merit or ability over the course of a career. Inevitably over time these annual evaluations widen the gap in pay and responsibility between workers who began their careers as equals.

Was the competitive orientation of these workers forced upon them by managers wielding the threat of poor evaluations? Was it an internally generated commitment? This distinction is difficult to make. The fundamental problem in the consciousness of Japanese workers lies in the fusion of self-motivated action with a compulsion of which they are only dimly aware. Organized workers in the postwar years have not hesitated even to take managers to court to fight discrimination for political activity. They have also protested vigorously against discrimination based on educational background or gender (although less vigorously in the latter instance). They have resisted excessive workloads or harsh working conditions.

But unionized workers have raised no fundamental objections to the ways in which flexible personnel deployment and work assignments incited intense competition among themselves. Indeed, as long as they perceived a fair opportunity to compete and a fair evaluation of their ability and "gung-ho spirit," workers not only failed to protest, they actively competed to show their ability, raise their social status, or improve their living standards. This was considered the behavior of a serious-minded worker. This behavior, I would argue, was the way of life inevitably chosen by the grandchildren of Fukuda Tatsuo, the embittered blacksmith of the early industrial era. His descendants during and soon after the war faced a gap between the ideal of interclass mobility and the difficulty of actually moving up in the world. When they saw that rapid economic growth offered a chance to realize this ideal, they embraced the new constitution, which for them embodied the principle of developing individuality in accord with ability.

The strange beauty of the *nenkō* system of seniority and merit lies in its close fit with such a perception of postwar democracy. Because workers faced no more of the arbitrary discrimination common before the war from the moment they entered the company, they came to believe that ability and effort determined success or failure. Those who hustled and stood up to the pressure succeeded. Those who were exhausted in mind or in body fell by the wayside. As differences in work assignments, promotions, and pay increases emerged between the successes and the failures, most workers considered this sorting out to be a *natural* process. Hardly aware of the structures that led to this perception, Japanese workers naturally came to think this way. In Japan, the standard for each and every personnel assignment is length of service plus an evaluation of ability and performance. Seniority may determine the pool of those who are eligible for a position, but a merit evaluation determines who actually qualifies for a particular job. That the majority of workers accept the results of these assessments without protest is due to the hegemony of a perception that the process is natural.

Am I too harsh or one-sided in arguing that organized workers in postwar Japan have mainly considered democracy a simple instrument to provide the opportunity to compete freely? After all, the new constitution includes a guarantee of the "right to a minimum standard of wholesome and cultured living" (Article 25). Unions have sought certain guaranteed minimum standards to realize this right.

And yet, I must admit the following: The minimum standards sought by unions may constitute a guarantee for those who inevitably fail in the intense competition among workers, but this guarantee does not extend to the kind of job they must perform. Consider the case of a female telephone operator afflicted by muscular ailments of the neck, shoulder, or hand. A conscientious union would attempt to protect her livelihood by reassigning her to a less strenuous job. But an even more conscientious operator might contend that anyone who took her place would develop the same injury. Such a worker would demand that her job be redesigned and made safe. She would claim both the right to cure her illness and the right to remain on the job to redesign it and make it safer.[4] Such a stance goes far beyond the competitive ethos of meritocracy. At the present moment, it represents a way of thinking that few Japanese unions and, indeed, few healthy fellow workers are willing to accept.

In the competitive *nenkō* system, one can assume that in any group of workers some will fail at their jobs in their own eyes and in the opinion of others. Labor unions need not accept this as unavoidable; they could dra-matically reduce the proportion of workers who fail. They could fight to establish performance norms that could be achieved readily by the over-whelming majority. They could seek to equalize job assignments by a sys-tem of rotation or straight seniority. But unions in postwar Japan have made few such efforts. As a result, the many workers who are not up to the competition are miserable at their jobs. Even if these many men and women are guaranteed a minimum material existence, they will inevitably harbor a sense of inferiority toward the few who achieve great success on the job. In sum, any guarantees of livelihood that are pursued without regard for the nature of work or the relations among fellow workers will not readily lead to the ideological autonomy of workers.

The problem goes further than this. I would suggest that the behavior of workers who dealt with flexible deployment by meritocratic competition, and a unionism that accepted this competition, has preserved, indeed strengthened, the hierarchical structure of labor in Japanese workplaces since the 1960s. This hierachy refers to the widened gap in the responsi-bility and rights of workers assigned to upper- and lower-level jobs. As the gap expanded, the more numerous ordinary workers were deprived of the right and the chance to exercise judgment in the course of their daily work. Their jobs became increasingly routine. From roughly the mid–1950s through 1970, Japan's large manufacturers phased out group work and jobs demanding workers with general purpose skills; they had their employees carry out diverse but simplified, individual tasks. Further, management introduced technologies that combined computerized controls and automa-tion. Together these changes created a framework of hierarchical work organization, and the changes themselves constitute a large part of the postwar history of Japanese workers.[5] But the issue that concerns me is the hardship brought about by this hierarchical structure, a result of the behav-ior of workers under the *nenkō* seniority and merit system.

The mechanics of this system are easy to explain. Work at the bottom of the hierarchy is carried out by regular male employees at the start of their competitive career trajectories, or by women workers or part-time workers who are rotated in and out of the workforce. Both employers and employees expect that individuals undertake such work for a limited dura-tion. Precisely for this reason, the workers can tolerate simple, repetitive tasks. The more senior regular male employees believe it to be a matter of course that, so long as they demonstrate competitive ability and a gung-ho spirit, they will escape from such simple jobs. Actually, the pyramidal struc-ture of job assignments makes it certain that a fair number of these men will fail to advance far up the hierarchy, but to the extent that they accept the competitive process as natural, they must take a resigned attitude toward falling behind. Such a consciousness makes these men hesitate to fight for change in the working conditions and job content at the bottom of the workplace hierarchy. They remain silent because they accept the assurance that, despite their inadequacy, "at least they still have a job."

In other words, one distinctive feature of work in Japan since the 1960s, and today, is that work groups at the production site lack a sense of autonomy in the face of decisions made by top managers.[6] Work procedures, job boundaries, work pace, staffing levels, and job assignments are ceded to management as part of the flexible deployment structure. Even workers of relatively activist unions that seek the right of self-rule or extended local negotiating rights accept this flexible structure as a given reality. Worker organizations on the shop floor do not see the right to regulate such workplace matters as a foundation of labor unionism.

The attitudes of unions in Britain and the United States are far more assertive.[7] Organized workers in Britain and America retain rights in the workplace to regulate the speed of the conveyor belts to a degree or to negotiate standard times and rates for output-based pay, and they invoke straight seniority rules in deciding job transfers or layoffs. In comparison, the workplace voice of Japan's organized workers is barely audible. This has become all the more true since high-speed growth ended in the middle of the 1970s, as the fierce meritocratic competition has eroded solidarity among employees. Common wisdom under the prevailing meritocratic orthodoxy dictates that if a worker wants some power to decide matters of daily work, he or she should gain that right individually by winning promotion out of the ranks of ordinary workers. After all, no institutional barriers prevent such advancement. A trade-off has apparently been made between the ability of individuals to move up the corporate hierarchy and their ability or will to transcend or overcome hierarchy itself. Ultimately, flexible deployment and competition based on perceived merit and ability have enabled management to preserve unchallenged rights and technocratic control by turning the workplace into an arid land and withering the solidarity of ordinary workers.

Escape from the Bottom of the Ladder

> The problem here is an attitude of contempt for workers which prevails even among the workers themselves. . . the passive vocational consciousness that simply considers the life of a worker as fate. . . . We can sum this up as an "underclass consciousness," a view of one's existing plight as immutable fate, coupled with a forlorn dream of a better status. . . for instance, the life of a salaried staff member or the prosperity of a self-employed businessman.

The pioneering labor economist Ujihara Shōjirō wrote this passage in 1954 to conclude his analysis of a survey of workers in several major factories in Tokyo and Yokohama.[8] The image he presents of workers nine years after the end of World War II differs little from the portraits of prewar workers drawn by Matsuzawa Hiroaki. Yet if one shifts the view to the 1960s or later, one discovers what seems at first a very different "postwar" situation in which workers compete on the basis of ability, encouraged by (and reinforcing) equality of opportunity and a hierarchical division of labor.[10] In what ways did this lingering "prewar" image of self-denigration change, and in what ways did it remain constant, in this new postwar condition?

The ability of Japanese workers to consume material goods and partake of a national culture approached the level of other segments of society beginning in the 1960s. Whereas workers in large firms enjoyed a higher standard of living than others, all had acquired the right to a minimum of social security. Postwar workers gradually shed the stigma of membership in an "underclass of factory workers," a status that may have been forced upon them, but one that they had internalized as well. To this extent, by the 1960s the prewar worker consciousness evaporated. The male blue-collar worker who received a monthly salary had in many respects become a "company man" like his white-collar counterpart. Newspapers no longer referred to these blue-collar men as "laborers," choosing to reserve the latter term for day laborers on construction crews.

But a continuity with prewar attitudes lurks beneath the surface and poses a serious, ongoing problem for any ideology of labor unionism. A workers' consciousness of "lower-classness" still persists in their appraisal of the labor that inheres in their occupations. This attitude lingers because the more workers fall behind in the competition for better jobs in a company hierarchy the more their daily tasks seem meaningless and leave them powerless. And because technological innovations generally have tended to cluster high-quality skilled work at the apex of a pyramid of job classifications, one actually finds increasing numbers of workers who share this negative view of their labor, stuck as they are in jobs at the middle and bottom of the pyramid that offer little satisfaction or pride. A worker was no longer derided as a "smith's blackie," but working in the factory remained a sad fate.

Although workers from the mid-1960s through the mid-1970s became consumers who enjoyed unprecedented material stability, a sense of alienation simultaneously spread in Japanese workplaces. Precisely because managers noticed the stirring of these sentiments, which could flare up in active or passive forms of resistance, they initiated labor-management programs such as "job enlargement," quality control circles, or "small group activities" to address the problems brought on by the deskilling of work and the atomization of workers. But these corrective measures themselves under certain circumstances merely intensified competition among the workers.

Given their negative feelings about the jobs that allow their families to lead seemingly middle-class lives, it is no surprise that many workers in the period of the 1960s–1970s, and to this day as well, do not discuss the every-day conditions at work that make this lifestyle possible. They do not bring home stories about their jobs, the machinery at the plant, or their fellow workers. They cannot talk with pride to their families about overcoming difficulties at work. They have no desire to have their children enter the same jobs. In attitude surveys since the 1960s, middle-aged Japanese work-ers have consistently responded that they live for their work. But even more workers have claimed that they live for their family. In fact, I think these two responses are flip sides of a single train of thought: "When I think that I can make it possible for my family to lead a life like other families, work becomes worthwhile, even though I take little pride or pleasure in the work itself."

A so-called underclass occupational consciousness desires to escape from that class; when an opportunity to actually escape arises, the desire is all the more intense. A middle-class consumer consciousness that can, in fact, coexist with an underclass self-perception of the work itself arouses the same wish to escape from this lower-class occupation. For workers in Japan, the era beginning in the mid-1950s saw the flowering of such desires. In the high-growth decades, the tendency to view membership in the working class as a transitory phase revealed itself in the efforts of those within the corpo-ration to escape from the rank-and-file category. Even blue-collar men in large companies seriously sought promotion to positions as supervisor or manager. When these prospects appeared dim, these men transferred their ambition to their children. In so doing, these men and their families faced a difficult reality: educational credentials and the "prestige" of one's school largely determined one's point of entry and subsequent trajectory in society's rank order of occupations; working-class families were thus swept into the heated race to enter their children in the right school.[11] Driven to place their children in jobs better than their own, both white-collar and blue-collar fam-ilies pushed their offspring into prolonged and arduous competition to excel in entrance exams.[12] From 1960 to 1975 the percentage of youngsters going on to college rose in a straight line from 17.2 percent to 34 percent, a trend that surely reflects the aspiration of blue-collar families to make their mem-bership in the working class a passing phase in their family's history.

This aspiration was only one factor making rates of interclass mobility higher in Japan than in most other countries, and it is difficult to separate out and measure the impact of such attitudes. Quite independent of the strength or weakness of worker motivations, changes in occupational struc-ture and the demand for labor also influenced interclass mobility. And even if the children of blue-collar workers suceeded in joining the white-collar ranks, this upgrade may not have conveyed the same sense of achievement to common people as it once did.

Japanese sociologists have made some noteworthy contributions to the understanding of this postwar social mobility.[13] Even though the fuzzy boundaries between skilled, semiskilled, and unskilled workers inevitably limits the clarity of mobility studies in Japan, they suggest the following conclusions:

1. From a comparative perspective, mobility within generations is low in Japanese society, but intergenerational mobility is high.
2. In the decades of rapid economic growth, many youths from farming and fishing families, as well as from blue-collar families, became white-collar workers.
3. The main avenue of status formation is a route from *educational aspiration* to *educational credentials*, thence to a *first job* and perhaps on to *a current job*. The impact of class background in directing a person on this course is limited.

In sum, one is presented with an "underclass" occupational consciousness, reflecting the pyramidal structure of workplace job assignments; a competitive ethos legitimated by a perceived equality of opportunity; and a traditional aspiration to escape one's class status, intensified by these first two factors. As the lifeways and behavior of organized workers in postwar Japan have been molded by these mutually reinforcing social values, they have failed to develop something important: a desire to continue in the status of worker and improve their lives as such.

Had such a desire been powerful, it would have sparked a drive to break down the division of workers into a small core of arrogant quasi-elitists and a large body dogged by an inferiority complex about their efforts. To make it possible to "continue as workers," unionists would have had to generate collective practices to control the nature of their work and relationships among fellow workers. Even if such self-governing workplaces were beyond reach, the workers at least needed to build a solidarity in the workplace upon which to negotiate with management over such matters. Only by creating such a factory community would workers have been able to defend a mode of living and working founded on a concept of security through equality, a philosphy different from notions of free competition and equality of opportunity.

Such an alternative mode of thinking would have enabled a critique, from the distinctive cultural position of organized workers, of an existing national culture that exalted meritocratic competition. Such a critique would have appealed powerfully and persuasively to unorganized workers forced to engage in a debilitating competition in which their chances of succeeding were even slimmer than those of organized workers. If the postwar reformist forces had found a way to reach people with these alternative ideas, they would have retained their independence and popularity even in the years of postwar affluence; they would not have seen their trademark calls for "peace and democracy, and affluent lives" co-opted by the ruling class.[14] In contemporary Japanese history, only a direct, critical examination of daily life at the production site and, through that, a strong critique of the competitive meritocratic ethos prevalent throughout society would have truly legitimated the progressive forces.

Such critical ideas have enabled workers in some labor unions to retain their independence in the face of the capitalistic system. For example, consider the common wisdom of sociologists in Britain, where blue-collar labor unions constitute a forceful presence. George Bain and his colleagues have posited a difference between blue- and white-collar worker values, as illustrated in Table 4.1. As the authors recognize, these are "ideal types," and the differences between the two groups are not immutable. Taking account of the work of other scholars, it is perhaps more accurate to say that in recent years the lower-level white-collar workers have been tilting strongly toward blue-collar unionism, though traditional blue-collar workers have shown increasingly individualistic tendencies. Nonetheless, in this socio-

TABLE 4.1

Comparison of Blue-Collar and White-Collar Workers

Point of View, Philosophy, and Value System	
Blue-Collar Workers	*White-Collar Workers*
solidarity, fraternity	egoism, pursuit of success
collectivism	individualism
class ideology that recognizes class conflicts	status ideology that sanctions class cooperation
social mobility means raising one's entire class standing by sacrifice made by other classes	social hierarchy is open to everyone. Merit and effort determine one's class affiliation based on competition
Opinion About Unions	
Blue-Collar Workers	*White-Collar Workers*
restriction on competition among coworkers (competition breaks down unity, and cooperation)	unions are means used by individuals to preserve dignity, prestige and control
	philosophy of competition is sanctioned
collective instrument for collective goals	collective instrument for individual goals

Source: George Bain, David Coates, and Vallerie Ellis, *Social Stratification and Trade Unionism* (London: Heinemann Educational Books, 1973), chaps. 1 and 2.

logical common wisdom, the unionism of blue-collar workers contrasts sharply with individualism, leading toward meritocratic competition and a drive for higher social status. This understanding ought to shock Japanese scholars and union leaders who simplistically conclude that the labor union movement is weak in Japan because individualism is weak. In the terms of this British analysis, Japan's blue-collar workers of the high-growth era and beyond, including unionized workers, have for better or worse become strongly individualistic and "white-collar."

How might such "modernized" Japanese workers react to the following statement by Hyūga Hōsai, at the time the president of Sumitomo Iron and Steel Company and clearly a man who has succeeded in life?

> I believe Japan's vitality stems from the fact that we have no class system. This constantly arouses the people's desire to advance in life, producing a straightforward sense of respect for successful people and sympathy and consideration for those who have fallen behind. Indeed, compared to the rest of the world, Japan can be seen to have succeeded in sustaining a superior degree of social harmony and development. . . . Moreover the principles of liberalism have functioned well in Japan, and the nation has created an egalitarian social system with a high degree of class and regional mobility. The fact that graduating from a good college serves as one's springboard in life reflects our society's systematic fostering of mobility and equality. . . . "Can we not conclude that our nation has the character of both educational credentialism and meritocracy?"[15]

A typical critique of this statement by postwar Japan's mainstream unions might claim that because society still rewards educational credentials more than true ability, the goals of mobility and equality have not been realized as fully as Hyūga claims.[16] Or it might argue that "sympathy and consideration for those who have fallen behind" remains inadequate. In other words, the mainstream of the postwar progressive forces is not intellectually prepared to challenge Hyūga's financial world value system head on from an independent position. In this sense, ours *is* truly a "classless" society!

Although postwar democracy did give rise to a certain type of class conflict in the immediate years after surrender, the thought and behavior of workers who experienced a Japanese-style take-off eventually shifted as it acquiesced to the status quo. As the postwar economy matured, workers became less and less willing to seek "security through equality" and struggle to encroach on managerial prerogatives by regulating work and relations among workers. This acquiescent attitude was of course amenable to the managers. A consensus had been reached: The good society was governed by free competition among individuals. How would the retreating Japanese unions respond to the dilemma of the "classless society" brought about by postwar democracy? Perhaps by concluding, "If you can't beat them, join them," and dismissing an active unionism on the shopfloor based on an organized workers' culture as an anachronism.

Dilemmas and Solutions After the Oil Crisis

Twenty years of dramatic economic growth under a special conjuncture in the history of Japanese and world capitalism came to an end in 1975. In a context of a labor shortage and the need for stable industrial relations, managers had been relatively generous to workers, but in the recession of the mid-1970s they suddenly changed their labor policies. First, managers refused simply to accept the annual "going wage" in bargaining every spring; they more firmly insisted on their need to set pay in accord with a company's financial capacity. A second change came in employment policy: Managers streamlined their payrolls and focused on eliciting superior performance from fewer workers. They shifted the balance between seniority and merit in the existing *nenkō* system, giving less weight to seniority and more to merit. Their overall goal was to cut back on total wage costs and the total number of employees.

The critical point here, so often overlooked, is that the *nenkō* system had always used merit evaluations to goad employees to work hard and compete with each other. This system was never intended to offer every worker a secure and comfortable niche in the company. The *nenkō* system, in practice, has always embraced a tension between its two aspects: the offer of some minimal protection via seniority-linked rewards to those who lagged in meritocratic competition and the unsympathetic treatment—even the outright dismissal—of these laggards. The balance between these aspects of the *nenkō* system has varied over time, reflecting the health and growth of the economy and corporation, and the vigor with which Japanese-style unionism pushed to turn formal principles of equality or community into material practice. Needless to say, when high-speed growth ended, and Japanese capital further anticipated an increase in older and well-educated workers, managers stressed the second aspect of *nenkō* at the expense of the first. The end of rapid growth also ended the generous treatment of ordinary workers who fell behind physically or intellectually in workplace competition, and this ungenerous treatment has accelerated in the 1990s.

After 1975, ordinary workers thus faced new dilemmas. Unions no longer won large wage gains in the annual spring offensive, and the employee's certainty that "at least my job is safe" began to crumble. Many companies stopped offering workers over age thirty-five even a portion of their annual pay raise on the basis of seniority; the larger part of the raise came to be determined by a merit evaluation. Employees beyond a certain age were divided into those likely to remain and those to be eased out. In this "up or out" system, some career workers were urged to take early retirement, and corporations placed a ceiling on years of service in lower-level managerial positions. Companies introduced systems of so-called self-assessment and counseling to enable employees to figure out on their own whether they should continue to compete to advance or resign themselves to second-class treatment. The practice of requiring employees to submit self-assessments is of particular fascination. It is both highly modern and typically Japanese, and it merits further examination.

The details differ from place to place, but in general terms the system works as follows: First, individual workers complete a personal report in which they record the nature of their job assignments and personal goals for that job, evaluate their ability and qualifications for it, and make note of future goals, hopes for job rotation, transfer, or promotion.[17] Second, individual employees' supervisors fill out a form, designed by the personnel office, which demands a truly comprehensive review of the worker. The form asks for assessment of employees' job performances and abilities or aptitude for their particular job, evaluation of their characters, potential for growth in abilities to perform their current jobs, and the potentials to develop new skills or abilities through retraining or transfer to new positions. Third, with reference to these data, supervisors and personnel staff conduct repeated interviews with each worker to further explore the limits of his or her potential, examining how the employee has demonstrated his or her ability and under what circumstances these capabilities can be developed further. Through this process, the worker's future course is charted.

One can imagine the following interview scenario as this rigorous assessment takes place:

"I've worked this hard. And I can still accomplish this much more."
"Well, I wonder. The company is expecting more of you. Do you really think you can accomplish more?"
"I will try. Please let me try!"

So the worker makes a promise. He or she is definitely committed to do his or her best. If the worker falls short, his or her own words provide management with grounds for harsh treatment in the future.

What strikes me as most distinctively Japanese about this system of motivating labor is its stress not on an employee's demonstrated capacity to achieve fixed goals or fulfill clear norms for a particular job, but rather on the employee's potential for developing latent ability. The ultimate goal of the exercise is to assess a worker's will and potential to increase the scope, or raise the standards, of his or her work.

Apologists for the system use lovely rhetoric. Today in the Japanese workplace, they tell us, we are exploring and expanding the potential of human beings. But clearly this system of personnel evaluation via self-assessment compels workers who aspire to secure and stable livelihoods to "voluntarily" make sales pitches about themselves and compete to work at a furious pace to live up to their promises. If they fail to make good on these commitments for any reason, they cannot count on their continued job security. Moreover, this system functions to persuade those who cannot live up to or endure the conditions to which they have agreed that their unfavorable treatment is justified. No space remains for a worker consciousness that even questions, much less attacks, meritocracy. The previous system of top-down evaluations at least left workers the freedom to be angry at managers and complain they were being evaluated unfairly. Now, in the name of participation, they are implicated in their own negative evaluations. Which method gives the workers greater freedom?

Finally, one of the most important measures to tilt the balance of the *nenkō* system decisively toward meritocracy was the drive to "cut the fat" by streamlining the workforce. From about 1977, numerous companies adopted so-called employment adjustment measures, such as in-company transfers, transfers of workers to subsidiaries, hiring freezes, and firing of part-time workers. In addition, companies implemented temporary layoffs of regular workers, placed workers on idle status at reduced pay, pending recall, and recruited employees for voluntary retirement. The unemployment rate in 1977 rose to 2.4 percent (a total of 1.26 million people). A 1977 government survey of people who had recently left their jobs indicates the gravity of the situation. In the 45-to–54-year-old age group, the largest number had "left due to personnel cutbacks or bankruptcy."[18]

These cuts targeted people who had fallen behind in merit-based competition. Labor unions had raised no fundamental objections to meritocratic practice as it had evolved in the high-growth era, and they were powerless to address the dilemma of those who had lost their jobs. Organized workers were accustomed to the increased abundance of life in the high-growth era, a time when the dark side of workplace competition remained largely obscured. They were no longer excited by or committed to the idea that their union's activating principle should be to restrict competition among workers, or even committed to the notion that they should use the union to protect their livelihoods. Such attitudes combined with resigned views that "the economy's in such trouble, it can't be helped" to cripple struggles against miniscule pay hikes, heavier workloads, and dismissals. When companies called for voluntary retirement, the quotas were often met or exceeded, even though the middle-aged and older workers (the main target of the call to retire) faced the worst chance of finding other jobs, and despite the fact that the fall-back employers of the past, agriculture and small business, were in no shape to take in such workers. Did these employees retire so readily because unemployment benefits had been improved over the years? This was merely a secondary, facilitating factor. These senior workers volunteered to retire because they fundamentally accepted the ideology of meritocracy and told themselves that "the company has judged my ability to be unsatisfactory. Many of my fellow workers seem to agree. So if I resist, the union will probably not defend me. If I retire now, I get a bonus in my retirement pay. That will be of some help."

To argue that labor movement leaders failed to develop any new strategies at all during this watershed era of the mid-1970s would be unfair. Beginning in the early 1970s, the Joint Committee on the Spring Offensive addressed numerous emerging problems that went beyond the framework of individual corporations. The committee developed what it called a "livelihood struggle" into a "people's spring offensive," which focused on a so-called institutional strategy at the national level. The committee called for tax reform, improved pensions, and higher minimum wages. It addressed such issues with considerable energy and produced some credible results, in particular by winning more generous unemployment insurance. At least in the conception of some of its proponents (Takagi Ikuo and Yamada Yoichi), this strategy's intent went beyond what I referred to in the previous chapter as a third stream of postwar union endeavor, to assist those who had met with misfortune or failed in competition among workers. By offering societally based guarantees, these advocates hoped that the institutional strategy would make workers less dependent in the first place on the corporation and its company-based welfare measures.

Yet, so long as unions did not even attempt to restrict workplace competition, the institutional strategy was destined to betray these hopes. Indeed, to the extent that state social policies provided sustenance to those cast out as failures by large firms, the success of the institutional strategy made it easier for corporations to intensify merit-based competition at the workplace.

After the crisis of the mid-1970s passed, unions did not address the problem of competition among coworkers. Those employees who managed to survive in a streamlined company by winning recognition of their merit and gung-ho spirit willingly accepted raised production norms in work sites with fewer people than before. They increased their pay by working overtime.[19] They received unprecedented bonuses from companies that cut their "fat" and restored profitability. Their small-group activities produced ideas that were likely to intensify the work pace or further reduce the number of workers. (For example, in the truck assembly line at the Toyota Auto Body Plant, one quality control group turned to industrial engineering to devise improvements that in a very brief span reduced the seventeen workers in that work process to ten, without any capital investment.)

Further evidence of the hands-off stance toward competition in big business unions lies in the treatment of society's weakest members. The institutional strategy did succeed in imposing some legal obligations that corporations hire handicapped people and the elderly, but the biggest companies, which are the most densely unionized, have the worst rates of compliance.

Working overtime, accepting cutbacks, and embracing quality control were steps taken by *successful* employees desperate to defend their jobs and livelihoods in the face of minimal pay hikes. Needless to say, many people behaved differently. They were judged deficient in the workplace, and they endured a lonely impoverishment. To be sure, compared to other countries that ran into severe "stagflation" during the oil shock, relatively few Japanese suffered extreme distress in these years. Nonetheless, numerous wretched scenes were played out between 1975 and 1978: unemployed workers, suicides of the elderly or an entire family, the hell of debt to a loan shark, and the largest number of homeless in modern Japan's history. These desolate phenomena foreshadowed the fate of those without special privileges in a world where competitive democracy had eroded collective systems of mutual assistance and protection and a prosperity in which a "rising tide lifts all boats" had come to an end.

Taking Off Once More

The bright light of postwar democracy promised to liberate workers from the prewar ideology of "knowing one's proper place." But lurking in the shadows of democracy was the incomplete formation, or indeed the destruction, of a communal society able to reconcile the clash of private rights.[20] Yet one must not simply resign oneself and conclude that any bright light casts shadow, but must face and oppose the phenomena that lurk in the shadow at the present moment. To achieve this, I still cling to a faith in the self-renewing power of the union movement.

Labor unions are still capable of protecting people's livelihoods by standing on a principle of equality that transcends the "national common sense" of bourgeois society. They possess a latent potential to challenge that merit-based competition at the production site that erodes the solidarity of Japanese workers. In contrast to the institutional task of ensuring the social security of the people, which can be undertaken by political parties and other organized interests, such reforms of the workplace can only be achieved by unions.

But to build in Japan a labor union movement up to this task will require a kind of cultural revolution. In the internal logic of the Japanese working-class take-off, postwar democracy was defined as equal opportunity to compete to demonstrate ability. Today the ideology of organized workers as such has lost any autonomy and any reforming impulse it once might have possessed. It has fused completely with the national common sense of neoliberal Japan.

Indeed, between the late 1970s, when I prepared the original version of this chapter, and the present year, Japanese labor unions have declined further. In 1989, the major industrial federations and national centers of the union movement merged into the Rengō federation of 7.6 million working people, but this did nothing to bolster unionism in the workplace.

Japanese-style management in the mid-1990s enjoys almost perfect freedom from union regulation. One sees examples of this in managerial practices such as the personnel cuts referred to as "restructuring," the shifting of regular employees into nonpayrolled positions, the temporary or permanent transfer of employees to positions in affiliated enterprises (*shukkō*), increases in the standard workload shouldered by employees, the requirement that employees offer unpaid "service overtime," and the expansion of wage differentials among employees of similar experience at similar jobs due to a more rigorous merit assessment. Female workers are increasingly relegated to the ranks of nonregular employees whose working conditions are entirely unprotected. At the same time, regular employees belonging to enterprise-based unions continue to throw themselves, now more desperately than ever, into a competition with their fellow workers to display their abilities and "enthusiasm" in order to obtain a limited number of managerial posts, maintain job security, and receive steady pay raises. The total effect of such conditions has been to reduce the rate of labor union organization from 34.4 percent in 1975 to 24.1 percent in 1994.[21]

In response to this situation, what must workers do to realize a cultural revolution? Clearly, something radical is needed. One must reinterpret postwar democracy as a workers' endeavor to achieve ideological independence and self-governing lives. Workers who mount a determined drive at the work site to realize more thoroughly the publicly sanctioned principles of the existing system can gradually overcome the dependent mentality that regards principles concerning how to work as granted by someone else. The ultimate result could be to construct a workers' society, within the corporate society, founded on a strong consciousness of "our own principles." That is, workers can take off once again. Workers must collectively pursue authority over, and meaning in, labor itself. They must regulate and thereby control competition among fellow workers. In so doing, they must challenge the foundations of the meritocracy, which is rooted in the production site and which permeates the entire society. The pursuit of these goals would contribute much to the ideological endeavors not only of organized workers but also of common people in general.

In order for labor unions to renew themselves, of course, they must attend to new trends among people so far ignored in mainstream union activities. For example, one social critic, Kagoyama Takashi, in 1977 identified a new antimainstream mode of thinking that was taking root among the urban lower class of day laborers, artisans, and employers and employees of tiny businesses.[22] These people are reportedly resigned to "live as [they] can work." They reject conspicuous consumption and do not enter the competition to advance in education or win promotions at work. Kagoyama concluded, "These people who have been prodded forward by the salaried elites—Japan's economic animals—have finally begun to build a separate identity and way of life."[23] Nearly twenty years later, I remain unconvinced that such common people in Japan have turned their backs on competition and the ambition to rise in society or have rejected the struggle to scrimp and save and somehow join the ranks of the mainstream. Nor am I confident they have constructed a new way of life founded on powerful communal ties. I suspect the people described by Kagoyama, the nonunionized lower classes, were then, and remain today, quite anxious and insecure in their way of life. But even if his observations provide no more than limited hope, the situation among these people may give pause to organized workers who for so long have accepted the competitive ethos of the elite salary-man.

Toward the end of the 1980s, the phenomenon of salary-men literally working themselves to death (*karōshi*) emerged as a social problem in Japan. At the same time, this workaholic tendency came to be viewed internationally as the reason for the extraordinary export strength of Japanese companies, and resistance to Japanese exports mounted in various countries. At this point, people in Japan increasingly recognized that something had to be done to stop the "vicious cycle" of trade surpluses, a rising yen, and further pressure on employees to cut costs. Leaders in the labor movement, political parties, and even a part of the business and financial world paid lip service, at least, to the need to reduce working hours and increase the margin of leisure in Japanese society. A number of government advisory committees developed proposals reflecting this sentiment.[24] However, such pressures from outside and above will not suffice to defend workers' lives, without simultaneous pressure from the workers themselves.

In the search for potential means to transform the consciousness of working people in Japan, one might focus attention on the social phenomenon called "small-group activity" in the workplace. Though certainly guided by management, these activities are nonetheless organized and implemented in large measure by ordinary workers. On occasion, one sees in these activities an authentic worker consciousness that renders productivity a secondary priority and gives primary emphasis to the autonomy of the work group in controlling its labor, for example by insuring that work group members have equal access and training in new skills or an egalitarian rotation of jobs. Is it truly impossible to nurture these tendencies and create a workplace society with a sense of independence from managerial intentions? I am intrigued by this question because I am quite suspicious of the thinking among some on the left who call for the creation of an autonomous citizen outside the workplace, in society at large, as a prerequisite toward nurturing independent thinking among employees within a firm. My own commitment is first to manifest the potential for a worker society inside the enterprise. In the following chapter, I examine whether such potential exists.

Notes to Chapter 4

1. For more on these cases, see Ōkōchi Kazuo, Ujihara Shōjirō, and Fujita Wakao, eds., *Rōdō-kumiai no kōzō to kinō* [The structure and function of labor unions] (Tokyo: Tokyo University Press, 1959), especially part 1, chapter 3, sec. 2, part 2, chap. 2; and part 3. This voluminous study examines the *nenkō* system and Japanese-type workplace unionism both theoretically and empirically.

2. On this process see Hyōdō Tsutomu's essay, "Shuntō no shisō to shokuba tōsō-ron" [On the spring labor offensive concept and struggle at the workplace], in Study Group on Labor Movement, ed., *Rōdō kumiai undō no kiki* [Crisis in the Labor Union Movement] (Tokyo: Nihon Hyōronsha, 1977).

3. For detailed discussions of flexible deployment, see Koike Kazuo, *Shokuba no rōdō kumiai to sanka* [Participation and labor unions at the workplace] (Tokyo: Tōyō Keizai Shinpō-sha, 1977), Iwata Ryūshi, *Nihonteki keiei no hensei genri* [The organizational principles of Japanese management] (Tokyo: Bunshindō, 1977) and Takeuchi Hiroshi, *"Jū-kōzō" no Nihon keizai.* [The Japanese economy's flexible structure] (Tokyo: Asahi Shimbunsha, 1978).

4. On this matter, see Konaka Yōtarō, ed., *Tōron: Seinen ni totte rōdō to wa nani ka* [Debate: What does labor mean for young people?] (Tokyo: San'ichi Shobō, 1978), pp. 196–197.

5. On technological innovation and transformation of labor there are numerous noteworthy theoretical and empirical studies in Japan. For a good introduction, see Hippō Yasuyuki, *Gōrika mondai no sangyō-betsu tenkai* (1) [The problem of rationalization and developments in various industries], *Kikan rōdō-hō*, no. 109. I shall not discuss his analysis in detail here but simply note that I adhere to what he calls the theory of "work simplification," or deskilling.

6. On this point, see Okamoto Hideaki, "Rōmu-kanri to rōshi-kankei" [Labor management and industrial relations], *Nihon Rōdō Kyōkai Zasshi*, no. 100 (July 1967).

7. For the United States, see Koike, *Shokuba no rōdō kumiai to sanka.* For Britain, see my *Kokka no naka no kokka* [A state within the state] (Tokyo: Nippon Hyōronsha, 1976).

8. Ujihara Shōjirō, "Daikōjō rōdōsha no seikaku" [The character of the workers in major factories], in *Nihon Rōdō Mondai Kenkyū* [Studies in labor problems in Japan] (Tokyo: Tokyo University Press, 1966), p. 365. This essay was originally published in 1954.

10. See the remarks by Matsumura Akihiro, in Hazama Hiroshi et al., eds., *Wareware ni totte kigyō to wa nani ka* [What does business mean to us?], vol. 1 (Tokyo: Tōyō Keizai Shinpōsha, 1976), pp. 33–34, 113.

11. Mita Sōsuke, *Gendai Nihon no shinjō to ronri* [Sentiment and logic in contemporary Japan] (Tokyo: Chikuma Shobō, 1971). Mita characterizes the educational fervor of Japanese parents as an "extension of desperation."

12. Sakurai Tetsuo in his "Minshu-shugi to kōkyōiku" [Democracy and public education], *Shiso* (December 1975) analyzed the linkage among social class, democracy, and education. He noted the striking similarity between the situations prevalent in Japan at that time and that present in the Third Republic of France. It is very instructive from today's perspective that he sees the rise of syndicalism as a mode of thinking that rose to challenge the emphasis on performance and drive for upward mobility under a democractic system.

13. I draw here on the work of Tominaga Kenichi and Andō Bunshirō, "Kaisōteki chii keisei katei no bunseki" [Analysis of the process of social class status formation], *Gendai Shakaigaku* (August 1977). In English on this topic, see Ishida Hiroshi, *Social Mobility in Contemporary Japan* (Stanford: Stanford University Press, 1993).

14. See Mutō Ichiyo's "Hokaku taikō hōkai no ato ni" [After the collapse of the conflict between the conservatives and progessives], *Tembō* (February 1977), where he discusses the progressives' loss of identity. For a general survey of the movements for "peace and democracy," see John Dower, "Peace and Democracy in Two Systems," in Andrew Gordon, ed., *Postwar Japan as History* (Berkeley: University of California Press, 1993).

15. Statement of Hyūga Hōsai, *Nihon Keizai Shimbun* (December 19, 1977). His citation is taken from Kōsei-shō (Ministry of Welfare), *Kokumin Seikatsu Hakusho* [Whitepaper on the people's livelihood] (Tokyo, 1977 edition).

16. Of course, emphasis on educational credentials is one aspect of an emphasis on ability. These two should not be placed in opposition.

17. Most of the employees who participated in these assessments were men on the career tracks, but especially in the 1980s, increasing numbers of women were covered by this system as well.

18. Sōrifu (Prime Minister's Office), *Rōdō ryoku chōsa* [Survey of the labor force] (Tokyo, 1977 edition). These unemployment percentages will not strike American readers as high, but it is important to note that this was a significant increase from levels of the 1960s and early 1970s, and that methods of counting unemployment are more stringent in Japan. Using U.S. methods of calculation, the rate would be roughly double.

19. As a point of reference, a typical example of a position on unemployment taken by organized workers with a far different conception of unionism is the resolution adopted by the 1977 conference of a British engineers' union. "Shop stewards of each company must increase the number of employees in their grade in a proportion equal to the percentage of the unemployed in their region. Otherwise they must be notified that all the overtime work in their grade will be prohibited by the union." *AUEW* (Amalgamated Union of Engineering Workers) *Journal* (July 1977).

20. For a fine criticism of postwar democracy along these lines, see Morisaki Kazue, "Sengo minshushugi to minshū no shisō" [Postwar democracy and the thinking of the masses], *Dentō to Gendai*, no. 30 (1977).

21. Rōdō-shō, *Rōdō tōkei yōran* [Handbook of labor statistics] (Tokyo, 1995). One small, hopeful sign, especially since 1983, has been the appearance of so-called community unions, formed mainly through the dedicated efforts of individuals who experienced the student movement of the late 1960s before turning to union activism. Anyone who works in the region covered by one of these unions may join. In contrast to enterprise-based unions, these community unions take as their main organizational target workers in small enterprises, part-time workers, and others who lack a guaranteed livelihood due to the existence of the major corporations. At present, there are only about seventy of these unions, and their combined membership is no more than 10,000 people. Yet although their present influence is weak, when one considers the bifurcation of the labor market into relatively secure regular employees in large firms, and huge numbers of men and women in

the sorts of workplaces targeted by these unions, the potential importance of these unions in the revival of the Japanese labor movement is considerable. For more on these unions, see Komyunichi yunion zenkoku nettowaaku, *Yunion, ningen, nettowaaku* [Union, humans, network] (Tokyo: Dai-ichi Shorin, 1993).

22. Kagoyama Takashi, "Shomin seikatsuha no kurashi to iken" [The life and opinion of proponents of the common people's livelihood], *Chūō Kōron* (April 1977).

23. Ibid., pp. 107, 111.

24. Characteristic is an interim report edited by the Economic Planning Agency, "Kokumin seikatsu shingikai sōgō seikatsu bukai chūkan hōkoku" [Interim report on the overall national life, by the working group of the advisory council on national life], *Kojin seikatsu yūsen shakai o mezashite* [Toward a society that prioritizes individual life], (Tokyo, 1991), pp. 7–8.

5

J53, MII, JAPAN

Light and Shadow
in Quality Control Circles

Why Talk About Quality Control Circles?

Beginning in the late 1960s, a variety of so-called small-group activities began to develop in spectacular fashion in the big business workplaces of Japan. The best known were the Zero Defect (ZD) movement and Quality Control (QC) circles.

The great majority of small-group activities were initiated with the encouragement of managers, and at times with their de facto coercion; they were at base ingenious tools to *manage* production and labor. But somewhere in midcourse these small-group activities came to constitute an autonomous *movement* of conscientious workers. Working people created informal circles on their own initiative, and they used them to devise means to improve job skills, prevent injuries at work, reduce the percentage of defective products, increase productivity, reduce costs, and more. Small-group activities are therefore sometimes called "self-management activities." In the steel industry, by the mid-1970s one finds self-management activities in fully 169 plants, which reported the existence of 30,000 circles and 230,000 participants, and a participation rate among the workers of 83 percent.[1] Although the extent of small-group activities in the steel industry has declined in recent years, largely due to sharp reductions in total workforce size, in 1994 one could still find 162 enterprises reporting a total of 19,000 circles with 113,000 participants. Since the 1970s, for Japanese workers the term "self-management" no longer referred to a new form of socialism; it instead came to signify this kind of small-group activity.

To describe this phenomenon using the language of the British working class, "we" (workers) are doing what "they" (managers) should be doing, as if "we" had the same values as "they." In this respect, the extraordinary spread of small-group activities is a distinctive phenomenon of contemporary Japan.

When the realms of worker and managerial culture are separate from each other, even if they are not in sharp conflict, such activities in which workers act independently to develop their skills, establish work standards, or modify production facilities are likely to obstruct managerial objectives; in such cases, managers cannot know or predict what the workers might do. For managers to encourage a self-managed movement of workers, then, would appear to be a truly perilous maneuver. But in Japanese production sites since the 1960s, managers have been safe to ignore this potential danger. Indeed, they can issue confident proclamations that self-managed small-group activities are the very essence of worker "participation." Underlying this confidence is the development discussed in previous chapters: Particularly beginning in the mid-1960s, unionized workers in Japanese big business enterprises adopted the norms of management as their own.

In this chapter I introduce a number of Quality Control circles. Analysis of self-management activities is essential for anyone concerned with the future of the union movement among ordinary workers. Such an inquiry should convey a clear image of the "incorporation of labor into management," a process that is being carried out by the employees themselves as they transform their mode of working. But the truly important question arises after presenting this image. Are there indeed no obstacles and no limits whatsoever to the incorporation of labor into management?

In his meticulous analysis, Nitta Michio concludes that incorporation is not total, that workers preserve a sphere of autonomy. He claims that self-management activities in the steel industry have been widely practiced because "they have intrinsic meaning for the workers on the job." He argues that these activities foster mutual understanding within work groups, satisfy the workers' "mental desires" by enlarging their jobs, provide ongoing education and training, and "make work easier to perform."[2] Nitta also asserts that the norms and feelings of the work group have a "transformational function." Workers, that is, reinterpret management's formal concept of the purpose of small-group activities. For example, when workers actually put in place improvements desired by management, they do so in a way that restrains the managerial desire to pin down individual responsibility and that prevents any increase in the workload or any reduction in staffing levels. In my reading of his work, Nitta is not clear about whether this "transformational function" is something he hopes for or something that has actually been achieved. Notwithstanding this, I find Nitta's overall analysis to be excellent. To sum up his thesis, Nitta points out that small-group activities may not have exerted such a profound impact on workers' lives, but that they are nonetheless beneficial to workers and that they could possibly develop to pose a latent threat to managers. In this chapter I examine this last possibility.

My inquiry also begins with the following hypothesis: Since the mid-1960s labor unions in Japan have retreated from any endeavor to restrict competition among coworkers. This retreat reinforced, and was reinforced by, the psychology of ordinary workers, who identified the meaning of postwar democracy as the opportunity to compete on the basis of merit and ability. It also provided the backdrop for the convergence of the cultures of the workers and of managers. But despite this retreat, I assume that as long as employees in Japan remain subject to managerial control, they will possess desires concerning their work and their relations to other workers that are in some sense independent from the intentions of management. In addition, one must consider the fact that this retreat of labor unions took place simultaneously with the advent of small-group activities. Combining these two points leads to my hypothesis: Although its purity may be compromised, a certain logic of labor that in other instances might have manifested itself in the activism of a union local is likely to be alloyed with self-managing QC activity.

My intention in this chapter should now be clear. In a book seeking to paint a portrait of organized workers in Japan, I am studying QC circles—formally speaking, not at all the concern of unions—because I suspect one may discover an independent logic of labor manifest in everyday work-place activity not in the union local but rather in the QC circle. I wish to test this possibility. And beyond this empirical investigation, I am investigating Japan's distinctive pattern of self-management activities in a search for a subversive potential embedded in the logic of capital.

My method is to use reports signed by the workers, where the responsibity for authorship is clear. These reports are found in several journals edited and published by the Japanese Union of Scientists and Engineers (JUSE), an organization devoted to the promotion of the QC circle movement.[3] In light of this, they can only read like compositions of model students. Even so, I am convinced that a close reading of these reports reveals problems that cannot be hidden fully by the stirring words of model students. Except for the last two, every example in this chapter has been selected from these more-or-less official sources.

My criterion for selection was the specific detail of changes in the workplace resulting from so-called improvements (*kaizen*). I also sought reports that conveyed what struck me as an authentic worker voice. For this reason, my sixteen examples do not necessarily present a proportionally true sample of the major topics addressed by QC circles. I include relatively few technically detailed reports on facility improvements to raise the rate of operation. In addition, I have sought to be as specific as possible. Wherever feasible I have identified the company names, the name of the work site and the work process, the composition of the QC circle or the work group, and the period in which the activities took place. I have used the exact wording of the original reports in presenting the specifics and the conclusion of each case.[4] As these case reports were originally prepared by workers for presentation to their peers, they assume familiarity with the work situations and may be somewhat opaque to outsiders. But to examine them closely is worthwhile, for the experiences and atmosphere conveyed by these records is likely to be close to the experience of many blue- and white-collar workers in contemporary Japan.

Activities to Improve Technical Skills

The examples to follow have been grouped in terms of the objectives of the QC groups. I begin with QC circles convened to improve the technical skills and knowledge of the workers.

Example 1.   This group consists of the foreman and thirteen male workers (average age of thirty-three) at the ship repair dock of Mitsubishi Heavy Industries' Kobe Shipyard. The year is 1974. The objective is to develop the versatility of all the workers and up-grade their skills to enable them to handle all possible fitting tasks.

I. Action Taken: The group composed a "grading scale" and classified workers into classes 1, 2, or 3 based on their skill in the tasks of marking, spot-welding, and operating gas-powered plate-cutting machines. This process uncovered considerable differentials in individual skill levels. These differences resulted from the tendency to assign difficult tasks only to the veteran workers, since no mistakes could be tolerated given the short cycle-times for our tasks. In addition, the supervisors tended to use only those who had proven records of performance for harder jobs. Therefore, we made a "graph for a plan to upgrade skill levels," with a goal of raising the current overall level by 50%. For each job we identified the problematic aspects. In spot-welding for example, the method of deciding on the block size and correcting for stress on the metal, and in marking, the task of making vertical and horizontal markings on the ships under repair. The chart was used to determine the instructor, the trainee, the method of instruction (either on-the-job training [OJT] or one-to-one instruction). Through OJT, each worker began to undertake a number of tasks he had not performed before.

II. Summary: In working with marking and spot-welding, the goal of a 50% average increase was not achieved, but in general the accuracy and speed of our work improved. Our resolve to allow newcomers and inexpert workers to undertake important tasks produced positive results. The old-timers who had until then complained "I've had enough of studying" or "I don't have to learn difficult tasks" began to say "I'm not going to let the young guys beat me. Teach me how to use the automatic gas-powered cutter." We are now experiencing for the first time the pleasure of working at this "general hospital for ships."[5]

This example strikes me as an unproblematic instance of an autonomous worker consciousness. The objective of the endeavor was to improve the skill of all workers, to make them equally competent and able to perform all the tasks in their division, thus building a foundation for solidarity among the workers by equalizing their capability. If meritocratic competition differentiates workers able to perform tough jobs from those limited to easy ones, the latter are "naturally" viewed and accepted as targets for layoffs or so-called voluntary retirement in times of streamlining. Though perhaps not consciously intending to do so, this group in effect acted to prevent such a situation from developing. Moreover, these workers put productivity on the back burner, if only temporarily, by giving priority to on-the-job training, which inevitably slows operations. Overall, this case shows us a group of experienced, skilled workers whose objectives are those of workers the world over. Compare this state of affairs with the next report.

Example 2. Toyota Auto Body's Truck Plant. Equipment Maintenance Section of the Sheet Metal Shop. Murata Circle. 1968–1972. Objectives: to acquire the know-how to work with new equipment such as large specialized machines and to reduce assembly line stoppage due to equipment failure.

I. Action Taken: Our QC circle activity entailed four steps: 1) Create a QC circle among maintenance men who are "lone-wolves" guarding "specialized skills." These men feel little need to participate in quality control activity, and their circle must somehow lead them to shed their "artisanal mentality." 2) Divide into groups by product (driver's seat workers, truck bed workers) and eliminate maintenance problems on their own as much as possible. 3) Aiming at greater exchange of information and knowledge between maintenance workers and assemblers, introduce a rotation system across different work groups at the plant, and refine the improvements in "combat teams" that include "visiting students" from assembly groups. 4) In addition, to broaden the perspective and scope of the undertaking, initiate joint circle activities involving engineers in the production technology and purchasing sections, and convene an assembly of "Preventive Maintenance Circles" drawing in all relevant divisions. Behind these efforts lay the company-wide objective of promoting QC.

II. Summary: Henceforth, by making full use of the capabilities we have begun to nurture, we plan to contribute to the prosperity of the Toyota Auto Body Plant by creating a system in which we undertake tasks traditionally in the domain of technicians, thus enabling the technicians to concentrate on work at a higher plane.

This report does not discuss the resulting changes made in the work itself, but the "maintenance men" clearly shed their craftsmen mentality and adopted a perspective beyond their assigned jobs, ultimately arriving at a "perspective that encompassed the entire company." To abdicate specific controls in a particular trade, to follow a straight line path to become a company man with a company-wide vision, that is, to become a good "Toyota man"—perhaps this is how a Japanese worker matures. But I am skeptical of the value such maturity adds to the life of a person who will continue a given job for an entire career. The maintenance man will in some sense commit himself to a company-wide perspective; at the behest of managers, he will learn to readily "adjust" his expectations of a once familiar workplace and job. As he is thus integrated into the corporation, the maintenance man loses his workplace autonomy.

I now turn to a workplace of so-called office ladies.

Example 3. Tachibana Metal Mfg., Yōrō Plant, business office, accounting unit. Okubo circle. Three women. 1971–1973. Objectives: to address disparities in individual ability and the inability to perform work beyond assigned tasks, and to overcome sectionalism.

I. Action Taken: Each individual completes a "self-evaluation chart" divided into 13 major categories with 79 sub-categories and sets objectives of doubling the number of categories assessed to be "A level" (understands it well) and cutting D-level categories (don't understand at all) by two-thirds, through OJT. Specifically, we each designed a "weekly work plan" that included our poorly understood tasks (categories C and D). We undertook these by relying only on the work standards manual and we re-assessed our results on the "self-evaluation chart." Mistakes and other problems were explored in meetings of the circle. We expected our supervisor to trust us as subordinates and delegate 90% of the work to us, and to foster our individual development as a human being, we hoped for the assignment even of such "heavy work" as the difficult tasks of processing direct-deposits of monthly wages and preparing reports on outstanding bills. Because K-san lagged behind the others in developing her capability, we gave her the middle of our three seats to facilitate her training.

II. Summary: Not only did each individual achieve her objectives in full, but we were able to reduce overtime to zero even in the busy season at the end of the fiscal period. In addition, each of us reduced by about 30 minutes a day the time needed to complete our jobs. Moreover, as we came to understand the relationships between various jobs and their importance, our motivation increased and our eyes began to sparkle.

These women seem to have achieved a nearly complete command of the entire array of jobs in the accounting office and have come to enjoy their work in the process. One should evaluate this highly. Perhaps the small size of their office enabled this achievement, but it may well be through such a process that career women are born. Yet the problem in this example is the system of checking the results of each individual's performance. One can well imagine that with a less generous group leader or a more stressful workplace atmosphere, Ms. K might have received harsh treatment. In this particular case, the deficient worker was dealt with gently, but some later examples will show that individual performance assessments can facilitate fierce and threatening managerial control.

It is worth noting, in this context, that JUSE recommends the use of statistical data, such as the number of slips processed, the time spent on phone calls, the number of errors, the number of claims processed, in efforts to assess and improve office productivity. In "hawkish" Quality Control circles, which aim to improve productivity and reduce standard job times (hours per person), the basic methods are none other than industrial engineering and time-and-motion studies.

Security and Reduced Hardship at the Workplace

I now turn to quality control activities seeking to improve safety in the workplace. According to a 1977 publication of the Iron and Steel Workers Union Federation (Tekkō Rōren), safety issues account for about 20 percent of the themes addressed by the industry's Quality Control circles.[6] This reflects the natural strength of worker concern with safety.

> **Example 4.**   Mitsubishi Steel Mfg., Nagasaki. Cast iron products repair shop. Joint circle of ceiling-crane operators and *tamakake* workers (floor workers who hang objects on the crane). 1972–1973. Objective: To meet mill-wide safety targets by eliminating injuries to *tamakake* workers.
>
> *I. Action Taken:*   Upon analysis of the causes of injuries and near-accidents over the past year and discussion among crane operators and *tamakake* workers the following measures were adopted. An illustrated manual was prepared for inexperienced *tamakake* workers, showing the center of gravity of oddly shaped objects and the best way to hang them. To deal with the tendencies to "forget to confirm (that an object was ready for lifting) and to convey incorrect hand signals," the *tamakake* workers took turns riding with the crane operators to get their perspective on the best position and method for effectively conveying signals and guiding the crane operators. As a result, new work standards were established. In turn the crane operators took turns at the tasks of the *tamakake* workers so long as this did not slow down operations unduly. Also we more clearly indicated the proper storage places, usage, and weight limits for hanging objects, to eliminate wrong

decisions. However, even as we implemented these measures another accident occurred. To put a stop to this, we took the following measures. l) Each crane was provided with a chart on loading procedures. When a procedure departed from the chart, crane operators were to stop the procedure. 2) The entire work group took a review course on standard *tamakake* procedures. 3) At the morning assembly each day, the entire work group recited the standard work procedures and rules. 4) In discussion sessions involving the two work groups, participants reported to each other on whatever errors or procedural violations had occurred and agreed to strictly observe procedures. 5) We agreed that when loading objects on a crane, the *tamakake* worker would call out "O.K.?" to his assistant and wait for a verbal reply of "O.K.!" before giving the go-ahead signal to the crane operator.

II. Summary: Since these steps were taken, no accidents have occurred. Team work has improved and everybody is delighted.

Here is an excellent example of worker activity. The crane operators identified inadequate training of new *tamakake* workers in the hanging of oddly shaped objects as the cause of poor performance, and the *tamakake* workers retorted that "We've all completed our training course, and everybody is well qualified." The crane operators insisted that some members were nonetheless unfamiliar with special procedures and unusual *tamakake* work. Out of such heated discussion, the chart for standard procedures was created. The report presents a rich picture of this entire process, in which the workers on their own initiative questioned the formal qualification standards and proceeded to acquire information and set standards truly essential to their work. The *tamakake* workers on the floor boarded the high-ceiling cranes with the operators and helped determine the position where hoisted objects should be deposited. The crane operators were not to operate the crane until the *tamakake* workers were ready.

Here, one sees a recognition by workers engaged in two different tasks that they are joined together by their work; this recognition led to cooperation in setting safety rules. Can one not conclude that a worker society was (re)discovered here? Neither worker self-hood nor work group autonomy is possible if the workers place all the blame for disasters on managers and fail to cooperate and to investigate matters for themselves.

In the next example, unfortunately, a very different situation prevails.

Example 5. Komatsu Manufacturing, Awatsu Plant. Sheet metal processing and welding division for main components of press machines. Twelve members representing all work teams. 1970–1977. Objective: zero accident rate.

I. Action Taken: We examined the nine accidents of the past three years and categorized the causes as "basic individual actions," "disorderly storage of materials and tools, sloppiness," "poor facilities," etc. . . . We then formulated and implemented the following plan of action. 1) All circle members are to check the work of their co-workers. Workers not following safety standards were sharply warned whenever a violation was noted. The time and date, place, name of violator, nature of the violation and the caution were all recorded and then discussed at circle meetings. Initially, "we disliked this plan because reports which identified individuals by name could harm the persons concerned." But realizing "the goal is to protect these individuals," and encouraged by our supervisors, we continued this practice for six months. We learned as a result that many unsafe actions stemmed from [improper] use of protective clothing and crane operation. We also discovered that the workers M, T, and O required special attention and reported this to the section chief. All work procedures of these three persons who "required special safety warning" received continuous monitoring by supervisors for three days, and they were persistently warned about their work clothes and actions. A further measure was to require them to attend all the safety training sessions conducted by the company. (This safety education apparently was effective for the three workers concerned.) 2) We worked on keeping things neat and orderly, properly arranging and stacking steel plates, etc. 3) We made minor improvements in facilities and materials. 4) We compiled a manual for the education of new employees. These were the measures adopted.

II. Summary: After the circle, the accident rate fell to zero, and we received the Factory Director's Award. Further, our efficiency rose by 20 percent.

Even though this undertaking began with the good intention of ensuring safety, I find it most troubling. Its primary focus was to identify "persons requiring special safety warnings." The group dealt with these people by ceding to the supervisor the responsibility for closely monitoring them and imposing compulsory guidance on them. This resembles the behavior of honor students who target inferior students and have the teacher scold them. The work group shows no inclination to ease up on assessing individual blame or protect somewhat problematic coworkers from management. Almost certainly, the three workers targeted by their peers will suffer low pay raises and delayed promotions for years to come. Quite possibly they will quit or be eased out of their jobs. Of course, in examples 1 and 3, the possibility also existed for discrimination to fall upon workers identified as lagging behind their peers, and in this kind of workplace, such practices certainly predate the advent of QC circle activities. But QC circles gave a new public sanction to such targeting and helped the practice win common acceptance among the workers themselves. This case shows that even circles that begin with the fine intention of protecting workers can end by harming individuals.

In addition to circles seeking to improve safety and skills, I count among the well-intentioned circles those hoping to "make our work easier." My strong impression after reading numerous cases is that women workers more often undertook this endeavor, so relevant to their immediate work lives, even as they remained rather indifferent to the "big" theme of raising productivity. When it came to making work more pleasant, they frequently and quickly decided: "We must put a QC circle to work on this." The following is one fine example.

> **Example 6.** Kobe Steel Co. Welding Rod Department. Operations Planning Room, Data Processing Center. Nine punch-card operators, dubbed the *"Kikkai* Team." 1971–1972. Objective: Raise efficiency, with primary focus on "making our work easier and more pleasant."
>
> *I. Action Taken:* We decided to inform the factory about poorly filled out forms and invoices (illegible, incorrect) which they send to us and call on the factory to improve this situation. We composed a "data processing section guide" describing the purpose of various forms and the proper way to fill them out. We distributed this to all the factories. In addition we sent a copy of an incorrect form, with corrections marked on it, to each individual recording clerk in the factory, together with a "properly feminine letter" asking the clerk to improve his work. We called this our "love letter strategy."
>
> *II. Summary:* We obtained results beyond our expectation. The number of faulty invoices and forms decreased dramatically. As a result, our own key-punching errors decreased as well.

As might be expected the Taylorites of JUSE commented that this group could have obtained even better results by focusing on so-called management targets, such as the percentage of faulty invoices submitted or the key-punchers' rate per minute. But this *"Kikkai* team" (their name was taken from a comic book hero who generates out-of-this-world ideas) would likely have rejected such a hawkish QC agenda. The activities of the women reveal a playful spirit, and the men who received their letters probably did not mind such an attempt to assign individual responsiblity for errors, so long as managers were not drawn in.

> **Example 7.** Pentel Co. Factory in Soka City, Saitama Prefecture. Pastel Crayon Packing Line. QC circle members: 2 males, 10 females (average age: 28). 1974. Objective: to improve factory procedures to make work easier.
>
> *I. Action Taken:* QC circle members previously believed that a so-called good QC circle raised company profits, and we had addressed

such themes as increasing output per capita or reducing defect rates. Circle members felt these themes were forced upon them by the company, and they showed little enthusiasm for them. Some even said it was best to take a vacation day when a QC meeting was scheduled. QC activities could in no way be regarded as worker self-management. So we decided that we should change things and undertake activities for our own benefit, such as improving work conditions, work procedures or the workplace environment. We resolved to solve problems that we would identify, without using any money but by using discarded or idle equipment. For example, by using six plywood boards and a roller-conveyer stored in the warehouse, we improved the packaging process by reducing the number of times we had to transport individual boxes each day. And we eliminated the job of carrying empty boxes by making use of the overhead conveyer, installing sideboards to keep the boxes from falling off when thrown onto the conveyer.

II. Summary: These changes not only eased our fatigue at work, but we were able to reduce the number of persons required for this job from two to one.[7]

If it is true that women workers are better able than their male counterparts to separate their own concerns from managerial objectives and focus seriously on problems in their immediate work environment, then the workers in this crayon factory exemplify such a female stance in a most refreshing way. The decision to make changes without spending money suggests a desire to avoid troublesome negotiations with supervisors, and the high value the summary placed on easing fatigue seems far more typical of female than male workers in Japan. Can one not say that for Japan's workers in general, so inclined to sacrifice to management the autonomy needed to sustain their ongoing working life out of a commitment to the greater good of the company, such a feminine perspective is a most necessary ability?

But many QC circle activities challenge precisely this "female" ability to maintain distance from company goals. Even in this example, one result was to reduce staffing needs and, presumably, lower the overall number of employees in the factory. The proud call in the title of this report to "look at what we accomplished!" may signal an incipient shift in the thinking of these women toward a closer identification with corporate needs.

Operating Rates and Defect Rates

In processing industries, stable operation of the plant's equipment is the decisive element in any plan to increase productivity. For this reason, many QC circles in the core workplaces of processing plants make improving the rate of operation their primary concern.

Example 8.   Asahi Chemical Industries, Bemberg Plant. Hank thread finishing shop. 1970. Objective: achieve operating rates of 95 to 97% on the continuous refining machines.

I. Action Taken: When we analyzed the reason for the existing low operating rate of 86 to 89%, we found the main causes to be in the equipment itself. We decided Team A would tackle problems with the dryer machine openings, Team B would work to improve the method of cleaning the rollers, and Team C would try to make the packaging of different fibers more efficient. We knew our effectiveness would be limited if our endeavor were confined to production workers with poor knowledge of machinery, so we asked a maintenance staffer to join each team. By sharing our information and knowledge, we sought to improve the facilities and our use of them. For example, when "spindles with mottled thread come from the slubbing section through the star-wheels, and move on to the dryer conveyer chain, many spindles entered the wrong hole." The circle members stayed on after hours in 40 to 45 degree centigrade heat to examine the entrance to the dryer closely. We learned that the diameter of the star-wheel was too small. The rate of operations was improved spectacularly by enlarging the wheel.

II. Summary: We achieved our goal of raising the operation rate. We gained confidence by solving this problem. We hope to continue working on this "system of production management by our work group."

In some factories the pace is so intense that workers look forward to equipment failure as the only chance for a breather. But with the exception of such places, workers generally welcome improvements in the rate of operation. In this example, blue-collar workers went to a great deal of trouble to identify and correct problems in the equipment. They gained knowledge of complex, hitherto mysterious equipment and the self-confidence to operate it. To perfect a "system of production management by our work group," these workers must engage in a high level of intellectual activity; they were forging the skills and the subjective determination to accomplish this. This is only one of many examples that reveal to us the high degrees of knowledge and skill possessed by blue-collar workers in Japan.[8]

The second concern of this section is the effort to cut defect rates. It may not matter to managers whether money is saved by increasing operating rates or by reducing defect rates, but for workers, the impact differs sharply. Especially in the machine manufacturing industry, QC circle activity to reduce the rate of defective products inevitably brings intensive scrutiny of worker behavior and attitudes.

Example 9.   Mitsubishi Heavy Industries, Hiroshima Plant. Drilling machine shop. 24 workers. 1971–1972. Objective: to prevent incorrect measurements.

I. Action Taken: Upon examining the 19 cases of faulty measurement of the past 9 months, we found that 70% of the problems resulted from failure to check the markings before drilling. Therefore, after constructing a proper "climate" of workplace opinion in favor of reforms, we took the following steps. 1) Even the most skilled worker must be certain to engage in self-inspection by checking his own work against the drawing. 2) The pitch and the dividing points in the markings [on the objects to be drilled] must be checked against the standard lines of the drawing by using a compass. 3) Workers must improve their understanding of the drawings with a thorough familiarity with plane geometry and trigonometry. 4) The supervisor should examine drawings beforehand and should prepare an operational guidebook that identifies the key points.

II. Summary: As a result of these measures, workers who had tended to stick to their own idiosyncratic work procedures ceased doing so, and a spirit of cooperation welled-up. Workers began to consult the supervisor about unclear points, no matter how minor. Formerly frequent simple mistakes virtually disappeared. In place of a general operational guidebook addressed to the whole shop, we now had a manual addressed exclusively to our concerns and created by us.

In this shop, "most of the drilling work was performed by following the markings, so that jigs and other corrective instruments were used in just 20% of the jobs." In such a workplace, where diverse pieces are produced in small lots by skilled operatives, the demand placed on workers pressed to reduce the defect rate is not particularly stringent. They are simply asked to perform their work more conscientiously, using more scientific techniques. Toward the end of the report, almost as an afterthought, as follow-up to the measures just described is the comment, "In order to reduce mistakes even by a single case, all the group members put into effect a nearly fool-proof corrective plan, with the support of the supervisor." I agree with the comment appended by the JUSE editors: "We wish they had elaborated a bit more on the specifics of the corrective plan." Any effort to apply standard procedures to a job has the potential to simplify that work. In this case, for example, what if a foolproof plan means an aggressive push to enable defect-free work "even without thinking," combined with a push to reduce the cycle time for the job? The result will be to eliminate the need for skilled machinists.

What, then, is the situation when the workers from the outset are semiskilled operatives?

Example 10. Fuji Electric, Fukiage Plant. Electromagnetic switch assembly shop. 1972–1973. Objective: to reduce the defect rate.

I. Action Taken: In accord with a section-wide program to reduce the defect rate to less than one percent, we designed four sets of plans.

1) We used industrial engineering (analysis of task components) to revise the time needed for each process along the conveyer line and to improve the tools used. 2) To cut down on defects resulting from "absent-minded" behavior, we compiled a Pareto diagram indicating the defects produced during the course of a week by each individual. Some people did complain about creating a color-coded chart identifying each worker, saying "I don't like this" or "It will be used to target the people who produce defective pieces." But we persuaded them that "If we are careful, defective work will decrease. And if we are absent-minded, it is our fault." 3) To guard against defective pressed plates (from scratches or dirt), we changed the layout of the plate area. 4) By these means we reduced "our defects" significantly, so we followed up by turning to defects originating in other work sections and organized a discussion group to exchange ideas with other sections.

II. Summary: The defect rate dropped from 1.7% to 0.22%. The number of defective pressed plates dropped from 42 to 2 cases. The tact-pitch of the conveyer belt was reduced from 45 seconds to 40 seconds. We achieved an efficiency improvement of approximately 14%. "We are delighted that output has risen."

As the report itself suggests, the heart of this case is the second step. Without reservation the promoters of this QC project suppressed the natural workplace voices of those who sought to protect each other and set out to identify "absent-minded" individuals. They also increased the conveyor belt speed. Though their tools were reportedly improved to some extent, the pressure on the operatives at this workplace undoubtedly intensified. This example makes it abundantly clear that defect-reducing QC activity in a mass-production engineering plant frequently ends up placing even greater pressure on individual operatives.

The editors from JUSE, however, rate this example highly. They state that QC circles dealing with routine assembly line tasks are "easy to talk about but hard to implement." Why, then, was it possible to overcome the difficulties in this case? My guess is that not only the author of the report (Nakajima Tōru) but also the vanguard leaders of this particular circle were male workers, though many of the "rear guard" circle members, whose voices expressed some doubts at first, were female workers.[9] The men in the vanguard eventually will be recognized by management for their QC achievements. They can expect to ascend from the newly "improved" workplace to better, higher-level jobs. The rear guard circle members knew they were unlikely to escape from the workplace in this fashion, so they were not likely to take the lead in QC endeavors to intensify the pace of their job. At the same time, these women rarely plan to spend a long career working at Fuji Electric Company, so they are not particularly stubborn in defending whatever "pastoral" quality may prevail in their jobs.[10] This sort of QC circle could succeed during the era of high-speed growth precisely because both male and female workers saw themselves as transient residents in this particular workplace; neither vanguard nor rear guard felt a need to ask whether a given change "will allow me to continue working at this place for a long time."

Finally, I take a look at women workers with somewhat different personalities. These women living in the foothills of Mt. Yatsugatake hold two jobs, as wives in farming families and as factory laborers.

Example 11. Kyōwa Optical Instruments, Nagano Prefecture, Suwa County. Zoom lens assembly plant. One man (supervisor) and five women (average age 41). 1973–1974. Objective: In preparation for the start of mass-production of product M, to reduce the defect rate and the standard assembly time.

I. Action Taken: We began by inviting the supervisor to serve as lecturer and we studied the basic concepts and goals of QC circles themselves. Next we turned to analyze the causes for the existing defect rate of 9.3%, and we found the most common defect to be "poor operation of the zoom mechanism." We then implemented six improvements to overcome this problem. Two typical examples follow. We stopped using a paint brush to grease the zoom ring's bore, and instead devised an automatic greasing mechanism taking a hint from the brush used to wash a baby's milk bottles. And we introduced a mechanism that would grease both sides of the zoom lens's washer simultaneously, by incorporating the principle of a washing machine wringer.

II. Summary: The defect rate fell to 2.1 percent as a result, and we shortened the zoom lens assembly time from 24 to 18 minutes. This allowed a reduction of overtime work, previously needed for us to reach our daily production quotas, from an average of 12 hours per person per month to zero just six months later. This eliminated our one "big headache." We came to realize how wonderful it was to work by constantly thinking about ways to improve our work rather than doing only what our supervisor told us to do. Now, even if someone is absent, we are able to meet that day's quota. Everyone tries not to be absent, so as not to cause others trouble, and when a worker knows in advance that she has to take the day off, arrangements are made so that work at the plant can proceed as usual. These are the watchwords of the "Mom's circle." We would like to continue working toward the goal of "making our jobs easier and enjoyable, so that we mothers on our own initiative create conditions where we manage our working processes."[11]

These self-styled "farm-village moms" add, "Even now, we check the water in the rice fields before going to work, and in the evening we hurry home to work in the fields." As might be expected, their initial interest in

QC activities was low. They wondered, "Why do we have to study like this?" This example shows us a group on the margins of company society (to be sure, their sense of being outsiders was none too strong, as we see in their willingness to work overtime to meet the "daily quota") who come to accept managerial objectives at the prodding of their supervisor. It indicates the power of the employee culture of Japanese companies to incorporate the surrounding society. Yet one must recognize that in the very process of their incorporation, these women were able to create a workers' society with its own rules. If they can preserve a value system that keeps a distance from corporate objectives, this workers' society may develop into a self-governing body that manages the work so as to "make our jobs easier and enjoyable," even if this means challenging the company and its supervisors. One cannot know if this will come to pass; and one can detect an outer limit to any potential challenge in the fact that their promise not to "trouble" each other by missing a day accepts the need to meet the daily quota as an unshakable premise.

Thus far I have presented QC circles that raised what I call "dove" issues. In some of these activities, workers in fact achieved benefits such as increased versatility at work, more equal access to and mastery of skills, reduced pain and difficulties at work, or fewer accidents. In others, workers addressed issues—such as improving the rate of operation or reducing the defect rate—whose basic character was unlikely to provoke peer resistance. Overall, these dovish QC projects hold the potential to raise workers' productive morale, improve their skills, and heighten their solidarity. Nonetheless, depending on the manner in which they are promoted, even these well-intended QC activities can bring direct harm to employees. Perhaps even more likely in the real world of labor-management relations is that the benefits of a particular improvement bring with them even greater costs to workers. For example, the endeavor to make workers more versatile is intended to enrich their working life, but for management a multi-skilled workforce is often prelude to, and condition for, staff reductions. In the forest of QC circles, light and shadow mingle in complex ways.

Diverse Patterns of Efficiency Enhancement

In contrast to the QC circles examined thus far, one also finds hawk circle activities. In this section, I explore their dark habitats in the QC forest. Hawkish circles seek changes that a labor union would typically fight as part of a struggle against rationalization. They openly take increased efficiency or reduced staffing as their direct objective, goals that were only indirect or unintended effects of the dovish circles.

> **Example 12.** Sawato Electric, Tokyo, Itabashi ward. Bus and truck starter shaft processing shop. Circle members: 7 males (average age 27). 1975. Objective: To reduce time required for tooling changes and sim-

plify the job. This was absolutely necessary in order to adapt to the *kanban* method of the parent auto company.

I. Action Taken: The main machines at the shop are four lathes, each operated by one person. The time required to retool a lathe was 80 minutes for rough turning and 120 minutes for finishing. We adopted a plan to reduce this by 50%. We analyzed the causes of the slow change-over by having someone other than the person in charge of the re-tooling conduct a time-study of the process. We implemented improvements addressed to each component of the job. We decided to: 1) standardize dock adjustments rather than rely on the worker's intuition or experience; 2) make it unnecessary to run around looking for tools and models by keeping these at a fixed place for each machine tool; 3) simplify "measurement adjustment" by making the diameter of the model in each case 20 millimeters bigger than the diameter of the finished shaft, thus ensuring that the space between the stylus and the bending tool's tip remains constant; 4) simplify "adjustment of the model's position and tappet adjustment" by making the length of the model uniform. As in step 3), we asked the production engineering division to remake the model. These measures enabled us to reduce the assembly line down-time during re-tooling by 80%. That is, the total time required for a change-over was cut from 200 minutes to 40 minutes. Moreover, we made the job itself very simple, and ordinary workers were now able to perform it.

II. Summary: Now we can even cope with the *kanban* system. Up until now we had simply assumed that tooling change-overs were naturally time consuming. But upon reflection we feel that the current, post-improvement situation is the normal state of affairs. We are truly ashamed at how long we previously took to do the job.[12]

Is it possible to dramatically exceed the initial goal and reduce down-time by 80 percent without intensifying the pressure or pace imposed on workers (see Table 5.1)? Certainly I am no expert in engineering or labor science, but I am still very dubious. But even setting this point aside, the fact remains that the workers themselves simplified their jobs in order to cut back on the hours required to perform them. This endeavor allowed them to exercise their creative intellectual capacity, but the result was to render this capacity useless in the future. They frankly concluded that "now anyone can do the job."

At first glance, this outcome resembles that of the first case presented in this chapter, but the impact of the QC activity on workplace life in fact differed decisively. In the first example, "anyone" became able to do the work because the employees undertook to upgrade all their skills; in this case, the job was simplified and requisite skills downgraded. Decision-

TABLE 5.1

Reduction of Time Required to Retool

	Before Improvements		*After Improvements*	
	Rough Turning	*Finishing*	*Rough Turning*	*Finishing*
Adjust model position	12 min.	12 min.	2 min.	2 min.
Set dock position	8 min.	8 min.	1 min.	1 min.
Adjust tappet	5 min.	10 min.	2 min.	2 min.
Adjust measurement	10 min.	25 min.	0 min.	10 min.
Look for tools & models	5 min.	5 min.	0 min.	0 min.
Total	40 min.	60 min.	5 min.	15 min.
	(2 lathes:	(2 lathes:	(2 lathes:	(2 lathes:
	80 min.)	120 min.)	10 min.)	30 min.)

Source: FQC (May 1977), pp. 54, 56.

making authority on the job was ceded to management, and the QC circle members turned their coworkers or successor workers into persons readily replaceable. These young Tokyo machinists were remarkably indifferent to the importance for workers of preserving control over skills in order to retain power in their relationship with management. Contradicting conventional wisdom on the impact of QC activity, this circle ultimately reduced the skills of the workers.

Another action of these circle members that violates typical norms of the world of labor is their decision to call in workers from another section to carry out a time-study of the changeover process. These QC circle members refused to believe the claim of the men who normally handled this retooling, that "we are not wasting time in what we are doing."[13] Finally, when these workers concluded that they were now "ashamed" of the situation prior to their reforms, one can only lament that they seem entirely unaware of those aspects of work that must be protected.

Example 13. Matsushita Electric Works, Tsu Factory. Switch assembly plant. Workers engaged in the same job, 9 women. 1969. Objective: in line with an early 1969 section policy, increase productivity by 20%.

I. Action Taken: When we compiled a "self-management work chart" indicating each individual's hourly output, we found a range from a high of 213 units to a lowest of 143, with an average of 185. Based on each worker's own self-declared goal, we set an objective of raising average output by 25 percent, to 231. We designated people to take charge of solving the various problems that were obstructing this goal, and we adopted the following corrective measures: 1) strengthen the workers' morale and the spirit of teamwork; 2) centralize the greasing process; 3) change the layout of our work-site; 4) re-measure the standard time required for the job; 5) rearrange the placement of the jigs.

II. Summary: As a result of these improvements, average output rose to 233 and the defect rate dropped. The most serious difficulty was the tension in relationships between experienced and inexperienced workers, and between older and younger workers, resulting from the difference in the individual objectives set by the workers.[14]

This type of QC activity was common in mass-production factories during Japan's high-growth era; workers performing jobs on mounts near a conveyor line sought to raise their output norms. In this case, measures 2 and 5 might have reduced the pressure on the workers. If not, this circle's activity can only have increased the work intensity. To the extent that "section policy" and monitoring by coworkers was part of this QC process, on one hand, the plan to increase output goals through workers' "self-declarations" cannot be considered the result of free choice. On the other hand, the effort to pin down individual responsiblity appears gentler than that of the switch assembly shop at Fuji Electric (example 10).

The JUSE editors commented on this case that the "discussion of time-and-motion study hardly appears in the report. . . . How about mastering such techniques more thoroughly?" The editors made a point of adding as a subtitle to the report, "Increased Productivity by Using Industrial Engineering Practices." Such comments are interesting reflections of the federation's ideology, and it indeed appears to be the case that hawkish QC circles often begin by learning the techniques of industrial engineering, the most reliable weapon for achieving material results.

The Carnage of Staffing Cuts

Although QC activities of the high-growth era frequently sought to increase productivity and usually did raise individual output norms, these efforts only rarely led to cutbacks in the number of workers. They surely helped create a climate in which "excess" workers could be discharged, however, and when the season of streamlined management began in 1975, QC circles readily turned to the task of lowering costs by cutting back staffing. Certainly manpower-reducing QC circles greatly aided Japanese big business in eliminating "excess" workers in the mid-1970s, and beyond. Michimata Kenjirō and his colleagues carried out field studies of the steel industry in the 1970s, and they approvingly cite the claim of left-wing workplace activists that "workers will never engage in suicidal 'self-management' activities that reduce the numbers of workers required for a job."[15] But is this claim credible? I fear they are too sanguine in their judgment of Japanese employees.

Example 14. Toyota Auto Body, Kariya Plant. Passenger car painting, finishing process. QC circle: 14 males (average age 26). 1975. Objective: Improve black-out painting work to reduce the time and manpower required for the job.

I. Action Taken: Our goal represented the specific plan of our sub-section (*kakari*) to implement the section-wide program to cope with the rising costs of material and labor. At the start, passive voices were raised in the workplace, claiming that "we can't possibly reduce the workers needed on this job from two to one" or "where will the excess workers be transferred to?" or "this will mean more intensive work." But we persuaded them by arguing that "if we study industrial engineering techniques, even if we cut one worker, we'll be able to make the job easier. And moreover, Mr. H, the seasonal worker, is about ready to quit." They were also spurred on by Mr. U's experience. He had just returned from a training workshop at T Company. He told us, "T Company's workload is double ours. If we try, we can do it!"

In order to enable one person to do our current two-person job, and still keep the same conveyer line speed of 1.6 minutes per unit, we had to reduce the job time from 302 DM [1 DM = 1/100 minute] shared by two men, one each on the left and the right sides of the line, to 160 DM performed by one man. To meet this challenge, the entire crew studied industrial engineering and re-examined every aspect of the work process. We decided we could skip black-out painting entirely when the outer plate in any case was black or nearly black. We replaced paint brushes with paint guns. And we introduced a bigger parts box (this made it possible to throw parts into the box from a distance). By these and other such changes, we reduced the job to 162 DM. Over a one-week trial, the highest figure was 172 DM and the lowest was 157 DM. Some workers concluded that "there are even some steps that can be done faster than the new standard time. Once we get used to it, each of us can do the job alone." Finally, "to make it possible to do the job quicker and easier," we introduced an improvement in the placement of the paint hose, and achieved a rate of 155 DM.

II. Summary: At the end of the process, the IE staff gave us detailed instruction in the new procedures and motions to be followed, and we were able to accomplish the job without changing the line speed of 1.6 minutes. Further, we revised the manual on job procedures, methods of work, painting conditions, and different model types.[16]

In this fashion, the Toyota workers implemented a program of rationalization so rigorous that "the defect rate increased a bit," and one of the two workers on this line disappeared, as if by magic. Even the JUSE editors commented, "The report says little about the hardship involved in cutting down from two workers to one." Was it acceptable because the dismissed person was a temporary worker? Such thinking is naive; the impact of this change is not simply to eliminate one seasonal worker from the line. The remaining regular workers have surrendered whatever slight respite had been embedded in the existing work process; clearly, the intensity of their work increased. Compare the pre- and post-improvement job sheets (Table 5.2 and Table 5.3). All of the waiting time and tool-change time has been eliminated. Rather than waiting for the automobile body to come to the worker, now the worker chased after the car. What a pain to have that eager young beaver come back from the "training workshop" at T Company! Is it possible that such young workers have no appreciation for the moments of respite so crucial for making work tolerable, to make it possible to survive in a given workplace?

TABLE 5.2
Job Sheet Before Improvements

Job Procedure and Elements (right side worker)	Time (DM)	Job Procedure and Elements (left side worker)	Time (DM)
1. Remove cover, hang on shrouds	9	(same as right side)	9
2. Wait for arrival of the body	5	(same as right side)	10
			(for 2
3. Take up gun, spray grill part (A)	14	wait for right side to finish	& 3)
4. Wait for left side to finish	5	take the gun and spray grill (A)	25 (for 4
5. spray grill part (B)	12	(same as right side)	& 5)
6. Remove cover, put it & gun down	9	(same as right side)	9
7. Remove hoodcap, put in parts box	7	(same as right side)	8
8. Pick up brush, paint installations	28	(same as right side)	32
9. With gun, spray installations from below	22	(same as right side)	22
10. Spray the floor	11	(same as right side)	13
11. Remove door pin and put in parts box. Put down spray gun	5	(same as right side)	5
12. Paint quarter corner with paint brush	16	(same as right side)	15
13. Remove rubber cushion and put it in parts box. Put down brush	6	(same as right side)	5
Right side work time	149 DM	Left side work time	253 DM

Note: Conveyor speed is 1.6 minutes per car. DM is $\frac{1}{100}$ minute.

Source: FQC (August 1975), p. 55.

TABLE 5.3

Job Sheet After Improvements

Job Procedures and Elements	Time (DM)
1. Pick up spray gun and cover	8
2. Spray right side grill	18
3. Move cover to left side, spray left side grill	23
4. Remove hood caps from both sides. Spray right side installations	11
5. Spray right side installations from below	14
6. Spray right side floor	11
7. Remove door pins, spray right quarter corner	15
8. Remove left and right rubber cushions, spray left quarter corner	10
9. Spray left side installations from below	15
10. Spray left side floor	12
11. Remove door pins and spray left side installations	13
12. Walk to the next body	5
Working time: 155 DM	

Note: Conveyor speed is 1.6 minutes per car. DM is $\frac{1}{100}$ minute.

Source: FQC (August 1975), p. 57.

Incidentally, it is worth noting that a further JUSE compilation of model QC circles, published at the height of the drive to downsize business operations, for some reason includes not a single example of this sort of man-power-reducing circle.[17]

I now present two slightly later cases of manpower-reducing QC circles, taken from reports presented at a November 1979 QC convention sponsored by the Y factory of X electrical machinery manufacturing company. The conference judges awarded the "Most Outstanding Circle" prize to workers in example 15 and nominated the circle in example 16 to represent the plant at the company's QC convention. The background of these two initiatives includes the persistence of slow economic growth in the late 1970s, an increase in the speed of the refrigerator assembly line, and a greater variety in the refrigerator models under production.

Example 15.   X Company, Y Factory. Freezer assembly line, station for placing the freezer into the outer body. Workers: foreman and 12 team members. 1979. Objective: to increase efficiency and reduce manpower in bolt-tightening work on the freezer bed, where numerous problems existed because the workers could not keep up with the line speed.

I. Actions Taken: When the number of freezers produced rose from 1350 to 1800, the number of workers on this job was increased from 2 to 4. This represented a 33% drop in output per worker. Therefore, we resolved to flush out the trouble spots by shooting for production of

1800 units by just two workers, and we put the following measures into effect.

Equipment changes: We improved the arrangement of the chair and air hose, which tended to impede work by getting in the way of the worker's legs. We adjusted the hose length and attached it to the back of the chair that the worker used for screwing bolts on the freezer bed. *Bolt driver:* Untreated air "blows out water," so we switched to dry air. *Parts:* We changed the length of the bolts and the number of screw piles. *Workers:* We changed working partners, adopted a rotation system, and changed from "monthly overall team norms" to "daily individual norms," raising the entire work crew's job consciousness by using a graph of the "distribution of individual defect rates."

II. Summary: We were able to reduce the time required to tighten the bolts from 4.6 seconds per bolt to 2.6 seconds. With three bolts on each bed, the time for each unit shrunk from 13.8 seconds to 7.8 seconds. Including related tasks, the two work processes which formerly took 36 seconds could now be done in 24 seconds. We exceeded our goal, making it possible for 2 workers to handle 1,900 freezer beds per day. We are now aiming to achieve 2100 beds. Moreover, the entire circle is working to upgrade both individual and group performance, to enable us to cope with any changes that may be introduced.[18]

In this case, workers were striving to make their job easier by improving the equipment (chair, air, airhose, bolts), but this QC circle was demanding a greater intensity of work from each operative. In a general context of pressure to raise labor productivity, the change from monthly group norms to daily individual quotas is likely to encourage competition among the workers and targeting of deficient individuals.

These measures ultimately cut the time required to tighten the bolts by several seconds and cut the staffing in half. How were the two "excess" workers selected, and where did they go? Most likely, the company followed typical practice in Japan and assigned them, for the time being, to some other department of the factory as "loan workers." This case offers a classic example of the sort of Japanese worker behavior found consistently in high- and low-growth eras. These circle members have no clear awareness of "that which should be defended" at the workplace. They adjust without resistance or complaint to the ceaselessly changing demands of the corporation.

Example 16. X Company, Y factory. Refrigerator assembly line, packing workshop. Circle members: 12 men, 1 woman. 1979. Objective: raise efficiency and reduce staffing.

I. Actions Taken: Current efficiency levels are as follows.

(A) automated line producing standard refrigerators: 2700 units with 17 workers (efficiency rating of 86%). (B) Non-automated line producing large models: 2000 units with 43 workers (efficiency rating of 43%). (C) Small models: 2500 units with 23 workers (efficiency rating of 60%). When rates are so "unspeakably bad," our section's policy is to use existing equipment in seeking out causes of the problem. We decided to examine thoroughly those aspects of the work process where improvement was possible, such as job time and work methods. We set case-by-case efficiency targets and implemented various measures.

Case A: 1) We constructed a board that would prevent the cardboard crate from knocking into the ventilation cage when we placed it over the product. 2) We made it possible to paste on the warranty envelope without removing our gloves by lengthening the envelope. 3) We attached a bag to the front of our aprons, to collect the backing removed from the self-adhesive warranty envelope (this eliminated the motion used to throw the wastepaper into the box behind the worker). With these changes we reduced overall staffing on the two automated lines by four workers, and we achieved an efficiency rating of 109%.

Case B: 1) We installed a rotating guide angle to simplify the 90 degree rotation of the refrigerator needed when we wrap a band around the box. 2) We improved the conveyer hanger and increased the hanger-pole's capacity, to reduce the time required to hook and lower the refrigerator body frame. 3) We combined some of the operations involved in attaching the band. As a result, we reduced staffing on these two lines by 10 people. The number of workers on loan from other sections in the plant was cut from 26 to 16. We achieved an efficiency rate of 99%.

Case C: With several improvisations, we were able to automate all but two of the processes involved in packing small refrigerators. We reduced the staffing level by 8 workers, allowing us to cut the number of loan workers to zero. We reached a 95% efficiency rate.

II. Summary: The staffing reductions in case A saved roughly 9,360,000 yen. All the circle members "gained the self-confidence that even in restricted circumstances, we can succeed if we try." We resolved that "from now on, we will take a managerial perspective and work to keep this a profitable shop."[19]

In contrast to the Toyota circle in example 14, the several creative innovations adopted here to lighten the workload offer no obvious evidence that work was intensified. But one cannot overlook the very substantial reduction in staffing, by a total of twenty-two workers. These reductions turned four of the seventeen standard line packers into "excess workers," who were probably transferred to some other workshop as loan workers.

On the packing lines for large and small types, the eight to ten loan work-ers suddenly became unnecessary. Would these people be able to find a spot in some other section of the factory? What if (as is quite likely) every shop in the factory was engaged in similar sorts of QC activity? Perhaps the increase in diverse refrigerator models will for a time generate a need for such loan workers someplace in the factory, but will these nomadic loan workers eventually find themselves "excess" to the needs of the entire fac-tory, with no place further to go? At the very least, one can be certain that as the heroes of this type of QC circle adopt a managerial perspective, they generate a latent job insecurity.

In presenting these sixteen detailed examples of QC activities con-ducted by the end of the 1970s, I have limited myself to rather brief com-ments and held back some harsher judgments. I now venture a more thor-ough assessment.

First, let me add a simple comment on trends from 1980 to the present. By the middle of the 1980s, QC circle activity in the production sites of major corporations seems to have reached a plateau, but new develop-ments in other areas have more than offset this. First, QC circle activity has spread to those small- and medium-sized enterprises intimately connected to major corporations. Also, in the name of rationalization (i.e., removal of waste), many companies are introducing QC circles for white-collar employees in their administrative and managerial sections. This trend is particularly noticeable in the banking and insurance industries.

As QC activities spread throughout the corporation, managers see the need to promote increased communication among the various sections of the company, each of which is to keep in mind a view of the company as a whole. This more intensely orchestrated activity is called Total Quality Control (TQC).

Finally, QC circles are being introduced in the overseas branches of Japanese enterprises. It may appear difficult to introduce these activities in countries that differ from Japan in culture or patterns of labor-management relations. Yet a recent study of Japanese automobilemakers operating in the United States reveals that in each of the six companies surveyed, the devel-opment of small group activities such as proposal groups and QC circles has met with "positive response." In total, approximately 30 percent of the employees are said to participate.[20]

The World of "Model" Quality Control

Groping through the forest of quality control, one eventually arrives at a set of worker characteristics that self-management activities seek to conquer. One object of QC conquest is a passive attitude toward work. The QC movement targets an instrumentalism that views work merely as a means to earn a living, restricts the output of mental and physical energy as much as possible, and refuses to seek meaning in work itself. The promoters of the QC mission assert that if workers simply have spirit and the will to improvise, they can make any kind of work a rewarding activity.

A second object of conquest is an individualism that lacks consideration for coworkers. In a production system based on a division of labor and cooperation, one worker's performance bears directly on the coworkers' jobs. Human relations at the workplace greatly influence the ease or the difficulty of everyone's work. A person who wishes to sink roots in a particular workplace can only realize the importance of a sense of moral obligation among coworkers. To the extent that they foster such a sensibility, QC circles are designed to re-affirm for workers the importance of collectivism and to overcome a mode of thinking that merely sees the workplace as a convenient place for a man or woman to earn a living.

In Japan's company society since the mid-1960s, a negative image of workers who embody one or both of these qualities became increasingly prominent. This instrumental, individualistic worker emerged along with changes in work due to new technologies of production. New technology generated a pyramid of jobs that was narrow at the top and quite wide at the bottom. Jobs worth doing, which demanded knowledge and experience, became scarce; boring jobs demanding neither became plentiful. Also, in many sites where people had worked in groups, talking and sweating together, jobs were transformed so that each individual now stood alone and operated large machines or complex instrument panels. At the same time, enterprises were expanding rapidly and generating demand for more and more workers at the bottom of the job pyramid.

In such a context, workers quite naturally came to take on negative traits. In particular, three sorts of workers came into more prominent view: (1) middle-aged and older men who had fallen behind in the race for promotion and had little interest in their jobs and merely sought a secure place in the company to insure the well-being of their families; (2) young workers who refused to commit themselves fully to any job or workplace; and (3) homemakers who took part-time jobs and maintained only a partial connection to the corporation.

Perhaps corporations can tolerate such workers so long as they mount no sharp challenge to the logic of capital. But the production systems of the present-day corporation demand tight synchronization of numerous processes and sites. If diverse values cause many employees to perform passively, a company cannot hope to outdo its rivals at home and abroad. The corporation must mobilize all employees to shed the detached mentality of a wage earner and cooperate with coworkers to make the greatest possible contribution to the company's productivity.

To achieve this goal, managers had to renovate their own practices as well as those of the workers by taking the following three steps: First, because negative work values were caused by a sense of powerlessness on the job as employees were deprived of the authority to make decisions, managers had to grant workers some space to improvise, so long as this did not strike at the roots of the Taylor System of centralized control.[21] Second, workers naturally and fundamentally value interesting work and solidarity with coworkers, so new management approaches had to respect such desires and allow small-group activities a degree of self-government. Third, the corporation had to devise powerful programs of guidance to insure that the autonomy and subjectivity encouraged in workers by these first two steps would be effectively directed at fulfilling company goals. Managers could have faith that such guidance would succeed in Japan, where a workers' culture has traditionally lacked a strong sense of independence.

In Western countries during these years (1960s–1970s), unrest among workers increased with their greater alienation at work, wildcat strikes broke out more frequently, and the frontier of union activities expanded to encompass themes traditionally the prerogative of management.[22] In some countries a new socialist theory of self-management began to emerge. But Japan during this period witnessed a "self-management movement" that might properly be called a managerial Cultural Revolution. Through this movement, Japanese managers revealed foresight; they adopted measures to prevent a Western-type crisis by taking advantage of the distinctive characteristics of Japanese workers.

Thus one arrives at a historic moment in 1980, when Ford Motor Company showed all its European employees a video that presented "a full picture of the dynamism and absolute dedication toward productivity and efficiency in Japanese automobile factories," and Ford managers then asserted, "We have two choices: either reduce the number of workers and increase productivity, or continue our inefficient ways and let Japanese auto makers destroy us."[23] We also saw Chinese leaders, who had repudiated their own Cultural Revolution and were promoting a program of modernization, present Japanese workers as a model in their QC activity, their competitive outpouring of labor, and their commitment to the goals of the corporation.

The world of model QC circles repudiates the instrumental, individualistic worker, whom I call the "lonely wage earner." When a model circle asserts a goal of enhancing the intellectual skills of workers, it does not seek to restore an artisanal spirit that seeks to preserve decisionmaking powers inherent in a given job. Its call for enhanced skill, instead, understands and redefines this job in a company-wide framework (as in example 2).

Some circles eliminated the margin or respite needed for a worker to make independent decisions. These groups standardized the work and reinforced the subordination of workers to their supervisor (as in examples 9 and 12). There are no cases in which model QC circles enriched the jobs of nonskilled workers. Instead, circles involving such workers frequently identified the individuals responsible for defective work, increased individual production norms (examples 5, 10, and 13), and either intensified work or reduced manpower through industrial engineering techniques (examples 14, 15, and 16). QC circles that tried to make the job easy were basically not model cases. The notion of enlarging the workers' knowledge of the job, so often given as the goal of QC activity, in effect means to understand managerial needs and shape one's mode of work accordingly.

A common claim among QC advocates is that the model world of QC strengthens solidarity among coworkers and eliminates the loneliness of those who work. But this is not the solidarity of a self-governing city in a corporate nation. A better analogy would be to the neighborhood associations in a fascist state. Readers who consider this to be an extreme polemical flourish should recall that fascism could not have succeeded without a semivoluntary organizing drive to incorporate people at the base of the society.

The QC circle as neighborhood association helps compel those comrades inclined to drop out to continue the march, but it does not defend those whom the nation considers to need careful monitoring, nor does it soften the demands of the nation on the individual. The norms of the QC work group demand submission to the needs of capital. In the small groups created by model QC circles, one finds no visible sign of the autonomy that typifies community organizations of citizens, no independence from the norms established at the top of the system.

Depending on the circumstances, both the resistance of workers to capital, as well as their integration under managerial control, can be strengthened by forming powerful workplace groups. Because Japanese workers rediscovered solidarity through a movement dominated by model QC circles, they were mobilized to follow the logic of capital even more fully than they had as lonely wage earners. Frequently, the most faithful and clever employees became the vanguard of the movement, and they expected the reward of promotions and pay raises for their meritorious service in model QC circles. But the profoundly problematic consciousness of Japanese workers lies less in this vanguard than in the rear guard. Ordinary workers not on the fast track were drawn into the QC movement actively enough to make the term "worker self-management" a fair approximation of the movement's substance.

Living as Residents of Workplace Society

If Japan's organized workers are indeed fully imbued with the logic of the corporation thanks to the powerful help of model QC circles, can the labor movement possibly construct an alternative vision of a worker able to maintain independence from the demands of capital and ultimately resist these demands? In this section, I discuss two possible alternatives.

One possibility is to resuscitate the lonely, or lone-wolf, wage earner, targeted for extinction by the model QC circles. Frankly, I find this a hopeless task. The attitude that work is simply a means to enable consumption offers no vision of the desirable workplace or desirable work. The stance of the worker-as-wage-earner provides no standard for "things that must be defended" in the face of QC initiatives to change the workplace. This very lack of a standard has made it impossible to restrain the powerful, model version of QC activities.

Further, because the isolated wage earner feels no sense of obligation to coworkers, he or she is unlikely to worry when competition builds up among them. This problem is important because of the contradiction inherent in QC activity, which, on one hand, promotes solidarity among circle members and, on the other hand, intensifies competition among workers as it promotes greater productivity. Managers can manipulate this contradiction by nurturing cooperation within circles and competition between them, but if workers recognize this tension and opt to cooperate rather than compete, this contradiction can be a lever to transform the behavior of the model worker. Of course, even these employees will not be completely free from competition among workers; there is long way to go before a publicly sanctioned code of concern for coworkers matures into a unionist determination to curtail decisively competition among the workers. But the instrumental, isolated wage earner is, from the outset, completely detached from any sense of obligation to coworkers. He or she can neither recognize nor build upon the deep and significant contradiction between the cooperation and the competition fostered by the QC movement.

Both the ability of the corporation to mobilize workers and the ability of workers to resist management depends on the prior formation of a site of cooperative endeavor. Workers can only attain independence from the firm on the basis of a workers' society, a community whose members believe that "here is a group that works together and struggles together, and I am part of that group." An isolated wage earner in the sense of a person lacking firm attachment to either a company or an occupation might possibly develop a sense of membership in a workers' society. For example, since 1983, even in Japan, activists have been forming regionally based "community unions" open to all comers.[24] But for the present, one cannot expect the isolated wage earner on the margins of a worker society to play a leading role in resisting the firm. That such people have held back from committing themselves to managerial objectives does not mean they possess the will or the power to restrain the behavior of the corporation.

A second possible source of resistance is the independent, specialized professional. Such a person could nurture an ethos as a kind of latter-day artisan whose needs are separate from the immediate needs of the corporation. He or she could take a detached view of the firm as a place in which one develops professional skills and could develop a sense of membership in society that does not depend upon membership in a corporation.[25]

Unlike a strategy placing renewed hope in the rebellious potential of the isolated earner, this approach takes a positive view of work itself and does so without exalting the behavior of the "company man." Nonetheless, I am not happy with this line of thinking. It fails to recognize that the skills and abilities of the great majority of ordinary workers today are more or less organically embedded in a cooperative endeavor at a particular work site. The professionalist strategy further ignores the fact that only rarely is the fruit of an individual's labor offered to society as an independent good or service; instead, it results from cooperative endeavor and is sold as the commercial property of the corporation.

Because their labor is thus anonymous and conveyed to society indirectly via the company's mediation, few blue- or white-collar workers can act as individualistic professionals. To gain respect as individuals, these workers paradoxically must embrace their anonymity as workers and recreate some form of community. If one fails to appreciate this, one cannot understand how natural it is for these workers to seek a stable job at a particular workplace with familiar coworkers. The individual independence of ordinary workers is achieved only by creating an independent workers' society with coworkers. For this reason, an image as an "independent professional" does not make sense to most ordinary workers.

Of course, some workers do possess skills that can be exercised in various settings; they do not depend on the support of a particular workplace. Such is the case with teachers, medical doctors, nurses, systems engineers, newspaper reporters, and others, and in their case the concept of the independent professional is appropriate. But even such men and women must create their own workers' society, a trade society outside of the bounds of the corporation, if they are to achieve independence from the logic of capital.

Even as they differ in their view of the value of labor itself, both the lonely wage earner and the independent professional agree on one key point. They both place high value on the independent individual, whether as human being, as citizen, or as professional, whose values are distinct from those of "company man" (*kaisha-ningen*). They share a critique of the collectivism of the Japanese employee that excessively fuses personal values with corporate ones. This critique issues ultimately in the following demands for ideological and systemic change. Japanese employees, it is said, must defend their individuality and take a relativistic, detached stance toward their companies. They should do this by nurturing multiple links with the broader society, so life as an employee will be just part of their existence. Further, they should demand a broadly based social security system that ensures their livelihood should they rebel against the company. And, this critique concludes, they should develop public norms capable of placing restraints on corporate greed from the outside.

I accept the value of this type of critique in correcting certain distorted features of Japanese working life. This critique converges to an extent with a labor movement strategy that despairs of generating struggle at the production site and seeks institutional reform outside the workplace. Quite possibly, this line of thinking will become the majority opinion of reformers in the labor movement. And yet, such a majority opinion with its focus on reforms external to the corporation will hardly make a dent on the everyday consciousness of the mainstream of organized workers active in QC circles.

In the everyday consciousness of most workers, the job is still the activity through which people (a man, in particular) most fully realize themselves; the workplace is an intimate world of social meaning, a place offering far more than just an income. Nothing shapes the extent to which such ordinary workers derive daily satisfaction than their familiarity with the workplace. Therefore, if theorists of workers and labor movements wish to have an impact on the daily life of the workers, they must offer a theory of activity that enables workers on their own to control work, the workplace, and relationships among coworkers. The subjects capable of exercising such control are none other than the inhabitants of a workplace society, those residents of workers' society for the moment so wholly assimilated to the logic and values of the corporation.[26]

By this roundabout route I return to QC circles with the following thought: The QC movement emerged just when union activism centered on struggle in the workplace declined; it drew upon the energy of workers who were seeking basic changes in relationships among coworkers and the character of work. For remaining activists to criticize the labor managers who launched the QC movement is quite easy. But is it enough for unionists simply to scoff at the manipulative goals of these managers and to distance themselves from the QC movement? Will such a response give birth to any constructive worker ideas? Those who seek to free themselves from managerial control have no choice but to infiltrate the QC circle movement. Reformers must redefine the substance and the intent of QC activity and transform the "model" QC circle from the perspective of those who continue at their jobs.

Three Standards of Evaluation

The boundary between hawk and dove circles, and between model QC circles and those transformed by the needs of workers, is truly paper thin. In such a situation, can QC activities be redefined from within? How might this appropriation of the circles proceed?

The boundary is both paper thin and permeable because Japanese workers even now retain the ambiguity of their dual status as both loyal employees and organized workers. In order to allow a union consciousness to triumph over corporate loyalism, one must revive union standards of an international character. Such standards reflect a cast of mind that remains latent and submerged among Japanese workers but that could enable a clear-headed assessment of conditions in the workplace and changes proposed by QC circles.

I propose the following three standards: First, will a particular "self-management" QC activity really allow the work group to expand its right to make significant decisions about work and production? Several of the cases presented previously conclude by suggesting that the members of a QC circle will no longer simply follow the directions of their superiors, that they hope to move toward collective management of work procedures and production (examples 8 and 11). Although a further train of thought (discussed later) is also needed to achieve a true workers' self-management, these cases are rich with potential. To somehow force the dominant Taylor System to retreat is without doubt the most urgent task facing today's workers. In addition, QC circle activities designed to raise the level of member skills to a common new standard (example 1) prepare their subjects to undertake work management by the workplace group, and managers' own formal commitment to versatile workers makes it difficult to resist moves in this direction.

Yet one must not forget that QC activities also hold the dangerous potential to reduce the decisionmaking authority of the work group by going too far toward an elevated managerial perspective and taking a so-called companywide view of the jobs in question. Such groups reason that "we can't do as we wish, for after all we are now aware of the company's circumstances." In a model QC circle, work group self-management means that employees of their own accord will adjust their work conditions in response to corporate needs. Major contradictions are certain to emerge between such a mode of thought and self-management that defends the daily needs of workers. As such contradictions inevitably surface in the course of QC activity, they will test the extent to which "production management by our work group" is an independent endeavor.

At this point, I must question with some care how much knowledge and of what sort is truly necessary for workers to make independent decisions. My own view is that workers whose perspective is narrow, but who truly know their own jobs, are in a better position to control the workplace independently than are employees with a companywide sensitivity to matters of corporate finance. I differ with analysts, such as Abe Shūichi, who criticize small-group self-management activities for focusing on work and the workplace without extending concern to companywide policies.[27] Such broad concerns can only serve workers if the realm covered by collective bargaining or other institutional forms of participation is first expanded to place a check on corporate policies. To be sure, an individual worker's subjectivity concerning his or her work can be stimulated by a fuller awareness of the company's condition. But this kind of subjectivity will not necessarily support the effort of the workplace group to increase its own decisionmaking authority.

A difference in the situation of blue-collar workers and one segment of the white-collar workforce is relevant here. For many blue-collar workers, to possess skill and decisionmaking authority on their job means to possess a certain control in bringing the principles of the natural sciences to bear on the object of their labor. For such workers, to become so-called specialists is to increase their control over nature and to achieve some degree of independence from capital or management. This is the independence of the artisan that gave trade unions their strength. In other words, in the world of blue-collar work, the desire to become a superior worker can be separated from the desire to serve the interests of managers. This separation can be widened by the intimate connection between workplace conditions and the social consciousness of these workers.

But for some white-collar workers, especially those engaged in marketing and sales in the broad sense of these terms, it is difficult to keep these goals separate. The links between the fruits of an individual's work and the achievement of business objectives are simply too obvious. For such employees, the act of working energetically with a sense of subjectivity can only bring acceptance of corporate goals, not independence from them. For these people, strict adherence to the remaining two standards is critical.

The second standard is this: Does a particular self-management activity bring the exclusive or absolute value of "efficiency" into question? Insofar as work has an objective and is not a game, it is natural for workers to be concerned with efficiency on their jobs. Even for workers armed with a politicized class consciousness, to attack productivity itself is an unusual step taken only in abnormal moments of struggle. In normal times, workers confirm their own abilities and power in a gratifying way when they manage to conserve materials or fuel, improve the operating rate, or reduce the defect rate. The act of becoming more skilled at work surely includes increasing one's ability to perform work quickly and cleverly without wasting time or material, in other words, raising productivity. At the same time, however, besides the joy of being a smart, effective producer, there are numerous other values important to those who seek to spend a long career in a particular setting. These include the ease of performing a job, the right to decide on one's method and pace of work, a cooperative mode of working in which, for example, one is able to converse with coworkers, and job security for the individual and his or her coworkers.

Model QC circles, especially hawkish ones, typically violate these values, which obstruct the sole and absolute goal of increased efficiency. The vanguard of circle leaders expect to move on to managerial positions when their workplace achievements in raising productivity are recognized, so they have little understanding of such values. Desires for comfortable, enjoyable work and control over its pace emerge mainly in the form of grousing among the rear guard voices of the workplace, and the persuasion of circle leaders apparently overcomes such concerns.

But is there in this very process the potential to turn circles into sites of struggle? As long as the QC movement remains founded on the premise of full participation by ordinary workers, the rear guard can defend their values as the credo of true workplace residents. They can thus push enhanced efficiency to the back burner, turning potentially hawkish reforms of the work process into improvements of equipment that will reduce the workload. They can argue that the true guarantee of productivity is respect for the workers, and they can force management to respect their concerns. Further, if such a logic of appropriation or transformation can be mirrored even slightly in the policies of the union local, the effect of this "guerrilla warfare" will be all the greater. And one can also expect that assertive women who are already seeking to manage the work process on their own but still retain a sense of themselves as outsiders in the firm will play an important role in bringing about this transformation.

Finally, I come to the third standard, this time a negative one: Will a given self-management activity intensify competition among the workers over wage levels, performance, job opportunties, or security? Will such intensified competition be used to screen workers for promotions or target them for cutbacks?

Within certain limits, QC activities generally reinforce equality and solidarity among workers by challenging the self-centered behavior of the isolated wage earner. Of course, I have presented several examples of model QC circles in which the tremendous value placed on increased efficiency led to more intensive micromanagement of individual performance, as measured in defect rates or production quotas. The potential for such scrutiny to accelerate competition among coworkers is more than clear. Moreover, the potential is obvious for this scrutiny to create a pool of expendable workers, those judged unable to keep up with tightened performance standards or unwilling to sign on to a frenzied mobilization to achieve some corporate goal. Thus, the "certain limit" within which a QC circle fosters solidarity or attachment to the workplace refers to the group imbued with a proper attitude as employees, candidates for the fast-track, perhaps seven or eight of ten workers. The remaining two or three people requiring so-called special attention will be removed from the circle of fellow workers and will find the workshop a more difficult place to remain in than before.

And yet in this regard as in others, QC activities possess a contradictory character. The very act of coming together at the workplace is the foundation for any true worker initiative; one formal principle of small-group activities is to respect the solidarity and integrity of the group, a principle at odds with the frequent actual result of promoting competition and screening workers. In this situation, the proper course for the rear guard is obvious. They must take advantage of this contradiction embedded in the QC movement to resist plans that promote divisive competition and to create a workplace society that respects the workers' own values of security and equality.

One can imagine a workplace in which, out of consideration for coworkers, unauthorized absences are few and the workers strive to polish their job skills; where crane operators are anxious for the safety of *tamakake* loaders, while the loaders work with an eye to the safety of the operators; in which all parties consider the welfare of their coworkers, and in return for commitments to high attendance and careful, high-quality work, the work group protects and helps its members to make sure that no one drops out or is left behind. If workers can make such a mode of living their own, then the workplace collectivity becomes a true workplace society, a community whose members have long-run security.

But in the mid-1990s in Japan, raising the "subjectivity and self-awareness" of workers quite often means tackling a job from the standpoint of management. Similarly, "strengthening solidarity" means consolidating a structure that forces the will of management on the individual workers. Nonetheless, if those who wish to cast their lot over the long run with a particular workplace take a hard look at their present conditions and future prospects in terms of these three standards, they should still be able to cross the line from loyal employee to organized worker. Even for Japanese-type workers, there is a ground upon which to build independence from managerial control. Even the "production management by our work group" as envisioned by the honor students of model QC circles possesses a latent power to challenge managerial authority, as long as the group members stringently examine their activities in terms of these three standards.

In our contemporary world of a gigantic, administered society, common people cannot simply barricade themselves in their community. But neither can they survive on the basis of individualism without community. Such an awareness lies at the base of the theory of an independent workplace society, developed in this chapter through examination of the QC movement; it has propelled my search for workplace residents who might transcend the state of the lonely wage earner. With hindsight, one can say that Japan's labor movement of the high-growth era and beyond generally has been unable to address the nature of work and relations among fellow workers, and has thus failed to develop a sociology of solidarity that addresses the life of blue- and white-collar workers at the point of production.[28] If the labor union movement rather than corporate labor managers had taken the lead in addressing these matters, I would not have had to undertake a convoluted search for a viable workplace unionism by using the language of the QC movement. The very need to critique the falsely labeled "self-management" activity of the QC movement amounts to a criticism of present-day unionism that remains silent and inactive in the face of this movement.

Notes to Chapter 5

1. See Nitta Michio, *Nihon no rōdōsha sanka* [Workers' participation in management in Japan] (Tokyo: Tokyo University Press, 1988), p. 34. These figures are as of June 1975. Also, according to a random survey of 4,722 employees of large firms conducted by the *Hitachi sōgō keikaku kenkyūjo* (Hitachi General Planning and Research Center) in fall 1977, as many as 18.2% responded that they were "actively involved" in small-group activities, 65.1% responded that they "participate[d] but not actively," and only 5.1% said they had "no interest in them and ignored them." Nihon Tekkō Renmei [Japan federation of iron and steel industries] *Tekkō-kai* [The world of iron and steel] (June 1994), p. 5. The 1994 data for self-management activities in the iron and steel industries also appear in the same source.

2. Nitta, *Nihon no rōdōsha sanka*, pp. 62–66, 69–76.

3. These journals are JUSE, ed., *FQC, Genba to QC* [The workplace and QC], and the supplement *QC Saakuru katsudō no jissai ni manabō* [Let's learn from the actual work of quality control circles] (Tokyo: JUSE, 1977).

4. Both Part I (Action taken) and Part II (Summary) of each example are Kumazawa's abridgment of the original reports. Even in cases where quotation marks do not appear, almost all of the terms used follow those used in the original report.

5. This report is included in a special issue of *FQC* titled *QC saakuru katsudō no jissai ni manabō* [Let's learn from the actual work of quality control circles]. The remaining cases are also taken from this volume, unless otherwise noted. The presentation format of *I: Action Taken, II: Summary* is the same in all cases. Although it is important to know what percentage of employees at a given workplace were members of the Quality Control circle, many of the reports unfortunately do not make this clear.

6. Tekkō Rōren (Iron and Steel Workers Union), ed., *Jishu kanri katsudō ni kan suru ankeeto chōsa* [Survey report of self-management activities] (Tokyo, 1977).

7. This case is from *"Mite kudasai! Watakushi-tachi no kaizen undō"* [Please look at what we accomplished with our *kaizen* campaign!], *FQC* (August 1975).

8. I have been criticized for stressing the high skill levels of Japanese workers by Kobayashi Ken'ichi in, for example, chapter 2 of his *Rōdō keizai no kōzō henkaku* [Structural changes in labor economics] (Tokyo: Ochanomizu Shobō, 1977). But I still maintain that the high levels of latent skills of the blue-collar workers in large industrial plants can coexist with the low level of skills that have hitherto been required in the performance of their daily work. The tension between their latent skills and their boring work is probably a major source of their energetic commitment to Quality Control circles.

9. This particular report is silent on the gender of the circle members. However, the overwhelming majority of workers employed in conveyor belt operations in the electromagnetic assembly industry are women.

10. For a discussion of the fact that the routes to escape from boring, routine labor are constructed separately for male and female workers, see Chapter 7. For a more detailed discussion in Japanese, see Kumazawa Makoto, *Rōdōsha kanri no kusa no ne* [The grass roots of the concept of workers' control] (Tokyo: Nihon Hyōronsha, 1976) chaps. 3 and 4.

11. This case was taken from *FQC* (August 1975).

12. *FQC* (May 1977).

13. Ibid., p. 54.

14. *Genba to QC* [QC and the workplace] (February 1971).

15. Michimata Kenjirō, ed., *Gendai Nihon no tekkō rōdō mondai* [Contemporary Japan's labor problems in the iron and steel industry] (Sapporo: Hokkaidō Daigaku Toshokan kō kai, 1978), p. 454.

16. *FQC* (August 1975).

17. The publication in question, *QC Saakuru katsudō no jissai ni manabō* [Let's learn from the actual work of quality control circles] (Tokyo: JUSE, 1977) merely mentions manpower-reducing QC circles at the Toyota Truck Body Co., at Chūō Hatsujo (Central Spring Mfg.), Aishin Seiki (Aishin Precision Machinery), Toto Kiki (Toto Pottery and Ceramics), and others in the notes.

18. This case is based on the mimeographed program of the "24th Convention of Y Factory QC Circles," 1979, as well as the author's interviews with participants.

19. Ibid.

20. Suzuki Naotsugu, *Amerika-shakai no naka no nikkei kigyo* [Japanese companies in American society] (Tōyō Keizai Shinpōsha, 1991), pp. 165–166.

21. Some Japanese managers claim it is necessary to overcome the Taylor System, which is based on the separation of mental planning and physical execution. Among those who during the period under discussion issued a call for "giving meaningful work to the workers" was Sony's Kobayashi Shigeru, the author of *Soni wa hito o ikasu* [Sony brings humans to life] (Tokyo: Nihon Keiei Shuppankai, 1966). A famous report by the Secretary of Health, Education, and Welfare, *Work in America* (Cambridge: MIT Press, 1973) issued a similar call. But such views have remained a minority position among Japanese managers. This chapter has introduced numerous examples of QC circles undertaking time-and-motion studies. Nonetheless, it is possible that small-group activities can lessen the all-pervasive dominance of the Taylor System. If capitalists permit the relaxation of some controls, it is because they have gained complete confidence that the employees have come to think just like managers. For the Taylor System see Frederick W. Taylor, *The Principles of Scientific Management* (New York: Harper and Brothers, 1913).

22. *Work in America*, introduced in the previous note, is the most useful source on the various actions of workers, which were widely observed in Europe and America during this period, who challenged the alienation of their work. During this time, the labor movement in Western Europe flourished. One aspect of this revival, as pointed out in C. Croach and A. Pizzorno, eds., *The Resurgence of Class Conflict in Western Europe Since 1968* (New York: Macmillan, 1978), was that labor unions expanded their functions in the workplace, and the resultant union encroachment into managerial rights carried with it a sense of triumph over labor's alienation, a process that might be called "the humanization of labor."

23. *Asahi Shimbun*, July 23, 1980.

24. Rōdō-shō, *Rōdō tōkei yōran* [Handbook of labor statistics] (Tokyo: 1995).

25. This position is taken by Tsuchiya Moriaki, an authority on management. See his article in Hazama Hiroshi et al., eds., *Wareware ni totte kigyō to wa nani ka?* [What does the corporation mean to us?], vol. 1 (Tokyo: Tōyō Keizai Shinpōsha, 1976).

26. Kurita Ken offers a different view of this issue, seeing opportunity for change in activity by workers to "more thoroughly establish their links [to the firm] as employees. . . thus, launching a movement to transform business into a self-governing society managed by employee organizations." See his "Sengo rōdō undō no keifu to kadai" [The lineage and themes of the postwar labor movement], *Jurisuto sōgō tokushū: kigyō to rōdō* [Special comprehensive edition of *Jurist: Business and Labor*], (1979). With some reservations, I accept his views.

27. Abe Shūichi, "Criticism of Japanese-style 'Self Management,'" *Jurisuto sōgō tokushū: kigyō to rōdō* [Special comprehensive edition of *Jurist: Business and Labor*], (1979).

28. In the 1970s and early 1980s, only in the unions of public corporation workers (Kōrōkyō) does one find some examples of efforts to regulate equality on the job and in relations among coworkers. See the research reports on workplaces of National Railway workers and Post Office employees, such as Endō Kōji and Hyōdō Tsutomu, "Shokuba ni okeru kumiai no kisei: kokutetsu unten shokuba no jirei" [Union regulations in the workplace: The case of the National Railway engineers], *Shakai Kagaku Kenkyū*, vol. 30, no. 4 (1981). Also Inagami Takeshi, "Rōdō kumiai to shigoto no kisei" [Labor unions and work rules], *Nihon Rōdō Kyōkai Zasshi* (December, 1979 and February 1980) and *Chōsa hōkoku: yūnai rōdō no jittai to kadai* [Survey report: Conditions and issues of workers in the postal system], *Zentei Jihō*, no. 183 (1978). In the years since these reports, however, the leadership of Kōrōkyō may have become less willing to defend the forms of workplace control described in these reports. After the defeat of the "strike for the right to strike" in 1975, the public sector unions felt the brunt of the government's so-called administrative reform drive of the 1980s, and both the National Railways and the Nippon Telephone and Telegraph Public Corporation were privatized. In the end, the public sector unions became in substance much the same as other single-company unions connected to private enterprises. For an analysis of the significance of the pivotal "strike for the right to strike," see Andrew Gordon, ed., "Contests for the Workplace," in *Postwar Japan as History* (Berkeley: University of California Press, 1993).

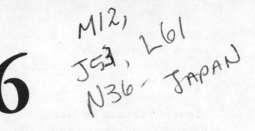

6

A Postwar History
of the Workplace

Management and Unions
in the Steel Industry

Themes and Perspectives

A workers' society is a place where working people share specific needs
and possibilities for living with each other. It is a place where coworkers
are able to nurture a tacit agreement to help one another in their work,
their earnings, and their job opportunities, while they limit competition
among themselves. The function of a strong labor union is to institutionalize such a workers' society, to make conscious and explicit the tacit agreement to mutual aid. Of course, labor unions—especially federations of
unions or joint struggle committees—often cross-cut or include several dis-
crete and varied worker societies, each with its own type of tacit agreement. But even in these cases, each workers' society asserts its individuality by retaining authority to regulate the core concerns of any union: the
nature of work and the mutual relations of workers.

This general perspective may prove helpful as one analyzes the historical changes in unions in a given period. One may further develop it by
positing three relationships between worker societies and types of labor
unions.

1. Skilled workers committed to a particular occupation, who constitute a
   trade society, which then creates craft or trade unions.
2. Workers committed to a particular employer, who constitute a workplace society, which then creates local workplace units of an industrial
   union.

125

3. Mobile workers with commitment to neither a particular trade nor employer, who constitute a general, regional worker society (among those who reside in a particular region for a while), which then creates general unions.

Two points must be added. First, the flow of causality in these three relationships can move backward from the end of each structure. That is, in some cases it is only after a union has been organized and has functioned for some time that the underlying workers' society comes into its own and its tacit agreements are codified. Also, I should note that in mass-production plants and offices with highly mechanized data processing technology, almost all employees can be considered semiskilled workers belonging to category 2, regardless of their designation as blue- or white-collar.

In terms of this model, I argue that workers' societies in Japan, especially as they have existed since the mid-1960s, are marked by two distinctive features. First, they lack a sense of independence from the corporation; the boundary between the world of the workers and that of the managers, between the needs of the corporation and the norms of workers' society, is unclear. Second, the first and the third types of workers' society and union defined above are not well established in Japan. In sum, in Japan over the past thirty years the dominant form of workers' society is that centered on the workplace and is so totally integrated with the company society as to be indistinguishable from it.[1] Of course, managers welcome this situation, for they regard independent workers' societies as obstacles to the efficient operation of a capitalist economy. The current situation signals the success of labor-management strategy and policy over the postwar era. In specific detail, how did these policies unfold? How did enterprise-based unions of regular employees respond to these policies? Did they resist labor-management policy at all?

Here, I approach these questions through a historical study of the steel industry, which should illuminate the general course of workplace history in postwar Japan. A comprehensive analysis of diverse industries would be ideal, but limits of time and space and the availability of rich materials on steel managers and workers lead me to focus only on this industry and, within it, on the Nippon Kōkan (NKK) corporation.

Management Strategy and Policy

I turn first to managerial policy, and then to the union's response and responsibility. As a window into the managerial mindset and approach, I primarily use the memoir of a labor manager at NKK, Orii Hyūga, who occupied a key position among the company's labor managers from the early 1950s through the early 1970s.[2] His memoir, *Twenty Years of Labor*

Management, indicates that, in the course of continual improvisation, the company adopted especially important labor-management policies on five occasions, in the years 1950–1951, 1957, 1959, 1963, and 1966. At each of these moments, a dramatic new managerial departure successfully responded to challenges of the previous years, and these new policies in turn shaped the workers' society into that which has since prevailed.

Using these turning points as markers, I divide the history of postwar labor management into five stages of roughly five years duration, beginning with the immediate postwar era (1945–1950) and concluding with the second half of the 1960s. Although there have been important new managerial initiatives since 1970, which I will discuss briefly in conclusion, I do not believe the basic pattern of labor-management relations has been altered in the twenty-five years since that time.

First Period

The chief question troubling managers in the late 1940s was how to regain their authority over the workforce, which they had ceded to unions in the numerous disputes of 1946 and 1947. At Nippon Kōkan (NKK), the labor union at the Tsurumi Mill won all its demands in a dramatic eighteen-day takeover of production in January 1946. The workers at NKK's main mill in Kawasaki launched a strike in October 1946, and after one week it won broad rights to a voice regarding personnel matters. Specifically, the company agreed to obtain union consent before taking action concerning "dismissals, transfers and change[s] in work organization, as well as standards and policies for hiring, punishments and rewards."[3] Further, the company agreed to adopt a grievance system to handle disputed cases of individual personnel decisions.

Offended by these concessions and determined to regain full control over personnel matters, in 1949 NKK managers demanded the union renegotiate the existing contract. When the negotiations stalled, the company declared "a state of no-contract." Further, NKK dealt the union a sharp blow in 1950 when it dismissed 180 workers who were Communist party members and union activists, as part of the nationwide "Red Purge." Such steps, supported by the shift in policy of the American occupation authorities, took place in most major companies around Japan.

Second Period

The first half of the 1950s was a period of transition in which the steel industry undertook its so-called first rationalization program. Some corporate labor managers advocated a new "scientific" labor management that would clarify job responsibilities, adopt more objective criteria for setting staffing levels, separate line supervisors from staff planners, and modernize wage scales. But this first postwar modernization drive did not go so far as to impose direct managerial control over the individual's work itself; a customary system of job assigments continued to regulate work group affairs, a system based on seniority and merit as assessed by work group leaders. In the early 1950s corporate managers continued to rely on an indirect control over rank-and-file workers; they granted the ranked members of the work group (foremen and crew bosses) the authority to apply standards of seniority and merit and direct their subordinates. For example, in 1951 NKK managers implemented a new companywide program to assess and define job standards in a so-called modern fashion. But this program involved no more than calculating appropriate workloads by assessing the rate of energy input (in calories) required for particular tasks; managers did not undertake any wholesale reorganization of the work process. The immaturity of management policy of these impoverished and "premodern" times is also seen in the company's New Life movement, which advised the wives of workers on birth control, child-rearing, and morality.

Third Period

In the second rationalization program of 1955–1960, the steel industry introduced new technologies and more modern equipment to the entire production process, and steel makers began the full-scale Americanization of labor management as well. In 1955, sponsored by the newly initiated Japan Productivity Center, the industry sent a team of managers to the United States to observe production techniques. In this foreign land they studied methods of industrial engineering, sophisticated techniques of internal cost accounting, and the "line-staff" system of managing production.

To apply these lessons, in 1956 NKK began to write a new manual of job standards at its Kawasaki Mill. In 1957 it set up the Efficiency Section to nurture a cadre of time-study experts and assess plantwide operations. For a time, the staff of the personnel division defended its practice of assessing workloads through calorie analysis and resisted new job assessments based on industrial engineering (IE), but as might be expected, the advocates of American-style IE won the day. In this same year, the wage system was reformed by introducing a job assessment factor into the formula by which group output premiums—these amounted to 44 percent of total earnings—were distributed to individuals. Previously, individual shares of this group efficiency payment had been distributed in direct proportion to a worker's base pay, which was calculated with reference to age, length of service, and education level. With this reform, the calculation of seniority and merit pay began to reflect, at least in part, managerial classification of individual jobs.

The rationalization project took a great step forward in 1959 when a state-of-the-art rolling mill began operations at Mizue, close by the old Kawasaki Mill. As it opened the Mizue plant, the company introduced a new hierarchy of supervision in the workplace. In accord with a plan to centralize managerial authority, which had been several years in the making, managers extensively revised the job of the foreman, now called *sagyōchō*.

The object of this reform was two-fold. Technicians formerly assigned to assist foremen in the production site were moved into a central "staff" office. From this newly elevated perch they were to rationalize production across the entire mill. At the same time, the *sagyōchō* (new foreman) who remained at each workplace gained a newly streamlined authority as the line supervisor of the production site. Although he lost some control over technical matters to the new central production staff, he now stood alone, with a broad range of authority over work and personnel management in his unit; this new foreman was now solely responsible for meeting the production goals of his work site while keeping down costs. The hierarchy of command at the workplace was reduced from eight to five layers with this reform.[4] Further, and of great importance, the new foreman was accorded white-collar status, although he had invariably begun his career as a blue-collar worker with limited education. For this reason, managers advertised their new system as "personnel management where the sky's the limit."

The advanced automated facilities of the new Mizue Mill did not require the skills of the old-guard steelworkers. The company thus staffed the plant by recruiting large numbers of inexperienced workers direct from high school, while it manned supervisory positions, such as the new foreman and crew chief slots, with senior men transferred from the old Kawasaki Mill. These reassigned workers were middle-aged men, typically crew bosses, frustrated because the road to promotion in the old plant had been closed, so they came to their new jobs with enthusiasm. By implementing transfers in this way, NKK helped institutionalize the distinctive postwar Japanese practice of interplant transfers for blue-collar workers.

I should note that in this same year the Labor-Management Division at corporate headquarters was beefed-up considerably. As it began interplant transfers, managers believed it important to extend uniform personnel practices, such as job assessments, throughout the company. In this fashion, various distinctive practices that were later systematized across the entire company, and more broadly throughout Japanese industry, first appeared in state-of-the-art facilities such as the Mizue Mill.

The impact of all these changes on workplace society should not be hard to imagine. Until the late 1950s, Japanese steelworkers identified themselves primarily as members of a particular workplace group, what I call the "workplace society." Their sense of themselves as members of a company society was mediated by their membership in these groups. Young workers accumulated experience and seniority within a work group that was clearly segregated from the white-collar world, and within their group they typically moved up the ladder from simple to more challenging tasks over time. Strictly speaking, long years of service were probably not required to perform the more difficult jobs, but seniority was still an accepted standard with which to locate a worker in the group hierarchy. The daily life of these blue-collar workers involved them in a cooperative endeavor of heavy physical labor, the smell of each other's sweat, and a shared social life. These workers typically spent their entire laboring career within the confines of a single work site.

Such a workplace order existed within a particular corporation and was hierachical in nature; these Japanese work groups of the early 1950s did not produce a strong consciousness of independence from the company. If, in the manner of the British trade society that encouraged powerful craft unions to emerge, the Japanese work groups of this era had been gathering places for people whose considerable skills were recognized by the society at large, their tacit shared understandings would have made them more independent from particular corporations. This was not the case. Even so, Japanese workplace groups of the late 1950s held some potential, under the right circumstances, to assert their independence from the control of the company.

In the late 1950s, a team of professors and graduate students at Tokyo University conducted a set of on-site surveys, including extensive visits to two NKK mills.[5] Today, their work is viewed as the definitive workplace study of that era. Their conclusion was that, in certain situations, the right circumstances might prevail and a Japanese style of workplace struggle could emerge from within. One such circumstance arose when workers felt the company made arbitrary decisions on matters over which the workplace group had no voice, such as wage levels. Another was found where workers with supervisory authority, those labeled as "bosses" (*oyakata*), themselves grew dissatisfied because their authority and pay fell short of that given to white-collar workers. A third circumstance conducive to work group independence arose when a pyramid-shaped hierarchy of job assignments was imposed on a work group whose members possessed similar skill levels. The contradiction between equal skills and unequal jobs produced frustration and antagonism toward the company.

These features characterized work groups in the iron and steel industry throughout the 1950s. They enabled steelworkers in numerous plants to carry out strikes every year between 1953 and 1956. This labor union offensive culminated in two major actions, an industry-wide strike staged in eleven waves in fall 1957, and a forty-nine-day strike at the NKK and Fuji Steel Companies in spring 1959. These acrimonious confrontations between management and labor cannot be understood simply as struggles over wage levels, but must be seen as responses to trends in the composition and organization of work groups. In particular, skilled regular workers, including ranked men such as crew bosses, played key roles in these disputes. Such men were the most active supporters of local units of the enterprise-based union. But the base for their activity was crumbling as customary patterns of work organization were beginning to dissolve in the face of technological innovation and new policies of operations and labor management. In the 1960s, management pressed forward with such changes on all fronts.

Fourth Period

In 1960 NKK invited a Professor Mandel from the United States to conduct an efficiency study. Following his advice, the company decided to apply industrial engineering to all of its operations, and it began to reassess its staffing levels at every work site. In 1963, the company made several major related changes in labor-management policy. The Efficiency Section, with its commitment to IE-based time studies, and the Labor Division, long-standing champion of workload analysis based on calorie requirements, reached a compromise that ended their several-year dispute over the best way to determine staffing levels. For the first time, NKK was able to set unified, companywide standards for assessing staffing needs, based primarily on industrial engineering and only secondarily on workload studies. In this same year, the new foreman system already in place at Mizue was extended to the old mills at Kawasaki and Tsurumi. In addition, the company introduced a system of "job wages." In the new wage structure, 49 percent of the average worker's income derived from his base wage and family allowance, 15 percent was distributed in the form of a "job performance wage," and 36 percent came from an efficiency premium now calculated on the basis of job evaluation points. The net effect was to link a portion of the worker's income to the company's assessment of the difficulty of his job. Also in 1963, as the company had come to rely almost entirely on high school graduates for its blue-collar workforce, NKK discontinued its training program for middle school graduates, which had originated in the 1920s and had been restructured in 1949. In sum, several measures first introduced in the late 1950s were fully implemented over the next few years.

The combination of a new plant, new equipment, and new modes of managing production and labor changed the workplace society in the steel industry in the following related ways: First, manual skills nurtured through long years of experience in a work group were no longer needed; the new automated production facilities for the most part required that the workers simply read meters and dials and push buttons. Second, skilled workplace veterans lost their customary voice in setting the work pace, dictating work methods, and assigning individuals to specific jobs; these matters were now set from above or from outside on the basis of the job manuals and standard job times dictated by the industrial engineers. Only a minimal amount of discretionary authority remained in the hands of the work group. Third, though the extent of heavy physical labor was reduced, the cooperative quality of the work decreased as well. Individual workers now typically carried out their jobs facing a huge machine in solitude, and reduced staffing further isolated the workers. In the account of one labor journalist who visited several steel mills in 1966:

> As production continues without interruption, the workers cannot take their lunch break in a group. They must eat in shifts, and their meal-times are thus irregular. One middle-aged worker remarked, "In the old days we enjoyed sitting down together and opening our lunch boxes." One union activist commented, "As things stand, we have no chance to discuss things with each other." The cohesion of the workplace group, that teamwork which was a special feature of the steel workers, has dissolved.[6]

The fourth important change was the weakening of the worker's sense of attachment to a specific work group due to more frequent and far-reaching job reassignments. Finally, the new foreman system turned a formerly powerful *workplace representative* into a *company spokesman* with broad authority and responsibility to impose the will of the company on his subordinates. The possibility that this "noncommissioned officer" might lead a mutiny of the troops was eliminated.

All the changes point in the same direction. The typical Japanese workplace, which had been none too independent of top management in the first place, further lost its independence. The importance of the work group in the employee's working life diminished, and employees became isolated from each other. One possible result of this change would be for the newly isolated worker to develop a heightened sense of belonging directly to the company, a sense of membership no longer mediated by the work group. Of course, this is the outcome that managers hoped for and sought to achieve with their policies of the third and fourth periods. Despite (or, indeed, because of) the standardization of skills at a lower average level, the managerial vision was one of a new companywide hierarchy of jobs arrayed in terms of their responsibility and authority, combined with programs to induce employees to compete to rise in this hierarchy and to pay the workers in accord with their success in competing.[7]

But a second possible outcome of this new isolation can be imagined. These atomized employees might end up as isolated wage earners with a purely instrumental attitude toward work and the company. For managers, this outcome was not an empty threat; although the young high school graduates who were emerging as the core of the industry's workforce might embrace meritocratic competition based on equality of opportunity, they also tended to place great emphasis on fulfillment in private life, a relatively new concept in postwar social thinking. One indication of a new, detached instrumental attitude among employees was the increase in job-hopping among younger workers during the labor shortage of the late 1960s.

At NKK, a sign of this stance came in the responses of workers to a companywide opinion survey undertaken in 1963, the very year that the full program of modernized labor management was implemented. If one compares the results to a survey of NKK workers in 1952, one sees that the proportion of workers professing "dual loyalty" to both firm and labor union dropped from 34 percent to 13 percent, but the proportion "critical of both" increased from 10 percent to 29 percent.[8] The report of the labor journalist cited previously concluded that industrial engineers were now controlling work, that individual merit ratings were of increased importance in setting wages and assigning personnel, and that competition among workers had intensified. It is hardly surprising that such a workplace will lower the morale of some of the workers and lead others to seek fulfillment and small pleasures outside the company.

For a corporation such as NKK, committed to companywide cost control, preventing the second outcome and involving the entire workforce in company-centered, merit-based competition was of paramount importance. In the second half of the 1960s, labor managers took steps to these ends.

Fifth Period
In retrospect, on the eve of the internationalization of Japan's economy in the 1970s, the following labor issues weighed most heavily in the minds of corporate managers: First, in order to increase productivity and hold down costs managers saw continuing need to introduce industrial engineering of a Tayloristic type, eliminate remaining paternalistic modes of management, and reject rigid seniority standards for promotions or raises. Although these goals implied increased reliance on meritocratic principles, managers feared that an unalloyed meritocracy would lower morale and provoke opposition. Instead, they hoped to devise a Japanized system to arouse a "fighting spirit" in all employees and reward them for developing their latent abilities rather than for achieving a specific norm. They were engaged in a delicate balancing act as they encouraged workers to discover the value of a new sort of work group, one in which coworkers would encourage each other as they competed to prove their individual abilities.

This view of managerial strategy reflects my interpretation of an ambivalent treatise published in 1969 by the Nikkeiren (Japan Federation of Employers' Associations) after more than two years of research, *Theory and Practice of Merit-based Management*.[9] The Nikkeiren sought what it called a "concord" between apparently conflicting objectives. On the level of theory, it hoped to reconcile economic rationalism and human respect. In practical terms, it sought a concord between rigorous policies to screen and motivate individuals and an older concern with group harmony.[10]

Resolving the problem in theory was not difficult. Forty-one percent of the managers studied by Nikkeiren maintained that "respect for humans" meant "offering treatment (pay and promotions) that reflected improvements in employee ability, thereby giving the workers hope for the future, and fostering in them a desire to excel." A further 32 percent defined this respect as "devising ways to develop each individual employee's ability to the utmost." These opinions overcame any blatant contradiction between rational management and respect for the workers. But when it came to the practical matter of reconciling individualized management and group harmony, the concord proved elusive, although the model QC circles described previously offered one possible solution.

Awareness of these dual, potentially contradictory, managerial concerns to maintain both efficiency and high morale helps one understand NKK's labor-management policy of the late 1960s. In 1966 NKK began operations at the new Fukuyama Mill, which remained its most important plant until the early 1990s. The company chose this as the occasion to reclassify all employees in the single status of *shain*, or company employee, eliminating the long-standing categories of factory worker (*kōin*) and white-collar staff (*shoku-in*). This change was described as "a fair means of managing rewards and promotion on the basis of the ability to perform assigned tasks."[11] (See Figure 6.1.)

Under this system, promotion up the ladder (on the right hand side) to higher qualification classes within each block depended upon length of service plus a managerial evaluation of the employee's ability and performance. Promotion from one block to the next required the employee to pass an examination and win strong evaluations, as well as accrue appropriate seniority. As the arrows in the pyramid portion of the figure indicate, as long as the worker demonstrated ability and a gung-ho spirit, the path was open even to blue-collar workers to rise to supervisory or other key positions, and even beyond that to managerial positions such as section chief. This reform can be seen as a grant of citizenship placing blue-collar workers on a par with their white-collar brethren; it institutionalized their direct membership in the company society.

This opening of career opportunity to regular blue-collar workers had an important, indeed, an indispensable, corollary. The only way to make the promise of open-ended career development plausible was to limit the numbers to whom the promise was made. The company had to somehow segregate the many people in lower-level or auxiliary positions whose prospects for advancing in this system were extremely remote, thus making it systemically difficult or impossible for these workers to demand equality of access or result. The trick, of course, was to exclude these people from the category of the "regular employee" eligible for promotion. NKK achieved this by greatly expanding the system of subcontracting. Several state-of the-art steel plants, such as NKK's Fukuyama Mill, began operations in the late 1960s. They all set up large numbers of affiliated subcontracting firms that handled what we might call the "three D" jobs: dangerous, dirty, and difficult.[12] In general, it appears that as many as half of the workers physically present in these new steel plants were in fact employees of subcontracting firms.[13] Thus, to integrate workplace society

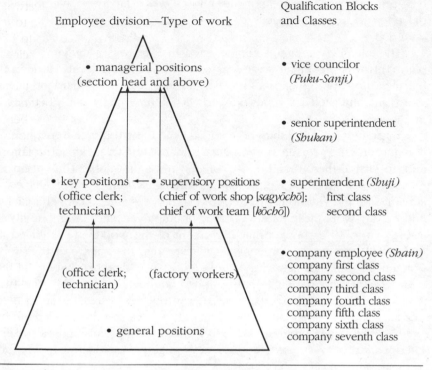

Employee division—Type of work

Qualification Blocks
and Classes

• managerial positions
(section head and above)

• vice councilor
(Fuku-Sanji)

• senior superintendent
(Shukan)

• key positions ←— • supervisory positions
(office clerk;   (chief of work shop [*sagyōchō*];
technician)   chief of work team [*kōchō*])

• superintendent *(Shuji)*
first class
second class

(office clerk;   (factory workers)
technician)

• general positions

•company employee *(Shain)*
company first class
company second class
company third class
company fourth class
company fifth class
company sixth class
company seventh class

FIGURE 6.1 New Employee System of Nippon Kokan

Note: Arrow signifies possibility for movement upward

Source: Orii Hyugā, *Rōmu kanri nijū nen* [Twenty years of labor management]
(Tōkyō: Toyo Keizai Shinpōsha, 1973), pp. 40–47.

into company society more tightly required that new boundaries be erected
around the former.

In addition to reclassifying and renaming workers, labor managers at
NKK in 1966 changed the pay system by introducing greater discretion (or
"range") into the setting of job rates for individual workers. The system of
job rates implemented several years earlier linked a portion of each
worker's pay to his job, which was graded for its inherent difficulty. Under
the new system, a range of so-called job-rates was created within a qualification class. Thus, a worker's "job pay" could be increased without changing either his actual job or his qualification class. NKK called this a system
of "range rates"; it gave management latitude to raise an individual's job
rate, even if he stayed on the same job, so long as his skill was deemed to
have improved. The company thus transformed job-based pay to merit-

and-ability-based, or qualification-based, pay. The loosening of the tie between individual job assignment and pay was a Japanese-style managerial effort to keep employees motivated even as they were stuck in the same job.

The third new program implemented in 1966 was a midterm staffing plan. This was a companywide reassessment of staffing levels carried out by calculating appropriate staffing levels on the basis of standard job times. The plan eliminated 2,200 positions in NKK's three major mills, beginning in October 1964.

What interests me is that these cutbacks in the workforce took place in conjunction with programs of job enlargement and systematic job rotation, and, to enable these, training of workers in multiple jobs. Thus management was constructing a mutually reinforcing system of three elements: streamlining the workforce, developing employee multifunctional abilities, and making work meaningful. A survey of employee attitudes in one major steel plant in 1972 showed that 28 percent of the workers felt fulfilled in their work because the supervisor had extended the sphere of their jobs horizontally and thus changed the jobs' substance. Another 35 percent felt their work was not fulfilling because it had not been expanded in this way. Although the survey suggests that the new policies were uneven in their impact, it can also be read to mean that all of these workers accepted the premise of the new program. Moreover, this system premised on a streamlined workforce was reinforced by a new wage policy to show that reducing manpower profits everyone.

NKK did more than just preach to its workers that the pie would not grow unless production increased. Beginning in 1968, major steel companies added a new element to the efficiency wage component of a worker's pay, a sum of money dubbed "staffing rationalization profit sharing." It was designed to return to the remaining workers a share of the savings accrued from workforce reductions.[14]

Orii's memoir ends its coverage with the previous matters, but I must examine two additional initiatives of these years by using other sources.

First, meritocratic management clearly expanded the role of individual personnel evaluation in all industries. According to surveys of 168 companies carried out by the Kansai Business Association, the labor or personnel sections of 134 of these companies had put in place some sort of formal assessment program for individual employees.[15] Table 6.1 shows the percentage of companies that used these progams in making various types of decisions in 1957 and in 1974.

During the seventeen-year period between the two surveys, the role of personnel evaluations expanded sharply, moving from a relatively restricted use in setting pay raises to a broad range of uses in personnel decisions. These assessments had become far more important in determin-

TABLE 6.1

The Percentage of Firms Implementing Personnel Evaluations
for Various Purposes (multiple responses)

Purpose	1957 (%)	1974 (%)
Raises	98.6	90.0
Bonuses	68.4	88.0
Promotions	59.6	81.0
Personnel transfers	38.0	44.0
Assignment	12.0	43.0
In-company education; retraining	16.0	24.0

Source: *Nihon romū kenkyūkai* [Japan Labor-Management Laboratory], *Romū nenkan* [Labor management almanac] (Tokyo: 1976), p. 220.

ing the short-term treatment and long-term careers of employees, and this change surely increased the intensity of competition among coworkers.

Another policy change that reinforced competition was the practice of requiring individual workers to file self-assessments as the basis for decisions about transfers or promotions. Nikkeiren conducted surveys that reveal that the proportion of all companies using self-assessments rose from just 27 percent in 1963 to 43 percent in 1968. Among companies with more than 1,500 workers, 60 percent required them.[16] It appears that such programs were aimed primarily at white-collar workers and that managers made their decisions on the basis of interviews and personnel evaluations, with the employee's self-assessment as a secondary factor. But even so, managers who required employees to engage in this practice of self-assessment and self-promotion were pushing employees to develop their competence in a competitive fashion. I see this practice as emblematic of the character of Japanese-style labor management of this era.

A second feature of the late 1960s not covered in Orii's memoir is the spread of small-group activities. Managers eager to prevent either individual employees or work groups from nurturing a sense of independence from the corporation encouraged the spread of small-group self-management activities (QC circles, ZD movements). Turning once more to the Nikkeiren surveys, one finds that by 1968 26 percent of companies had introduced Quality Control circles and 23 percent had introduced Zero Defect movements. For companies with over 1,500 workers, the proportions were 43 percent for QC circles and 42 percent for ZD movements.[17] The spread of these circles in the steel industry was particularly rapid and complete. NKK was a leader of the movement, launching its first circles in 1963. By 1969, twenty-nine steel corporations had introduced self-management activities in over 20,000 work groups at 102 plants, with a total of 175,544 individuals registered as members.[18]

As I discussed in the previous chapter, the corporate intent was to curtail an emerging instrumental orientation toward work among employees who were increasingly isolated at the production site by IE and new mass-production technologies. These technologies had curtailed the relative independence of work groups and destroyed the value of skills obtained through years of collective experience. Managers wanted to bolster morale and give workers some opportunity to develop and use their skills. Of equal importance, managers wanted workers to create a new form of camaraderie and a work group collectivity that virtually coerced workers to improve their performance and channel these gains toward measurable managerial objectives.

In my inquiry thus far I have drawn on the memoir of Orii Hyūga and have presented the history of labor management at NKK as a prototypical case in the postwar history of Japanese corporate management of the workforce. To sum up: In the first postwar decade, big business launched a counterattack on the immediate postwar gains of labor unions; from roughly 1955 to 1965 managers promoted massive technological innovation and introduced their version of American-style labor management; and from the mid-1960s through the first oil crisis, they made Japanese-style adjustments to encourage the workers to develop their adaptive ability and build new companywide solidarities. These measures generally succeeded. They brought into being the workplace atmosphere and employee consciousness desired by managers. But before simply accepting this conclusion, one must examine the postwar responsibility of the labor unions in enabling this outcome.

The "Postwar Responsibility" of Labor Unions*

Policies to "Oppose Rationalization"
I begin with the three-point platform concerning personnel rationalization adopted by the Japan Federation of Steel Workers' Unions. In 1953, the first stage of the iron and steel industry's postwar rationalization program was well underway. At this point, the central committee of the Federation stated, "We are fundamentally unable to accept rationalization measures which seek only to increase the profits of monopoly capitalism and do so by sacrificing both workers and small-to-medium enterprises."[19] The committee emphasized the need to struggle against job reassignments, "capitalistic wage rationalization," wage cutbacks, and "managerial control of the

---

*Kumazawa uses the notion of the "postwar responsibility" of labor unions in an ironic fashion here. The term is a pun on the concept of the "war responsibility" of the emperor, Japanese leaders, and the people at large, which has been the subject of fierce and continuing debate.

workplace which squeezes the workers dry and intensifies labor," as well as the massive layoffs expected to result from these rationalization plans. The Federation did not oppose rationalization categorically; in fact, it approved rationalization aimed at "the peaceful growth of the iron and steel industry. . . which is sufficiently planned and democratically managed."[20] At the same time, it is noteworthy that in resisting rationalization on managerial terms, the Federation assigned a crucial role to "workplace struggles" of local unions.

Contrast this adamant stand to the position, twelve years later, of the Steel Workers' Union Joint Struggle Committee on Rationalization. In September 1965, as one milestone along the road of high-speed growth, the major iron and steel firms were about to scrap old facilities, thereby cutting production of crude iron by 10 percent and cutting workforces by "natural" attrition. They also were planning the wholesale reassessment of manpower needs through industrial engineering and large-scale interplant transfers of the resulting surplus workers. The union response follows.

To combat programs that shift the burden of sacrifice to workers: Oppose plans to idle workers or lay them off. In cases of transfers, negotiate for company acceptance of the following four conditions. (1) The terms of inter-plant transfers must be agreed to by both the union and the person concerned. (2) Existing wage levels and working conditions must be maintained. (3) Transfers must have a legitimate reason. (4) Appropriate replacement personnel must be assigned to the workplace from which the transfer is made. In addition, we will struggle for job security in tandem with workers at sub-contracting firms and part-time workers.

❖ ❖ ❖

Issues for assertive action: (1) Early implementation of four crew/three shift work schedule and a 40 hour week [this would allow more days off and fewer hours than the existing three crew/three shift schedule]. (2) Add more workers to reverse the increase in our workload (staffing levels to be negotiated on the basis of union-run inspection of the workplace). (3) Take a long view and struggle to change "policies premised on the needs of monopoly capital which sacrifice workers and the general public's livelihood."[21]

Finally, fast-forward another thirteen years to 1978, a time of industrywide downsizing. Consider the following two items: a special report of the Kobe Steel Corporation Steelworkers' Union, presented in fall 1978 to a conference of delegates from the Japan Federation of Steel Workers' Unions, and the "guidelines for dealing with rationalization policy" that accompanied the report.[22]

Kobe Steel's rationalization plan proposed reducing the workforce by 4,000 over three years through attrition and a hiring freeze, plus transferring or permanently reassigning 700 workers to subcontractors. The union held, "We understand the need for rationalization because we believe that a firm foundation for the company is critical to assure us a secure livelihood in the future. But we think it important to somehow ease the transition of those who are transferred or reassigned. We also believe it crucial to clarify fair standards for selecting these workers which will satisfy all observers."[23] The union planned to seek these assurances through labor-management consultation, not collective bargaining.

The union's detailed proposals laid out the following position: In consultations concerning interplant transfers within Kobe Steel, the company should "clarify" the purpose of the transfers, the working conditions of the sending and receiving workplaces, the length of time in cases of temporary reassignment, and arrangements to help home-owning transferees dispose of their houses. If the union concluded that its members' needs have been met it would agree to the transfer. "On this occasion there is the question as to whose viewpoint carries greater weight, that of the individual worker or of the union. This issue concerns the union's organizational operations. . . so even though the opinion of the individual worker is an important element, the union must make the final judgment by taking all factors into consideration."[24]

The union at Kobe Steel may have been unusually frank in approving the company's strategy of rationalization. But by the late 1970s its basic stance was no different from that of the other leading enterprise-based unions in the steel industry. Their overriding concern was to make sure that no regular employees were subject to outright dismissal. On all other matters their "understanding" of the management position was complete.

Although documents such as these give only a surface picture of a union's goals and behavior, the contrasts among these union positions from 1953, 1965, and 1978 is sharp enough to convey how dramatically the union movement in the steel industry changed in this quarter-century. First, unions stopped resisting capitalist rationalization. Second, the workplace diminished in importance as a battleground between union and company. Third, the basic means to deal with labor-management issues shifted from collective bargaining to joint consultation. Fourth, resistance to transfers within the company weakened. And fifth, it seems that regular workers no longer felt any compunction about excluding workers who were not regular employees from the union and its remaining benefits.

Why did unions change in these ways? Few documents are available that speak to this issue, especially the transformation as it took place below the surface. In the rest of this chapter, I examine the substrata of change by looking into the way postwar unions thought about and acted in workplace society. The integration of workers into the corporation, as well as their ability to resist integration, depends on the way they come together in workplace society.

The Erosion of Customary Work Groups

The most important value sought by Japan's workers through the militant union movement of the immediate postwar years was equality as a (regular) employee. The specific demands that gave voice to this value ranged from job security to abolition of status discrimination between white- and blue-collar workers to elimination of differential pay raises and the call for a living wage reflecting need, not merit or rank. In other words, organized workers in the early postwar years demanded that corporations practice what they preached; they sought to realize in practice the promises implicit in managerial rhetoric of the prewar and wartime eras.

At the risk of imposing an external standard on these workers, I would argue that their early postwar agenda was not sufficiently attentive to the centrality of workplace society in the life experience of ordinary workers. For better or worse, the early postwar labor movement did not seek to democratize the work group or strengthen its autonomy from the corporation. It demanded equality for workers as company employees without much concern for the nature and role of the workplace group. To draw an analogy to political movements, the logic that drove postwar unionism drew on a concept of "citizens' rights" rather than one of "village self-rule." Strictly speaking, so-called workplace struggles in the early postwar era were not in fact struggles to control work or to regulate relationships among coworkers.

Of course, the emphasis of early postwar unions in part reflects the atmosphere of a desperate time, when workers did not have the margin to devote energy to such matters as the hierarchic quality of daily work life and the relationship between foremen, crew bosses and unranked workers. At a time when the struggle to eat and to survive faced foremen and even white-collar staff, these lower-level bosses joined workers in criticizing management. But the critical point is that, even in later years, a weak impulse to question the character of work, relations among coworkers, or the arrangement of the work group persisted as a negative legacy for Japan's union movement.

In the early 1950s (the second period treated previously), the early postwar crisis had passed, and labor movement activism declined. Management had succeeded in limiting the function of unions primarily to wage negotations at the company, and not the industry, level. Managers also sought to reinforce the customary workplace hierarchy of seniority and merit, the existing version of the *nenkō* system. To this end, they offered special benefits and authority to crew bosses and foremen. Managers hoped to impose their will on the unranked workers by bolstering the day-to-day authority of workplace bosses; they encouraged the latter to sustain their customary involvement in the personal lives of their subordinates. This strategy could succeed to some extent in restoring order precisely because the immediate postwar unions had not promoted a movement of internal democratization that might have attacked the authority of work group bosses.

Turning to another political analogy, this reaction of the early 1950s has much in common with the aftermath of the Cultural Revolution some years later in China. Once the situation calmed down, the people who had crowded the streets of Beijing hysterically shouting for the destruction of the bureaucracy had no choice but to return to their daily routine of village life dominated by old customs and human relations.

In the latter half of the 1950s, however, this decline in labor activism was reversed; this was a time of manifold opportunities for unions. Also at this moment, a group of professors and graduate students from Tokyo University, noted previously, conducted perhaps the finest of the many field surveys of postwar workplace life and unionism in Japan. They gave sustained and careful attention to the interactions between individuals and work groups as well as unions and management. In the first two chapters of their book Ōkōchi, Fujita, and Ujihara offer finely drawn portraits of several work sites between 1956 and 1958 at NKK's two major mills, and I will use these portraits to explore the opportunities of these years in more detail.[25]

New technology and management policy introduced two important changes to NKK's workplaces at this time. First, new production technology in the main sections of the steel industry sharply reduced the years of experience needed to qualify a man for higher grades of previously difficult work. Second, because the company had imposed a hiring freeze in the early 1950s, the workforce included a large number of men with eight to ten years of experience and the skills to undertake almost every job in their section. These two developments, the latter especially, destabilized the seniority- and merit-based *nenkō* hierarchy in the workplace, which had served both managers and workers well enough when years of experience had corresponded roughly to a hierarchy of increasingly demanding jobs, and increasing seniority in the firm seemed to both workers and managers one reasonable ground for determining wages.

And yet, the *nenkō* structure had been a firmly established aspect of the workplace social order; the crumbling of one of its pillars (the connection of job assignments to skill accumulated through experience) by no means led directly to its total collapse. Thus the persistence of *nenkō*-based hierarchies greatly frustrated senior workers who felt that their pay, based in large part on their seniority, lagged behind their latent ability to perform the higher-level jobs at their workplace. They complained about small annual raises for unranked workers, secrecy in the process of ability and performance ratings, extreme differentials in the allocation of efficiency pay, the essentially coercive nature of overtime for workers under constant review, and the arbitrariness of decisions to promote some workers to supervisory rank.

Because of the increase in such complaints, unions now had an opportunity to address them using a program to democratize the work group and bring a new equality to it. Unions could have pushed for a kind of self-rule by work group members as equals, ultimately affirming the independence of norms of the work group from those of the company. For instance, insofar as new technology and the hiring freeze had combined to make all the workers more or less equally skilled, the union could have sought to institute a system of rotating work assignments. It could have demanded that promotion to supervisory posts be decided strictly on straight seniority, instead of a combination of seniority and merit rating. It could have pushed to make the ability-performance rating process more open. It might have demanded that the authority to oversee work be shifted from the hands of foremen or crew bosses to a self-regulating body of the workers. On the basis of the workers' own standards, such a local union branch could have negotiated with management over workload, staffing levels, or overtime. After establishing this kind of equality in the workplace, the union could then seek to minimize wage differentials.

This scenario should not be dismissed as my utopian fantasy. In this same period, the miners at Mitsui's Miike Mine demanded and won many of these changes. In a situation in which all coworkers were equally skilled, they implemented a system to rotate assignments at the mine face, and they eliminated discrimination between frontline and auxiliary crews in job assignments and pay. The Miike union also restricted competition among workers to meet output norms, and carried out "work-to-rule" actions to enforce safety measures.[26] Coworkers challenged management and asserted their independence on the basis of membership in a stable, long-standing work group. The potential for steelworkers at this moment to raise similar challenges successfully cannot be denied.

But the historical record is sobering. The enterprise-based unions in the steel industry ultimately could not take advantage of this opportunity to challenge management and assert independence. To realize the Miike model required a conceptual leap past the prevailing notion among steelworkers that unions should provide "equality as an employee" and a decent livelihood without concern for the substance of the work. In the steel industry, and many other processing industries, two related factors combined to prevent this leap.

First, in the 1950s companies such as NKK began to shift labor-management authority away from supervisors at the workplace to plant-level managers and, beyond that, to corporate headquarters. This forced the union to make a corresponding upward shift in the level at which it undertook collective bargaining. The 1956–1958 field study at NKK found that authority to negotiate not only over base wages but also over the factors to be used in setting output premiums (standard output levels, staffing levels, and hours) had recently been shifted away from the union local (a section within the plant) to the level of the plant or above. Matters that remained as items for local union negotiation had been limited to individual job assignments, assignments to overtime and vacation days, and the allocation of output pay premiums to particular sections and then to the individual workers. The report by Kōshiro Kazuyoshi concluded,

> If we define the union's "workplace organization" as a negotiating unit that ought to deal with wages and the details of working conditions at each production site, then the plant union headquarters currently fits that definition perfectly. . . . The union local constituted at the level of a section within the plant has almost no room to bargain collectively, and it cannot be called a workplace organization. . . . This is all the more true of the union's sub-local unit at the level of a work team.[27]

In this case, the enterprise-based union was no longer an organization anchored at the site of production; it was a unit based at the site of financial management that took bargaining over average wage levels to be its major task.

Second, a large number of the union officials at the local level were supervisors, such as foremen or crew bosses. According to the field survey of NKK, these supervisors accounted for 50 percent of each union local's top three officers, 38 percent of the local steering committee members, 50 percent of the local delegates to the plantwide central committee, 25 percent of the representatives to the annual union assembly, and 66.7 percent of the union team chiefs (the sublocal leader). There are numerous reasons for this state of affairs. In a world of *nenkō*-based hierarchy, senior workers were the "natural" leaders. Unranked workers were seen to be weak in dealing with white-collar staff. Compared to foremen, they were too busy with day-to-day (or minute-to-minute) tasks to take time out for union activity. If an unranked worker were to become a union officer, he would hesitate to exercise his authority as a unionist over foremen who were also in the union.

In such an incestuous structure, would men who simultaneously ran the union local and served as low-level supervisors identify more with the company, or would they develop a union loyalty that set them uneasily against management? The outcome would depend on the degree and scope of the authority the company gave them.

The field survey of NKK describes this authority in detail in the case of the steel plate section of the Tsurumi Mill. The duties of the foremen and crew bosses during the late 1950s were numerous, but was their authority extensive?

1. They *transmitted* to the workplace the work plans and production directives issued daily by operations managers and supervisors.
2. They *consulted technical staff in making decisions* concerning oversight and supervision on the job, procedures to be followed, and assignment of workers.
3. They *advised their supervisors* on decisions to increase or reduce the staffing levels, fill vacant positions, transfer people within the section, assign trainees and temporary workers, promote unranked men to supervisory posts, or raise temporary workers to regular status.
4. They *assisted* labor division staff in recording worker attendance and absence.
5. They *considered and gave approval* to requests for days off, for break time, for temporary departure from the workplace for personal business, and they *designated* individual assignments of overtime.
6. They further *consulted technical staff* in making initial merit and ability ratings of their subordinates, leading to assignment of "merit grades" used in deciding raises, bonuses, and premium pay allocation.

It appears that these workplace bosses were unhappy because their authority was shrinking, and the Labor Management Division and other white-collar staff members were taking greater control over job operations and decisions about individual workers. It is impossible to know the exact degree to which this discontent translated into support for assertive union activity.

At times the anger of foremen could erupt in opposition to technicians and white-collar managers, and ultimately the company itself, as these men grumbled "what the hell does a white-collar guy know about steel work?" On occasion these frustrated low-level supervisors, foremen, and crew bosses strove to unite their workplaces in support of the union and against the company, and they supported decisions to strike for higher pay. But even when some foremen turned in a prounion direction, they did not call for democracy and equality in the work group as the first step in asserting the independence of workplace society from management. Their ultimate goal, after all, was to bolster their threatened status and their own skill as senior workers, a rather different agenda from that of the rank-and-file workers.

And of course, not all foremen or crew bosses supported the union. Because they still retained some authority over the jobs and the treatment of ordinary workers, they were fully capable of maintaining a procompany stance. Indeed, as their *formal* powers shrunk, these foremen realized that the more they turned in a procompany direction the more management was likely to respect their *informal* authority. If they were loyal, managers would conclude that they could "safely leave things to them."

In this situation, the issues that the union locals raised most vigorously were precisely those over which the ranked workers still retained some authority. These ranked men monopolized local union offices, and they wanted to use the union to reaffirm their ability to make decisions on their own; they did not wish to see the union win a decisionmaking voice to address the dissatisfactions of veteran unranked workers. The union did respond to the discontent of the latter by dispatching organizers from union headquarters to address local problems, thus bypassing the formal structure of the union local, dominated by ranked men.[28] This strategy revitalized the union at the grass roots somewhat in the late 1950s, but it ultimately did not change the way work group members managed their jobs and their relations with each other. The union headquarters could do no more than establish standards for output and personnel transfers. The main impetus to struggle to democratize the shop floor came from left-wing leaders in the headquarters of the industrial federation and NKK enterprise union. Local activists inclined to join hands with them had to detach themselves psychologically from the work group. The difficulty of making this break is a dilemma that has continued to characterize the Japanese labor movement.

The Response of the Atomized Worker

Workers can only find the strength to resist capitalist rationalization in the impulse to control work and relations among themselves, an impulse nurtured in a familiar workers' society. In the 1960s Japanese steel workers were unable to cultivate this impulse and so could not resist the company-wide rationalization programs of these years. The reason for this failure should be clear. At a time when labor unions had tried but failed (had failed, that is, to introduce much democracy or equality into the old-style work groups) to induce frustrated senior workers to view the work group as their "stronghold," the company's new labor management policies responded effectively to these discontents. They offered outlets for this frustration via commitment to a company society. Workers who viewed the prospects of constructing their own stronghold in the workplace as uncertain instead adapted themselves to the modernization programs of corporate labor managers.

The new foreman system (*sagyō-chō*) was one outlet created for the ranked men (foremen, crew bosses) whose customary authority had eroded.[29] The outlet for unranked senior workers took the form of the "blue sky" system introduced in the mid-1960s, to offer them hope of advancement in qualification classes. In addition, because changing technology had destroyed the rough correspondence between seniority, promotion, and skill acquisition and had made customary practices of job assignments and wage determination seem arbitrary, workers viewed the revamped system of job assignments and promotions, including the new job-based component in the wage structure, as a fair and "democratic" reform. In 1962 the NKK union leaders acknowledged the prevalence of such views when they responded to the company proposal for job-based wages. They agreed that new technology, changed skill requirements, and the increase in younger workers required the modernization of the older seniority-and-merit (*nenkō*) wage system, whose standards for wage determination were unacceptably vague.

In the matter of job transfers, there was a similar shift. Workers no longer sought local control through the union but accepted a system of companywide control on management terms. The union had first responded to the danger of dismissals during the hectic years of "scrap and build" of the late 1950s and early 1960s by demanding that workers at obsolete jobs be transferred to new ones. The union further insisted on a decisionmaking voice to insure that the company guaranteed the four conditions that would assure sufficient retraining and economic support to ease the transition. But from the mid-1960s, the company gained the power to make small-scale intraplant transfers without consulting the union.[30]

The practice of transfers offered job security to the regular worker, at a cost. It dispossessed him of knowledge of the job rooted in experience. It forced the worker, who sought to somehow adapt to his new workplace, to be more submissive to the dictates of technocrats and the imperatives of the machinery. This was especially true in new workplaces where little of the work was done on a cooperative basis. But for the senior workers frustrated by the poor fit between their job assignments at a recently modernized mill and their skills accumulated in the old-style work group, a transfer to an important job in a brand new, state-of-the-art plant was a welcome opportunity to develop a career for a brighter future, despite the increased psychological stress of that work. The large-scale relocations of the mid-1960s transformed steelworkers from laboring men who stubbornly stuck to familiar ways to "company men" who competed as individuals to adapt and advance in the corporation, free from the customary restrictions of the old work group.

In sum, the new foremen gained authority centered on their power to rate their subordinates; the workplace was completely integrated into the corporate hierarchy; and the trends toward meritocracy, competition, and individualism were accelerating. These mutually reinforcing changes eroded the union's antirationalization movement at its base, while simultaneously promoting a stronger company consciousness in the workers. The mid-1960s were also years of fierce interfirm competition in the steel industry. A worker's success as a company man hinged on cooperating to increase productivity and triumph in this competition. In the mind of the steelworker, the boundaries within which one pursued a career had expanded from the workplace to the corporation. As the employee became more competitive and individualistic in his behavior in the workplace, he developed a stronger company-conscious group identity. This conclusion may run counter to conventional wisdom about individualism, but it is logical enough for the experience of postwar Japan.

As workers thus changed, the union narrowed its sphere of activity. It came to serve primarily as a body that negotiated the average pay raise for the workforce as a whole. Enterprise-based steel unions were among the first to thus shrink their agendas, and the union presence in the workplace greatly weakened. In addition, even during wage negotiations, the union grew reluctant to strike. Beginning in 1959 with NKK, union after union decided to drop out of the previously unified, industrywide annual wage struggles. And, of course, as soon as a union at a competing company broke ranks and settled on a new wage level, pressure mounted on the other unions to settle without a strike, for fear that the firm lose market share to its competitor. Since the twenty-four-hour strikes at Yahata Steel, Fuji Steel, and Sumitomo Metal Industries in 1965, not a single strike has taken place at a major steel company in Japan.

With labor-management relations "stabilized" in this fashion, the left-wing leadership of enterprise unions and the industrial union federation fell from power. Even though I have presented left-wing activists as being, to some extent, responsible for the generally weak concern with the workplace in the Japanese labor movement, their demise was nonetheless a blow. These activists had sought to build upon the discontent of the ordinary workers with an organizing system that bypassed the work group bosses who dominated union locals. Further, they had promoted an ideological solidarity of workplace activists who drew strength from the union.

The new union leaders appropriated the label "labor unionists" in a remarkable semantic inversion of this concept as it is understood in the West. Since they gained hegemony in the 1960s, this stream of leadership has ruled with little change. They have cemented an incestuous relationship with management, embodied in their almost universally held dual status as both union officers and workplace supervisors (foremen or crew chiefs). These union officials no longer feel any tension or conflict of interest in these dual roles. Neither do they any longer fear losing their grip in the face of a challenge from the rank and file. Thus, stability has come at a price. Class solidarity has withered; once-sharp criticisms of the logic of capital have ceased, along with union drives to promote workplace activism. Feeling no pain or contradiction in their roles, workers in supervisory positions who identify profoundly with management have controlled these unions for three decades now.

And what of those workers who could not adapt to the brave new world of meritocracy and competition? They have turned toward an instrumental view of their jobs and a focus on their own personal lives.

Integration into the Company Society

From the mid-1960s to the mid-1970s, union members in Japan faced a thin array of choices. A Japanese-style practice of labor management had been designed, and was subsequently revised, in a manner that prevented or contained the spread of alienation among the workers. In the face of spreading Japanese-type meritocracy and related practices, unions posed no countermeasures of note. Thus one may characterize this decade in the history of labor management by recalling the following points:[31]

First, the activities and authority of labor unions in the steel industry came to be concentrated at the center and the peak of the organizational pyramid. Orii tells us that, in the early 1960s, the plant-level unions at NKK ceded much of their authority to the companywide federation, which reached a new unified labor contract with the corporation. After 1965, the sites for bargaining and setting of working conditions were centralized in similar fashion in virtually all big business unions in Japan, and the independent authority of factory-based or plant-level unions within corporations became noticeably weaker. Finally, in 1972, the formal structure of the union federation was changed to reflect the shifting center of gravity. Plant unions in multiplant corporations such as NKK no longer joined the National Federation of Iron and Steel Workers' Unions directly. Instead, a companywide federation of plant unions joined the national federation as a single entity representing all plants in the firm. This sharply eroded the autonomy of plant unions and their workplace locals. All important decisions concerning production, equipment changes, staffing, job assignments, or shift changes were made through formal negotiation or, more often, informal discussion between the companywide union federation and corporate headquarters.[32] The plant and local units of the union merely implemented and enforced these decisions.

To be sure, in the 1960s and 1970s, unions responded to the criticism that "there is no union presence in the workplace" by extending the system of union-company discussion or "joint consultation" to the plant and local levels. But in conception and in practice, this hierarchy of discussions prevented any segment of the union members from independently formulating demands and fighting for contractual agreements that were binding on both labor and management. In essence, joint consultation eroded collective bargaining. From the 1970s through the present, plant-level unions in the Japanese steel industry have in practice been unable to bargain collectively over basic labor conditions, and workplace locals do not even have a contractual right to do so.[33]

To a certain extent, this upward and centralizing shift in the union's decisionmaking function was an unavoidable response to a prior and parallel corporate centralization of managerial decisionmaking on labor issues. But even within this context, the union could have made some different choices. By abandoning antirationalization struggles that raised issues of control and coworker relations at the local level, by adopting the principle of wage negotiations that "accepted economic reality," and by turning away from the strike as a weapon, unions themselves eroded their local authority. Today, in their goals and in their daily operations labor unions in the steel industry are extraordinarily responsive in their "adjustments" to the situation as defined by management.

That ordinary workers have come to view these unions with cold detachment should be no surprise. Consider, for example, the 1970s survey of workers at New Japan Steel Corporation. As workers moved from assessing the most local to the highest level of the union, the proportion who felt that their "expectations [were] not [being] met" increased consistently, as did the proportion who answered, "I have no expectations in the first place."[34] The responses to the three questions presented in Table 6.2 suggest how alienated these workers were from their labor union. Nearly half of the respondents said, "We can't expect results even if we speak up." Such was the state of mind of steelworkers in the 1970s, and polls from the 1990s show that this alienation is even more widespread.

These workers probably have such low expectations because even the union local has abandoned any aspiration to regulate corporate treatment of individual employees. The survey just cited also examined "issues that directly concern the union local. . . and the company section, which became points of contention in the workplace" at NKK's Keihin Plant union

TABLE 6.2

Workers' Reactions to Union Activities

Survey Question	Response	Percentage in Agreement
A	Do you believe that your views are well represented in union activities?	
	They are represented well	2.6
	They are represented to some extent	22.0
	They are not represented very much	40.9
	They are not represented at all	25.9
	No response	8.6
B	Did you express your wishes or opinion in the current spring offensive?	
	I expressed my opinion and wishes	35.5
	I did not express my opinion	61.3
	No response	3.2
C	Why did you not state your wishes and opinion?	
	I did not feel the need to say anything	33.8
	I had some things I wanted to say, but there were no opportunities to place to do so	11.0
	Because I believe it would be useless to do so	46.4
	A climate of free expression does not prevail	4.3
	No response	4.5

Source: Rōdō Chōsa Kyōgikai (Labor Survey Council) and Tekkō Rōren (Federation of Steel Workers' Unions), eds., *Tekkō sangyō no rōshi-kankei to rōdō kumiai* [Industrial relations and labor unions in the iron and steel industry] (Tokyo: Nihon Rōdō Kyōkai, 1980), pp. 517–519. Survey A was conducted in 1974, Surveys B and C in 1977.

in the 1970s (the Keihin Plant union was formed with the amalgamation of the Tsurumi, Kawasaki, and Mizue Mills in 1970).

The survey found that the leaders of union locals (divisions), in close contact with the leaders of the plant union, did in fact discuss and reach mutual agreement with section managers on the following matters: calculation of production norms used to set output premiums and standards used in the annual merit ratings, staffing levels, and intrasection transfers. But the union's concern was with general standards, not with treatment of individuals. The local did not seek a formal voice concerning wage evaluations for individuals, the allocation of overtime to individual workers, the assignment of particular workers to specific jobs, or the appropriateness of selecting a particular person for a transfer or a promotion. These decisions were made on the basis of the personnel section's merit ratings, which were primarily based on evaluations prepared by foremen or assistant section chiefs, who were often officers in the union local but who acted in their capacity as supervisors, not as unionists. Thus, the union played no formal role in conducting or regulating the personnel ratings, which were critical in deciding a worker's raises and bonus, his promotion in rank and responsibility, his job and workplace assignment. Further, when a person did on occasion protest a supervisor's decision about his ability or attitude, the union would not necessarily support the complaint, and the unhappy worker could expect his actions to be factored into a negative view of his attitude in the following year's rating.

Thus, as both cause and result of the atrophy of the union's local authority and activism, the relevance of the union organization to the daily lives of employees steadily declined. With no help from the union, the worker had to balance his role as a member of the company society with the imperative that he compete with his coworkers. As a window on the attitudes that resulted, one may turn to further survey data concerning workers at two new cutting-edge steel mills in 1969 and 1976.

These men worked in modern plants with automated facilities, which demanded close attention and care. Compared to the average manufacturing worker, their wages were high. They enjoyed a substantial promise of long-term job security and generous company benefits provided through facilities located close by the plant, including housing, transportation, company stores and medical centers, and recreational facilities. Beyond these material benefits, they possessed a clear pride in working in an important "core" industry. They shared a competitive consciousness toward other companies, a willingness to accept technological innovation, and a strong sense of "corporate community" and unity as employees. On one hand, given this sense of community, they viewed both immediate supervisors and top managers as "us," not "them"; on the other hand, they regarded workers in other steel companies and subcontract workers to their own firm as outsiders. The survey concludes, "In their hearts. . . very few of these employees regard sub-contract workers as true members of their community."[35] Mutual understanding prevailed only among fellow company-men.

But this "community" was not an authentic workers' society, in which members cooperated and helped each other and restrained competition and rejected differential rewards in order to protect a common standard of living. The survey noted, "Many workers harbor some objections" to the specific method of merit ratings that caused workers to compete with each other. Yet, (the survey concluded) "they accept the system of merit ratings itself. Only a minority oppose the competitive system. The prevailing belief is that the company is itself a competitive society, so that employees should compete with one other. . . . Those who cannot stand up to the competition are either eliminated or cease to advance. . . ."[36]

As the Japan Federation of Employers' Associations (Nikkeiren) has itself recognized, a latent contradiction exists between membership in a "corporate community" and the desire to advance at a coworker's expense in a world of "merit-based management." The authors of these opinion surveys of the steel industry reluctantly acknowledged that a "community committed to promotion" had come into being by the late 1960s. What allowed its members to finesse this contradiction was the following, perhaps tortured, logic: "By driving myself to compete on behalf of corporate growth, I can increase the percentage of those who succeeded in this competition, for the company will prosper and be able to reward the effort of many or most of the workers." Or, perhaps, a more humane logic lay behind the striving of some or these aspirants for personal success in the firm: "My contribution to the success of the company would produce profits for it, which would protect the livelihoods of fellow workers who were not as successful in the competition."[37]

In any event, by some logic or other these latent contradictions were contained. They did not greatly trouble the 1970s system of labor management in Japanese steel. In retrospect, the workplace society of steel-making men in the 1950s possessed a slight potential to protect a realm of autonomy from the company. As these older workplaces were transformed, this potential vanished, and the steelworkers were integrated directly into the company as isolated individuals. Under the new system, the workers could throw themselves into a struggle to climb the ladder of career success in the "corporate community" or devote themselves to membership in a small work group reminiscent of the "neighborhood association" under Japan's fascist state, or they could do both. Whatever the case, the first commandment for the worker was to accommodate himself to a world of ongoing, thorough merit-ratings and compete to outdo his peers. And as this corporate world underwent successive waves of restructuring, an ever-larger number of men and women who should have been considered fellow workers came to be excluded from the workers' society of the "regular employee."

Labor-Management Relations in the Steel Industry Today

The function of unions in big steel companies in Japan has atrophied to the point of immobility. One could attribute this to a variety of factors, in addition to those stressed previously. Further, the process of atrophy differs somewhat in the workplace societies of light industry, mass-production engineering industries, and white-collar office work. But the following three points, illustrated here in the case of steel, are broadly applicable to the history of labor and management in postwar Japan. First, the union movement has been hindered by some particular "negative traditions," which are deeply embedded in the historical experience of the working class. Second, labor managers quite cleverly adapted their strategies to these historical conditions. Third, and related to both the first two points, enterprise-based labor-management relations, which are driven by the imperatives of corporate balance sheets, have not been transformed after all.

In the latter half of the 1950s a customary mode of organizing the workplace was weakening; this was the moment of greatest potential for democratizing the work process and the human relations of workplace society and for making this society a secure home for ordinary workers with a strong sense of independence from the company. But these three features of postwar history together prevented labor unions from succeeding in this democratizing initiative.

In taking such a position, I am arguing that unions should nurture a workers' society. It should be clear that I reject the view that equates unionism with modernism and individualism and ascribes its weaknesses in Japan to the enduring strength of a deep-rooted, traditional collectivism embedded in the company community. Precisely because the workers had been individualized, they engaged in merit-and-ability-based competition and were brought more firmly than ever under the unifed control of a company society whose norms had become the sole point of reference for its employees.

The historical analysis in the original version of this chapter ended with the mid-1970s. Even (or especially) with the added perspective of subsequent years, I find the decade from 1965 to 1974 particularly important. In these years basic patterns of labor-management relations and worker lifestyles crystallized, and these patterns continue to characterize Japan today. The conditions found in the steel industry today, in the mid-1990s, are little different from those previously described. But a few things *have* changed since 1975, and I close this section by outlining these changes.[38]

The greatest difference between the past twenty years and those preceding is the severe cutback in employment levels. Managers in the Japanese steel industry had to cope with the industry's "maturity," meaning an end to easy growth and more effective competition abroad. In terms of the causes and methods of corporate downsizing in the steel industry, the past twenty years can be divided into two periods of about ten years each.

The span from 1975 to 1985 was a time of adjustment to the oil crisis. Steel producers focused on conserving resources, energy, and labor, as well as maintaining export competition. In 1975 the total number of workers in the industry was 440,000; by 1985 this had dropped to 349,000. Blue-collar operatives felt the brunt of these cutbacks, which peaked toward the end of the 1970s. Workforce reductions were achieved mainly through cuts in overtime, employee transfers, and hiring freezes. Furthermore, in response to union and government pressure, and the aging of the society as a whole, companies agreed to extend the age of mandatory retirement from fifty-five to sixty. To compensate for this, they introduced systems to promote early retirement. The corporate goals of "versatile industrialization" and flexible workplaces were fully realized in this period.

The second decade may be called a time of adjustment to the yen crisis. Between 1985 and 1986, the value of the dollar suddenly dropped from 239 yen to 169 yen. By the middle of the 1990s, the dollar had sunk to 100 yen or less! This relentless rise of the yen in Japan's latter years as an economic superpower caused the steel industry to lose its ability to compete with producers in countries such as Korea. In this situation, all companies had to look to further personnel reductions as the only way to survive. From 1985 to 1993, the number of workers in the iron and steel industry fell by another 65,000. The first wave of these cutbacks, between 1985 and 1988, was accomplished by the closure of blast furnaces, transfers en masse to related enterprises, and a freeze on the extension of the retirement age. Such measures were implemented in addition to the steps taken during the previous decade of reductions. The second wave of cuts in 1993 and 1994 changed the status of those who had previously been transferred to affiliated companies. They were essentially stripped of their status as employees of the main company. Further, retrenchment policies were extended to white-collar workers in administrative and managerial positions who had never before found themselves the objects of personnel cuts. At present, the steel industry must be grouped among the nation's "structurally depressed industries," in which employment is most unstable.

In the face of this onslaught by capital, labor unions have only declined in their ability to resist. As early as 1977, Tekkō Rōren chose to abandon its struggle for large wage increases, which had been the overwhelming focus of private sector unions since the mid-1960s. Instead, it adopted a policy of "adjustment to economic conditions" in which wage demands were calibrated in deference to the financial situation of the industry and company. In the process, unions no longer even threatened to strike as they approached each negotiating season. Then, beginning in 1988, the level of so-called wage demands came to be decided in closed-door meetings between managers and union leaders. Unions called this the "joint information approach." The wage increases sought in the spring labor offensives of recent years are gradually shrinking to become no more than small seniority increments, with no margin for cost-of-living increases.

In addition, enterprise-based unions have been unable to resist personnel cutbacks. This was evident already in the 1979 policies of the Kobe Steel Company Union, discussed earlier. This union merely begged the company to "make every effort to utilize excess workers," and so long as managers made no outright dismissals, the union accepted all other forms of adjustment in employment. For this reason, the company now has a free hand to take steps such as encouraging early retirement, freezing new hiring, transferring employees temporarily to affiliated enterprises, and even changing their personnel status to that of employees of the affiliate, a step tantamount to dismissal for such workers. The unions have also failed to make progress in demanding "work-sharing" as a means to reduce working hours and defend employment levels. Although since the late 1980s unions have tried to link the demand for reduced hours to a demand for wage increases, they generally have settled for the first offer made by management, without even threatening any industrial action.

This may seem an all-too-gloomy ending to the historical inquiry into the relationship between labor and management in the steel industry. In the mid-1990s the corporate initiatives to survive the so-called structural depression have almost completely robbed enterprise-based unions of their will to resist. Such is the case in the steel industry, in which, at least for now, I see no hope of a revival of activities benefiting those of true organized workers. The most one can do is frankly to acknowledge and expose the travails of the steelworkers.

Notes to Chapter 6

1. For a detailed discussion of workers' society see my *Rōdōsha-kanri no kusa no ne* [The grassroots of workers' control concept] (Tokyo: Nihon Hyōronsha, 1976) and Kumazawa, ed., *Hataraku nichijō no jichi* [On self-government in daily work] (Tokyo: Tabata Shoten, 1982).

2. Orii Hyūga, *Rōmu kanri nijū nen* [Twenty years of labor management] (Tokyo: Tōyō Keizai Shinposha, 1973).

3. Ibid., pp. 6, 165.

4. In the old system, the line hierarchy ran as follows: division chief, section chief, assistant section chief, technician, supervising foreman, foreman, crew boss, unranked worker. The new system was: division chief, section chief, *sagyōchō* (new foreman), crew boss, regular worker.

5. Ōkōchi Kazuo, Ujihara Shōjirō, Fujita Wakao, eds., *Rōdō kumiai no kōzō to kinō* [The structure and function of labor unions] (Tokyo: Tokyo University Press, 1959).

6. Report of Rōdō mondai kenkyū kai (Labor problem research group), *Gekkan rōdō mondai* [The labor problem monthly], April 1966, p. 74.

7. On this point, see chapter 2 of the Yahata Steel survey of the 1960s: Meiji daigaku shakai kagaku kenkyūjo (Meiji University Social Science Research Center), *Tekkōgyō no gōrika to rōdō* [Rationalization and labor in the iron and steel industry] (Tokyo: Hakuchō Shobō, 1961). For the mutually contradictory aspects of "skill" and "responsbility and authority" see Kumazawa, *Rōdōsha kanri* [Workers' control], chap. 2.

8. Orii, *Rōmu kanri nijū nen*, p. 77.

9. Nikkeiren (Japan Federation of Employers' Association), *Nōryoku-shugi kanri: sono riron to jissen* [Theory and practice of merit-based management] (Tokyo, 1969).

10. For other works on Nikkeiren's "labor management based on merit and ability" see Tsuda Masumi, *Nihon no rōmu kanri* [Japanese labor management] (Tokyo: Tokyo University Press, 1970), Hazama Hiroshi, *Nihon-teki keiei* [Japanese-style business management] (Tokyo: Nikkei Shinsho, 1971), and Mori Gorō and Matsushima Shizuo, *Nihon rōmu kanri no kindaika* [Modernization of Japanese labor management] (Tokyo: University of Tokyo Press, 1977). The last two works fail to distinguish between merit-based management and ability-based management, and this mars their authors' understanding of Japanese labor management of the period since the mid-1960s.

11. Orii, *Rōmu kanri nijū nen*, pp. 40–41.

12. In Japanese these were originally called the "three 'ki'" jobs, *ki*ken na (dangerous), *ki*tanai (dirty,) and *ki*tsui (difficult), using the katakana syllable for "*ki*." Sometime in the mid-1980s, the reference was transposed into the romanized "three Ks."

13. Inagami Takeshi, *Rōshi kankei no shakaigaku* [The sociology of industrial relations] (Tokyo: Tokyo University Press, 1982), p. 110, has a table on the percentage of subcontracting in various steel plants. Other superior works on this topic are Fukada Shunsuke, *Shin-nittetsu no teihen kara* [From the bottom of New Japan Steel] (Tokyo: San'ichi Shobō, 1971) and Uchiyama Takashi, *Sengo Nihon no rōdō katei* [The labor process in postwar Japan] (Tokyo: San'ichi Shobō, 1982), chap. 3. In other industries as well, policies in the same years entailed using part-time and seasonal workers.

14. Orii Hyūga does not mention this progam, but it is discussed by Inagami Takeshi, *Rōshi kankei no shakaigaku* [Sociology of labor-management relations] (Tokyo: Tokyo University Press, 1981), p. 111.

15. Kansai keieisha kyōkai (Kansai Business Association), "Jinji kōka seido chōsa," in Nihon rōmu kenkyūkai (Japan Labor-Management Laboratory), ed., *Rōmu nenkan* [Labor management almanac] (Tokyo: 1976), pp. 220–223.

16. Nikkeiren, *Nōryoku-shugi kanri*.

17. Ibid.

18. Nitta Michio, *Nihon no rōdōsha sanka* [Workers' participation in management in Japan] (Tokyo: Tokyo University Press, 1988), p. 22.

19. Rōdō shō (Ministry of Labor), ed., *Shiryō: rōdō undō shi* [Documents: The history of the labor movement] (Tokyo, 1953 edition), pp. 437–439.

20. Ibid.

21. Ibid., 1965 edition, pp. 564–566.

22. The report was later published in *Sōhyō chōsa geppō* [The monthly report of Japan General Council of Labor Unions], February, 1979.

23. Ibid.

24. Ibid.

25. Ōkōchi, Fujita, and Ujihara, eds., *Rōdō kumiai no kōzō to kinō.*

26. On the Miike story, see Hirai Yōichi, "Mitsui Miike tankō no shokuba tōsō" [The workplace struggle at the Mitsui Miike coal mines] in vol. 23 of the annual report of the Shakai-Seisaku Gakkai (Social Policy Academy) (Tokyo: Ochanomizu Shobō, 1979). Also see Shimizu Shinzō, "Sengo rōdō undō shi ni okeru Miike sōgi no chii" [The place of the Miike strike in the postwar history of the labor movement], *Gekkan rōdō mondai* (October 1980).

27. Ōkōchi, Fujita, and Ujihara, eds., *Rōdō kumiai no kōzō to kinō*, pp. 76–77. This portion was authored by Kōshiro Kazayoshi.

28. See the report by Takanashi Akira on workplace discussions led by organizers from the union headquarters in the NKK Tsurumi Plant, Ibid., sect. 1, chap. 2, pp. 174–176, 215, 221–222, 240. He shows that the discussion in these forums was franker than that sponsored by the formal union organization controlled by foremen.

29. See Totsuka Hideo, "Yahata-seitetsu no sagyōchō-seido" [The new foreman system at Yahata Steel], *Gekkan rōdo mondai* [Labor problem monthly] (September 1964). The Yahata Steel Workers' Union accepted the new foreman system, concluding, "It is not desirable to constantly oppose whatever is new by enclosing ourselves in an old-fashioned, unchanging shell."

30. Rōdō mondai kenkyūkai, *Gekkan rōdō mondai*, p. 77.

31. Relations between labor and management in the steel industry during the twenty years since 1975 are examined briefly in the concluding section.

32. Inagami, *Rōshi kankei no shakaigaku*, pp. 94–98.

33. This process is discussed in detail in Rōdō Chōsa Kyōgikai and Tekkō Rōren (Labor Survey Council and Federation of Steel Workers' Unions), *Tekkō sangyō no rōshi-kankei to rōdō kumiai* [Industrial relations and labor unions in the iron and steel industry] (Tokyo: Nihon Rōdō Kyōkai, 1980), pp. 456–460.

34. Ibid., p. 512.

35. For surveys on workers' attitudes in cutting-edge steel plants I used data from Rōdō Chōsa Kyōgikai and Tekkō Rōren, and Inagami's work, all cited in previous notes. The surveys were conducted in 1976 at the New Japan Steel Company mill in Kimitsu, the NKK plant in Fukuyama, Sumitomo Metals in Kagoshima, Kobe Steel in Kakogawa, and Kawasaki Steel in Mizushima.

Further causes of the social situation in which workers have "no ties but to the company" are found in their ability to purchase houses with the generous assistance of the company, in the fact that these new houses are located in the suburbs away from the traditional working-class residential districts, and in that, from about 1962, the percentage of "workplace marriages" of male production workers and female office staff have risen. *Asahi Shimbun*, March 16, 1980, and *Nihon Keizai Shimbun*, February 19, 1981.

36. Ibid.

37. For a sensitive, perhaps overly sanguine, treatment of efforts of bank managers to deal with these contradictions, see Thomas Rohlen, *For Harmony and Strength* (Berkeley: University of California Press, 1974), especially chaps. 4 and 6.

38. The following paragraphs draw on these sources: Kimura Yasushige, "Tekkō-gyō no rōshi kankei to kenkyū kadai" [Research issues in labor-manage-

ment relations in the steel industry], in Hokkaidō Daigaku Kyōiku Gakubu Sangyō Kyōiku Keikaku Shisetsu, Kyōiku Hōkokusho, *Tekkōgyō no risutorakucharingu to jusōteki rōdōryoku hensei no gendankai* [The restructuring of the iron and steel industry and the present stage of stratified labor-force organization], 1995, pp. 1–8; Rōdō-shō, *Shiryō rōdō undō shi* [Materials on labor movement history], 1987 edition, pp. 509, 522–524; 1988 edition, p. 558; and 1990 edition, p. 489; Rōdō shō, *Rōdō tōkei nenpō* [Annual report of labor statistics], 1975, 1985, and 1993 editions; *Asahi Shimbun,* October 10 and 22, 1992; March 12 and April 22, 1993; and December 4 and 6, 1994; also, Ishida Mitsuo, "Nihon tekkōgyō no rōshi kankei" [Labor-management relations in the Japanese iron and steel industry], in *Hyōron–shakai kagaku* [Review of the social sciences], September 1989 and March 1995, provides a detailed account of labor-management relations in "type-B iron works" during the late 1970s, when the workforce was streamlined.

7

A Postwar History
of Women Workers

Perspective and Methodology

What kinds of jobs did women hold in the postwar years, and what kind of awareness did they nurture through this work? In this chapter I sketch the postwar course of women at work and offer a plea to eliminate gender discrimination in Japan.

To begin the inquiry, I present some statistical data essential to any discussion of women workers in Japan. Since my approach is historical, a long sweep of chronological data is desirable. But unfortunately, several key surveys have only been compiled in a form comparable to the present since the early 1960s, and the period before this can only be analyzed with fragmentary statistics.

According to the data in Table 7.1, first of all, women's overall labor force participation rate, regardless of age, has not changed dramatically since the 1950s (row 1), and the female proportion of the labor force (economically active population) has been even more stable (row 2). "Labor force" includes the self-employed, "family workers" (family members who assist in the work of independent family businesses), and "employees." These are all people who work outside the household to produce goods or services for the market. In sum, the data in the first two rows of Table 7.1 indicate that in the postwar years roughly half of Japanese women worked in society outside the realm of household labor, and these women generally accounted for 40 percent of the labor force.

The point is simple, but must be stressed. Women's labor has been extensive and significant. In addition to constituting 40 percent of the economically active population as previously defined, women performed almost all of the household work. Their housework alone is roughly equivalent to 25 percent of the gross national product (GNP), meaning that, altogether, women have performed well over half of the labor needed in Japan's society.

TABLE 7.1

Indices on Women Labor and Employees in Japan

	1955	1960	1965	1970	1975	1980	1983	1990	1993
1. Labor force participation rate (women)	56.7	54.5	50.6	49.9	45.7	47.6	49.0	50.1	50.3
2. Percentage of women in total labor force		40.7	39.8	39.3	37.3	38.7	39.5	40.6	40.5
3. Percentage of female labor force participants who are "employees"	31.2	40.8	48.6	54.7	59.8	63.2	65.7	72.3	77.0
4. Number of women employees (10,000 persons)	531	738	913	1,096	1,167	1,354	1,486	1,834	2,009
5. Percentage of employees over age 15 who are women	(15.6)	21.9	24.3	27.0	26.9	29.5	31.3	35.4	37.7
6. Percentage of women of total employees		31.1	31.8	33.2	32.0	34.1	35.3	37.9	38.6
7. Marital status of women employees as a percentage:									
single women	(65.2)	(63.2)	50.3	48.3	38.0	32.5	31.1	32.7	32.8
married women	(20.4)	(24.4)	38.6	41.4	51.3	57.4	59.5	58.2	57.8
divorced women and widows	(14.3)	(12.5)	11.1	10.3	10.8	10.0	9.4	9.1	9.4
8. Average age of women employees		26.3	28.1	29.8	33.4	34.9	35.2	35.7	36.0
9. Average length of service of women employees		4.0	3.9	4.5	5.8	6.1	6.3	7.3	7.3
10. Pay differentials by sex (compared to men: 100%)		42.8	47.8	50.9	55.8	53.8	52.2	49.6	50.9
11. Percentage of part time employees who are women		8.7	7.6	12.2	11.4	19.3	21.2	27.9	31.8
12. Percentage of unionists that are women employees	30.8	28.0	30.7	29.4	29.0	24.6	23.1	18.3	17.6

Sources: Rows 1 through 7 and row 11, Rōdō shō (Ministry of Labor), ed., *Rōdō ryoku chōsa* [Labor force survey]; rows 8 and 9, Rōdō shō, ed., *Chingin kōzō kihon chōsa* [Basic survey on wage structure]; and row 12, Rōdō shō, ed., *Rōdō kumiai kihon chōsa*. But figures in parentheses in rows 5 and 7 are from Sōrifu (Prime Minister's Office), ed., *Kokusei chōsa* [National census]. Information is from relevant annual volumes.

In addition to showing these continuities, the data offer evidence of important changes over the postwar era. Though overall participation in the labor force was fairly consistent, never falling below 45 percent or exceeding 57 percent, rows 3 and 5 of Table 7.1 specifically show that many working women shifted from the status of self-employed or worker in a family business to jobs as employees outside the family. In 1955 less than one-third of female workers were employees, but by 1993 employees accounted for 77 percent of working women (row 3). As a result, numbers of female employees rose dramatically, from approximately 16 percent to about 38 percent of all employees (row 5). In general terms, this shift can be called the modernization of the industrial structure and the working mode of women.

Second, crucial characteristics of this increasing body of female employees were changing. Their average age was rising, as was the proportion of those in middle and higher age groups who were married (rows 7 and 8). It was no longer unusual for a woman to work after marriage and after having children, returning to employment after a period as a full-time homemaker. By the mid-1990s, over 40 percent of women in their forties were wage earners. All of these changes are responsible for the controversy in recent years over the impact of working women on the family system.

In the following section, paying close attention to the concrete situation in the workplace, I will explore the significance of these trends rendered superficially visible by statistics. I adopt a prosaic chronological division of 1945–1955 (Shōwa 20s), 1955–1965, (Shōwa 30s), 1965–1975 (Shōwa 40s), 1975–1985 (Shōwa 50s), with some concluding attention to the late 1980s and early 1990s, the end of the Shōwa era and start of the Heisei era.[1] Because I consider the recent situation especially significant, I present more detail as the story approaches the present. Before beginning the discussion, some remarks on my premises and approach are in order.

First, three factors interact to determine the conditions of female workers. One is corporate labor policy, which I call the capitalist logic of labor demand. The second factor is the supply response, the work consciousness and behavior of women as they respond to this demand. The third factor of particular interest to me is the impact of so-called minority factions. These are active unionists and feminists inside or outside the labor movement who challenge the logic of corporate demand and seek to change the supply response. The mutual interaction of these three elements shapes the character of women's work; one must keep them all in mind.

Second, my primary concern here is with the *industrial* dimension of women's conditions and consciousness, not with the political or civic dimensions of women's lives. In other words, I examine the specific work that women perform at the production site, their treatment by the firms that employ them, their voice at the workplace, and their thoughts about these matters. Of course, the right to speak out in the industrial sector is related to political rights, such as voting and civil rights, such as those of women in family law. But the possession of such rights by women does not lead directly or inevitably to equality with men or freedom of choice in the workplace. To win the latter requires a specific mode of thinking and struggle concerning work as an employee.

I emphasize this point because it is my impression that in the discourse on postwar democracy, discussion of female labor is clouded by a relative indifference to the nature of work itself and to industrial struggles in the workplace.[2] This indifference, for example, led those fighting gender discrimination in the workplace to struggle for legal equality in the courts. The result, I believe, has been to ignore the workplace and push reformist discourse and strategies concerning female labor and activism on behalf of women in an excessively legalistic direction.

Third, the subjects of my analysis are mainly female employees in the lower strata of the working class. For actual workplace conditions and surveys of worker opinions, I cite primarily cases involving female factory workers in the electrical machinery industry, and female office workers (so-called OL, or "office ladies") in banks and trading companies. Office employees (clerks) and production workers in the factory are the occupational categories of the largest number of female employees.[3]

Let me reiterate the central hypothesis that the fundamentally unchanged position of female labor in postwar Japan results from a remarkably enduring, gendered division of labor that does not readily reveal itself in statistics. In this society, women carry the burden of household work and raising children, and Japanese common sense renders the idea of women working outside the household as of secondary importance. Female labor, not only for middle-aged part-timers but for the majority of university graduates as well, has for this reason remained concentrated on simple, auxiliary tasks. Despite the changes in women's labor force participation previously noted, this system has remained intact. So long as a fundamental gendered division of labor appears to be an immutable social fact, other changes will be hardly significant.

Nonetheless, there is no contradiction in recognizing this formidable staying power of a gendered division of labor and at the same time affirming the possiblity that this system will be undermined in the future by the combined force of numerous "hardly significant" changes. Focusing on both the stability and the instability of gendered differentiation at the production site, I explore the possiblity that the accumulation of change in the workplace might lead to broader social change. Just possibly, a drive for genuine equality of men and women in the workplace might inflict a heavy blow against the society's overall gender-based division of labor.

"Prewar" Conditions Under the Postwar Constitution: 1945–1955

For the first ten postwar years, the state of women workers was basically unchanged from their prewar condition. According to the first postwar census in 1950, of 13.7 million working women only 3.6 million, or slightly over 26 percent, worked as employees. Of this group, 70 percent were unmarried young women.[4] Blue-collar production workers accounted for 35 percent, the largest single category. And as in the prewar period, by far the greatest number of factory women were employed in the spinning and weaving factories of the textile industry. In 1914, women textile workers constituted 86 percent of all women in manufacturing jobs. In 1931 this proportion was 82 percent, and in 1938 it was 65 percent. Although the proportion continued to fall, in 1952 it remained fairly high, at 55.4 percent.[5] (The truly sharp drop came in the following ten years; by 1965 textile jobs employed only 18 percent of women workers.) The life pattern of most female workers in this first postwar decade was basically that of the prewar textile workers, young daughters of impoverished farm families. They were sent out to work to reduce the number of family members who had to be fed, or to augment the family's income, but it appears that most of them eventually returned to the village and married.

Needless to say, there are also key differences from the prewar situation. The new constitution of 1947 established the principle of "the basic equality of the sexes" and granted women political and civil rights: the rights to vote and hold office, equal rights to education, and equality of husband and wife in a democratic family system. These three, plus the end to licensed prostitution, constituted the "four great goals" of the prewar women's movement. Except for abolition of the public brothel system, achieved in 1958, these were all gained by the laws enacted in 1946–1947.[6] Further, the Labor Standards Law provided women with six weeks' leave before and six weeks' leave after childbirth, the right to request leave for taking care of a child, the right to paid leave during menstruation, a cap on overtime of two hours per day, six hours per week, and 150 hours per year, a ban on night work (from 10 P.M. to 5 A.M.), and prohibition of wage differentials based on sex. Without question, these measures prevented the exploitation that had endangered the lives and health of women workers. As early as 1948 employer federations began to seek revision of labor laws restricting overtime and night work; such efforts attested to the impact on employers of these provisions to protect women workers.

Nevertheless, when one speaks of the creation of a system providing for gender equality and the right to speak up in Japan, one finds that the civil lagged behind the narrowly political realm, and the industrial dimension lagged behind even further. Simply put, so-called postwar features were still not found at the production site in this first postwar decade. It remained the practice, as before the war, to employ submissive women at low wages. In factories their work required manual dexterity but little physical strength; in financial institutions they did "ordinary arithmetic work" that was "distinct from technical and managerial jobs entailing use of brains or special skills."[7] Personal relations at the workplace partook of a quality labeled "feudalistic" by Japanese critics. For example, in banks around the period 1953–1954 the male employees typically ordered the women workers to do all the cleaning, prepare tea for the men, go out to buy them cigarettes, bread, or milk, and wash their handkerchiefs and socks, and management viewed this as a "natural" part of their job. Male workers even had the women polish their shoes and wash out their lunchboxes.[8] To require the women workers to tend to male workers' personal needs as part of their jobs—with the men ordering the women to "get that for me" or "bring this here"—was justified by management as the bank's effort to nurture appropriately feminine virtues in young women considered by mainstream society to be under the bank's care until they married.

In response to such treatment, some female workers in this era launched struggles against discrimination, and they concentrated on practices that most blatantly violated the spirit of the new constitution. They fought for the abolition of wage differentials based on gender, the enforcement of laws protecting women, and the "abolition of feudalism" in the workplace. To some extent managers in public sector workplaces agreed to these demands, primarily raised by the "Young Men and Women's Division" of various labor unions. Also, according to back issues of *Forum*, a journal of activist bank workers, even in private banks women workers came to demand "compensation for early arrival" at the office to undertake the janitorial work required of them. Also, women protested against the common view that serving tea was a requisite of femininity.[9]

The most remarkable protest against "feudal" practices in those days was the series of industrial actions launched by the "factory girls" in a major silk reeling company. In 1954, the women workers in the Ōmi Kenshi Mill staged several lengthy strikes and finally destroyed the premodern system of labor management. The battles were landmarks in which the successors to the meek prewar "factory girls" changed into assertive female production and office workers who acted on their "orientation to natural desires."[10] The battle over issues of "premodern" or feudal treatment spread mainly to female office workers—for example, those in regional banks—and it became increasingly difficult for managers in these banks to impose their personal errands and miscellaneous tasks on women in the name of "socializing" them.

At the same time, women workers of this period still maintained a traditional frame of mind when it came to the question of *continuing work as an employee*. Most quit their jobs when they married. Indeed, this practice was so customary that business firms had no need to institute formal policies requiring retirement upon marriage. According to one study, the Bureau on Women and Youth of the Ministry of Labor in the 1950s held that enforced retirement upon marriage did not violate the Labor Standards Law.[11] Several factors supported this custom. This was not a period of affluence when numerous married women could be full-time homemakers with time to relax; the time required for household tasks and raising children was far greater than today. In 1940, the average Japanese woman gave birth to 5.2 children. Moreover, within many families women still held demanding and economically productive jobs that could not be separated out from household work or childrearing. The self-employed took in work on contract, performed at home. In the early postwar years, other homemakers commonly peddled a variety of goods in their communities. The most common work done by women assisting family businesses was helping out on the farm; next came working in a family's retail shop. Some middle-aged and older women did work outside the home, as day laborers in local food producing plants or in construction work, but the economically productive labor of many women took place inside the home. They often worked silently in the household for longer hours than the men, enduring mean-spirited criticisms by husbands and mothers-in-law.

Of course, a woman's right to a voice in family matters increased to the extent to which her labor was essential to the family's livelihood. The literary works of postwar writers such as Nakagami Kenji and Takahashi Kiichirō use their close relatives as models, and they introduce hard-working women who display a glorious independence in gender relationships. In general, my impression is that gender discrimination in language and in consciousness in both Japan and the West is stronger in the working class than in the middle class, but that in social behavior greater equality prevails in the relations between men and women in the world of the common people where the level of economic partnership of women with men is higher.

Yet, during this first postwar decade, the real strength of Japanese women, demonstrated in their economically productive labor and in their household work, was not recognized by society because these activities were subsumed in the family, which was represented to the outside society by the husband. The subsequent shift of women into paid employment outside the home was a process in which this strength came to be recognized, a modernizing process that remains significant in raising women's recognition of their worth.

Simplified Jobs and the Gender-Specific "Escape" Route: 1955–1965

The years 1955 to 1965 constitute the first of two decades of extraordinary economic growth in Japan. Technological innovation and a modernized employment structure had a significant impact on women workers. The number of young women employed in production, office work, and sales increased spectacularly. In the early 1960s women working as "employees" came to equal in number those engaged in family businesses or self-employed, and by 1965 the number of "employees" had surpassed the latter and constituted 48.6 percent of the female labor force (line 3 of Table 7.1).

Behind this labor force demand lay the expansion of unskilled and semiskilled jobs resulting from new mass-production systems in factories and high-speed data processing in offices. Women were in great demand for work as single-purpose machine operators, assemblers, inspectors, and packers in factories making electrical appliances, machinery, food, and pharmaceuticals, and so on. And huge service sector firms such as trading companies and banks valued the physical and mental fortitude of these women, as demand grew for people to operate simple clerical instruments or to serve at reception counters such as bank windows.

Although blue-collar women workers engaged in simple, repetitive procedures governed by machines that stringently regulated the substance and pace of their labor, the work of the "business girls" was a little more diverse. But in offices where many processes came to be mechanized, routine work began to predominate as well. For example, a survey of the personnel assignments in Kyōwa Bank's "IBM room" (the data processing office) in 1958 reveals that of a total of thirty-one workers, including two male supervisors, twenty-six were women. At least fifteen of the women did routine key punching.[12] In general, the tasks of these women consisted of using abacuses or adding machines, typing, duplicating, preparing invoices, organizing and filing documents, answering the telephone, plus working as receptionists or tea-servers. They performed a cluster of simple, auxiliary office jobs.

But these "business girls" were not merely restricted to routine tasks that were separated from jobs requiring discretionary judgments. They had another role to play, as the "flowers" of workplaces that were being rationalized. These young women had to create a pleasant atmosphere, on one hand, for the customers that the increasingly mechanized organization dealt with, and, on the other hand, for the male employees who occupied the key positions within the organization; in the "real" world where men did the main work, the corporation regarded their presence as indispensable. These young women told themselves that management believed "the work of the company [was] progressing well because [they were] helping out in various ways within the system"; they had convinced themselves that they were at their beautiful best when typing efficiently at their desks or cheerfully and competently answering the phones. These were women who trembled when male employees were being scolded by their superiors, but who feared to speak up in their defense. Banks and trading companies of the 1950s and early 1960s openly held docility, cooperativeness, and a beautiful and elegant appearance to be job qualifications for women workers.

One can analyze the employers' requirements for female workers from another angle. Between 1955 and 1965 the early postwar seniority (*nenkō*) system was being reorganized. The workforce was being thinned out at the top and expanded at the bottom. That is, corporations introduced technological innovations that redistributed work so as to concentrate decisionmaking and planning tasks in fewer hands at the top and increase simple, routine work at the bottom. To accomplish this, managers considered a gender-based division of labor at the point of production an absolute necessity. In the early years of their tenure, even male workers were placed at the bottom of a pyramidal structure of work assignments in both factories and offices. But the company could not count on these men to sustain high morale and corporate loyalty if it restricted them to routine work for their entire career. Managers felt they had to provide them a route not only toward higher wages but also toward increased status as their years of service increased. That is, in the *nenkō* system, a path had to be created along which they could rise (or escape) from routine work to supervisory positions such as foreman in a factory, or to managerial and planning positions in an office. However, *what securely opened this route for male workers was the removal of women workers from this competitive upward track and their permanent restriction to work at the bottom level.* Moreover, confining women to simple, routine work enabled management to justify their low pay in modern, functional terms as a result of their low-level work.

Thus, the following self-sustaining system emerged. Simple, routine work (point 1) and low wages with lower pay increases than men (point 2) weakened women's determination to remain at their jobs. Unlike men who aspired to escape by moving upward, women sought to escape their plight by moving sideways, that is, by quitting their jobs. The result was short workplace tenure for women (point 3), which in turn justified points 1 and 2. These gender-differentiated escape routes depended fundamentally on the mutual reinforcement of simple, routine work, low wages, and brief job tenure, and the separation of these two routes has remained to this day, although in somewhat changed form, the basic principle of Japanese labor-management applied to women.

On the other hand, changing circumstances and conditions in the broader society gradually emerged during this period to enable women to work as employees even after marriage. From 1955 to 1965, the agricultural and family business sectors continued to shrink, the average number of family members dropped from five to four, and at the same time Japan's households were electrified with the advent of washing machines, electric rice cookers, refrigerators, and vacuum cleaners. These appliances reduced time needed for housework and made it *more possible* than in the past for women to go out and work. At the same time, the rising cost of urban living and the very appliance revolution that opened the possibility of new forms of work created a *new need* for increased income to purchase these consumer durables. According to a survey conducted by the authors of *Business Girl Studies*, 29 percent of the "business girls" surveyed in the early 1960s responded that they would "continue working after marriage," 22 percent responded that they would "continue working until they [had] children," and 9 percent replied that they would "continue working until living conditions improved." Only 22 percent said that they would "quit working when they married."[13] Although the survey does not indicate precisely what types of women were interviewed, the results surely suggest that quitting work at marriage was no longer an obvious or automatic decision for women.

Also, 70 percent of these women considered themselves to be members of the "working class," and the largest number supported the Japan Socialist party. The contrast with opinion surveys of later decades in which 90 percent of respondents, both women and men, place themselves in the middle class is striking. It appears that even after they left the workplace and became household members they continued to remain a latent force for causes of "peace and democracy."[14]

Such attitudes surely lay behind a number of protests staged by women in these years against companies that forced them to leave their jobs upon marriage or dismissed married women. Despite the stance of the Labor Ministry's Labor Standards Bureau that "termination of employment upon marriage does not violate the Labor Standards Law," some unions continued to struggle against these policies. For example, in 1959 the union at Tokyo Electric Company forced the company to retract its policy requiring women to quit upon marriage. Landmark nationwide hospital strikes were staged in 1960 over wages, night work, the dormitory system, and compulsory retirement upon marriage. Through these struggles, nurses won the repeal of compulsory retirement rules in hospitals throughout the country during the 1960s. As a result, the proportion of married nurses shot up from just 2 percent of all nurses in 1957–1958 to 60 percent by the 1980s.[15]

In these same years, movements also spread to compel companies to respect laws protecting working mothers and to establish day care centers in particular regions. In the case of female bank workers, after the bank purchased electric tea kettles and subcontracted its janitorial work, activists felt less pressing need to oppose tea-serving and janitorial tasks. They shifted their focus to strategies to make the workplace more hospitable to married working women. A long-running "Debate on Working Couples" began in the popular press in 1956, framed in terms of the sharp clash between women's "need to continue working" and the lack of understanding shown even by "progressive" husbands.

A new era was thus beginning. If full-time women workers struggled insistently to continue working no matter what kind of jobs they held, companies could no longer force them to quit upon marriage. In fact, the percentage of female employees who were married nearly doubled between 1955 and 1965, reaching 38.6 percent at the end of this decade (row 7 of Table 7.1).

Yet, the "natural" choice for many young women in these years remained to escape. The mutually reinforcing, three-way system previously described continued to make the pursuit of long-term employment a problematic course. When a young woman imbued with the postwar democratic outlook decided not to endure the difficulties involved in continuing to work, married life in a nuclear family seemed a welcome option—an option of escape from the restrictions of the family system or the burden of tiresome service in a family business, plus the chance to live in a housing complex where housekeeping had been rationalized. And if this housekeeping was for the husband she loved, it was that much more gratifying than working at a company. In these years, marriage based on love was a form of ideology. Thus democracy in the *civil dimension* in some sense liberated women from the frustrations of inequality in the *industrial realm*. Until debate on the "need to continue working" turned to this industrial level, to question the nature of work itself and gender-based division in the workplace, a woman's decision whether to continue working would be determined above all by whether her husband's earning power met their "needs."

The Systemic Restructuring of Discrimination: 1965–1975

Qualifications and Labor

Beginning in the mid-1960s, labor managers in big business started to emphasize what has come to be called Japanese-style meritocracy. In previous chapters I introduced the background to this concept and the complex forms it has taken. Here, I consider the impact upon women workers of the new labor management policy, especially the new "qualification system" and the system of classifying workers by ability.

Broadly speaking, the new systems created a pyramidal structure of grades based on qualifications and ability. All employees could move from lower to higher grades in accord with their personnel assessments, with more stringent appraisal of employees' ability and "gung-ho spirit" the higher they rose. This grading system determined both promotions and raises. Two points were particularly relevant for women: First, women were generally restricted to low-level job assignments and were therefore concentrated in the lower grades. Second, even if women cultivated the ability to perform difficult tasks, promotion to upper grades was obstructed by the limit to the number of high-grade positions. Such a system relies primarily on what one may call "modern" forms of gender discrimination, and only secondarily on "traditional" forms.

The impact of this kind of labor management upon women can be observed in the workforce distribution by qualifications and job-clusters at Toshiba and the Seventy-Seventh Bank. These data are somewhat complex but deserve careful scrutiny. In the qualification system used by Toshiba, most women are concentrated between the ranks of employee second class and assistant superintendent or assistant engineer, with very few women assigned to higher qualifications (Figure 7.1). The workforce distribution among job clusters at Toshiba shows that in production jobs, the largest number of women work in the "D" rank (assembly-line operative) and in clerical work, the largest group occupies the lowest, "C" rank (Table 7.2). At the Seventy-Seventh Bank, nearly 62 percent of female workers belong to the fourth class (the lowest class) of the clerical staff, and only 26 percent are found in the third class. In comparison, male workers make up only about 7 percent of the fourth class, and only about 13 percent of the third class. Only 7.2 percent of those in positions of assistant superintendent or higher are women, but men make up approximately 53 percent of

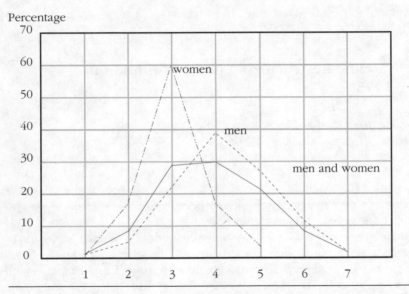

FIGURE 7.1 Workforce Distribution at Toshiba, Based on Qualifications (all junior members, 1973)

Job Categories
1. employee third class
2. employee second class
3. employee first class
4. assistant superintendent and assistant engineer
5. superintendent third class and engineer third class
6. superintendent second class and engineer second class
7. superintendent first class and engineer first class

Note: Promotion is based on evaluation of performance.

Source: Asada Takamasa, "Beruto conbeya no shokuba to rōdō" [Conveyor belt work-places and labor], *Gekkan rōdō mondai* [Labor problem monthly], December 1976, p. 39.

TABLE 7.2

Workforce Distribution at Toshiba, Based on Job Clusters Classification
(all union members, 1973)

Job Clusters	Male (%)	Female (%)	Total (%)
Production Work			
A	17.8	–	12.8
B	38.8	0.5	28.1
C	29.3	13.7	25.0
D	14.0	85.5	34.0
E	–	0.3	0.1
Clerical and Technical Work			
A	59.6	4.0	47.1
B	28.0	27.3	27.9
C	12.4	68.7	25.0

Note: Separation into job clusters was based on the nature of the work. The job-based pay was determined by the six classifications in each job cluster.

Source: Asada Takamasa, "Beruto conbeya no shokuba to rōdō" [Conveyor belt workplaces and labor], *Gekkan rōdō mondai* [Labor problem monthly], December 1976, p. 39.

this group (Table 7.3). In sum, a perfectly shaped pyramid is formed by concentrating women workers at or near the bottom.

Gender discrimination was redefined in this modern, functional way probably because managers could no longer effectively maintain wage discrimination based on older practices and concepts. For example, maintaining different pay scales for men and women was likely to run afoul of the constitution or the Labor Standards Law. The industrial actions of women employees at the Fukuoka Branch of a major bank in 1961 to force management to set a uniform pay scale for men and women failed because of the traditional mind set of male *union members*.[16] But if management had been faced with an all-out, united struggle, the bank could not have justified its position. In this sense, the long era in which gender in and of itself could be the basis for wage discrimination had ended.

Equally important, in the space of a few years after 1966, Japanese courts issued an extremely influential series of verdicts nullifying the traditional discriminatory practice of forcing women to retire at marriage.[17] The struggles of women at the following companies all ended in defeat for the company: Sumitomo Cement Company's policy of retirement upon marriage (Tokyo District Court, 1966); Tōkyū Engineering Industry's policy of restricting female employment to women under age thirty (Tokyo District Court, 1969); Mitsui Shipbuilding's policy of enforcing retirement upon childbirth (Osaka District Court, 1971); and Onoda Cement Company's workforce reduction policy, which provided for the dismissal of any "woman with a husband" and all "women over the age of thirty" (Morioka District Court, 1968).[18]

TABLE 7.3

Men and Women Personnel by Qualifications, at Seventy-Seventh Bank, in October 1976

Qualifications	Total (%)	Men (%)	Women (%)	Age Groups[a]	Men (%)	Women (%)
Fourth-class clerical staff	29.4	6.6	61.1	ages 18–21	7.1	61.9
Third-class clerical staff	18.1	12.4	26.0	22–24	13.2	22.7
Second-class clerical staff	9.9	13.0	5.7	25–28	15.0	5.0
First-class clerical staff	9.5	12.4	5.4	29–32	12.1	3.2
Vice superintendent (*Fuku-Shuji*)	11.1	18.7	0.6			
Superintendent (*Shuji*)	8.0	13.8	–			
Vice councilor (*Fuku-Sanji*)	3.7	6.4	–	over 33	52.7	7.2
Councilor (*Sanji*)	3.3	5.7	–			
Vice senior councilor (*Fuku-Sanyo*)	2.4	4.2	–			
Senior councilor (*Sanyo*)	0.3	0.5	–			
Laborer third class	0.1	0.2	–			
Laborer second class	1.4	2.0	0.6			
Laborer first class	1.8	2.6	0.6			
Chief of laborers	0.9	1.6	–			
Total (%)	99.9	100.1	100.0			
Total (N)	3,320	1,930	1,390	Total (N)	1,808	1,372

[a]There is no horizontal correspondence across qualifications and age group columns.

Source: Research Institute for Bank Employees (RIBE), ed., *Ginkō rōdō chōsa jihō* [Survey: Current report of bank labor] (July 1977), p. 24.

Note: Total percentage may not equal 100 percent due to rounding.

Some companies initially responded in stubborn fashion by formaliz-
ing hitherto customary practices of retirement at marriage. As a result, gender-differentiated retirement policies actually *increased* in number for a
brief time in the late 1960s. But the situation had changed to the extent that
if the issue was brought to the courts, the employer was certain to lose.

Once matters had reached this point, "modern" personnel systems
based on qualifications or ability became the method of choice in enabling
managers to control wage scales as they desired. When qualifications or
ability were linked to wages, women who were not promoted out of low-
level grades or jobs "quite naturally" or "legitimately" received low pay and
few raises. Even if a few women who had worked at their jobs over a long
period were promoted and given considerable raises in exceptional cases,
they did not greatly inconvenience the corporation.

Consequently, the policy persisted of using women in the ever-expand-
ing domain of simple, routine work. In a survey conducted by the Ministry
of Labor in 1968, managers in the manufacturing and financial services
industries gave the following reasons for "assigning women to newly introduced jobs": "We switched to using women because the work became
lighter and simpler due to mechanization" [32.4% of manufacturing firms
offered this as one reason, and 11.1% of financial services firms did so];
"Women were assigned to work requiring intricate use of fingers, and auxiliary work" [per 44.7% of manufacturing firms and 22.2% of financial service firms: 22.2%.]; "Women were assigned to positions where new machinery and new types of jobs were introduced" [per 39.1% of manufacturing
firms and 38.9% of financial service firms].[19]

During the same years, concern over the impoverished substance of
work at the site of production began to grow. A variety of observers published reports or analyses of labor conditions.[20] These studies provide specific descriptions of the extremely simple work performed by women in
factories and offices: soldering wires on televisions, making transmission
coils for television sets, inspecting tape recorders, work as a bank teller,
checking and bagging at a supermarket. To offer one typical example,
female blue-collar workers in an electrical appliance manufacturing plant
repeated a 60- to 90-second task all day, involving intricate assembly work
on stereos or radios.

There are few descriptive on-site accounts of the work of "office
ladies," or OL, but one can examine the content of their jobs by looking at
a major trading company's 1974 internal document titled, "Guide for New
Women Employees."[21] Their work was more varied than that of blue-collar
women, even though each particular task was simple. According to this
guidebook, the bulk of OL work involved preparing documents (32%),
delivery (11%), filing (13%), reception (15%), typing (9%), and calculating
(8%). Also, the introduction to the guide states that even though other tasks
may appear to be more interesting "all work is essential for the company."

It advises the women on the proper way to acknowledge work orders, proper posture, preparation of memos, and how to orally echo statements of advice on how to do their work. It further provides guidelines on "the pleasant style of responding [to a coworker]," "proper word choice and speech," how to prepare for and clean up after a meeting, the proper way to serve tea or to speak on the telephone, proper dress, makeup, greeting of customers, and bowing. The manual also instructs women that preparation (for work) must be completed by 8:45 A.M., and cleanup (after work) must not begin until 5:15 P.M. (The officially scheduled working day was from 9:00 a.m. to 5:00 p.m.!)

These OL, who by this time included recent university graduates, were *not* required to become familiar with the trading company's business affairs and exercise their judgment. Their training was completely different from that of male university graduates destined to serve on the front lines of business dealings. In the first place, the company did not hire women university graduates until it faced a severe shortage of female high school graduate recruits; the women university graduates posed an understandable dilemma: What should their job classification be? Should it be that of female high school grads or male university grads? (This indecision was a sign of weakness in companies concerned with preventing any blurring of the sharp dividing lines between different job clusters). The corporation's ideal was to hire "lively and gentle" OL, neither flashy nor abrasive nor plodding, who would abide strictly by the company's hierarchical order. Such young female helpers boosted the morale of both gung-ho male employees on the fast track and the less-ambitious "happy-go-lucky" guys. The ability and the will to do the work of the men who supported Japan Incorporated were heightened even further by the communal erotic fantasy supplied by this collective image of the office ladies.

Movement in Two Directions

A new development during the decade of 1965 to 1975 undermined this logic that was congenial to both the companies and their male employees; it disturbed the system that had restricted young women to efficient yet vivacious performance of simple auxiliary work. This development was the divergence in two new directions of the desired self-image of female employees.

First, career women emerged who took seriously the prevailing slogan of this period, that is, "merit and ability." After serving time performing simple tasks, these women sought to open a way toward more advanced work as a specialist or toward managerial positions.

There were actually two ways to become a career woman. One approach was to advance through the selection process for promotion by winning in a competition with men within the framework of the existing system, accepting the principle of "equality of opportunity." Each woman who chose this course had to undergo her own inner mental struggle. This path, however, was open mainly in local or national government bureaus that, because of their public character, had no choice but to respect gender equality, at least in principle.

The second option for career-minded women demands greater attention. This is the road traveled by women engaged in desperate struggles in private sector workplaces to end discriminatory practices in promotions and pay raises. One example is provided by the veteran female office workers of Japan Bank and Trust Company.

In 1970 this bank introduced qualification-based pay through an agreement with the mainstream union to which most of the employees belonged. The qualification levels in this new system were clerk, vice superintendent, superintendent, vice councilor, and councilor, and they were connected to a person's job assignment. Each qualification level was further divided into fifteen grades. Just as some people had feared, all of the women, including those with long years of service, were placed in the category of clerk.

At this point the struggle began. In 1971, forty-six women who were members of a minority second union at Japan Bank and Trust demanded fair standards of promotion for women. They staged a women-only strike for half a day, engaged in collective bargaining with the chief of the personnel division, and demanded that the branch manager, who was in charge of personnel evaluations and promotions, take responsibility for the discrimination. Not only did these efforts lead to promotions to the "vice superintendent" level for qualified women, but they also triggered a more broadly focused antidiscrimination struggle by the entire minority union, all of whose members had been subject to discriminatory raises and promotions. From spring 1974, this union staged a long struggle involving collective negotiations, appeals to the Labor Standards Inspection Bureau and the Tokyo Metropolitan Labor Committee, distribution of flyers at railroad stations, and a sit-in before the company headquarters of 111-days duration. After one year, a provisional settlement was reached, and the next year after that, the union won a promotion schedule in which the workers, both men and women, would be promoted to vice superintendent (work group chief) by, at the latest, age twenty-nine, to superintendent (deputy department head, auditor) by age thirty-five, and to vice councilor (department head, chief auditor) by age forty-three.

The 1976 union victory succeeded well in eliminating indirect pay discrimination; but this struggle against discriminatory promotions did not fully achieve its ultimate goal: an end to gender-based discrimination in work assignments. After the 1976 settlement, bank management began to accelerate the promotion of men and weaken the link between qualifications and jobs. Even among men and women of the same qualification rank, the men were assigned more important managerial jobs. Clearly, equitable treatment of men and women is more than a matter of pay equality. The women office workers who carried on this struggle have since initiated a renewed challenge to such job discrimination.[22] Through these types of actions in the 1970s, the collective activism of career women finally made its appearance in Japan.

I now turn to the second tendency in the self-image of female workers. If some women who began working in the 1960s began choosing diverse paths to become career women, many others who entered the workplace during these years seem to have turned their backs on work after taking a hard look at their true situations. According to a 1971 survey, young women, more than young men, were complaining that their jobs were simple-minded, boring, and meaningless because they were not given authority and could not develop their abilities.[23] In contrast to the men, they saw no evidence that might persuade them to endure, to continue working at a boring job because it could serve as a useful experience for the future. The single positive attitude toward work that the women in this survey showed more often than men was that "it's good because it's easy."

The mid-1960s through the early 1970s, when work was viewed in this light, was a period of affluence. Young women hardly felt compelled to continue working at unpleasant jobs, and in a time of labor scarcity, they believed there would always be a chance to make money someplace else. If one considers that this was a time of rising levels of education for women, and rising expectations, the conditions seemed encouraging for young women to reform the workplace by demanding jobs of more fulfilling substance. But no such movement took place, probably because of the immaturity of progressive thinking that hardly addressed the nature of work itself, and because of the atrophy of labor union activism at the site of production. The mini-skirted workers who had, after a fashion, absorbed this era's spirit of "opposing the administered society" turned their backs on labor. They rejected the "desirable image of the office lady" who dedicated herself to the managerial principle of efficiency. Instead some of them turned to the determined pursuit of leisure, telling themselves, "Anyway, for women it's not important to work" and quitting their jobs immediately upon an unpleasant personal interaction.

Citing examples from the journal *Anonymous Correspondence* (1959) produced by her own "circle," Morisaki Kazue wrote in 1970, "Women desire a state of affairs in which they can enjoy life without worries. . . outside the purview of wielders of power and controlling authority." They hoard and treasure "the freedom of a victim. . . who has never harmed anyone."[24] Can one not then say, following this astute perception, that young women were pursuing "the freedom of the discriminated?" After all, this was a time of numerous managerial laments, such as the story of an office where the entire female staff requested simultaneous vacations to travel abroad together. The day after the department head cautioned them to stagger their vacations, the women all submitted their resignations.

It is admittedly difficult to assess the scope and extent of such actions by Japanese women during this period, but their subtle acts of disobedience and frequent decisions to quit did pose a threat to employers who required a stable supply of workers to perform simple, routine tasks in a period of labor shortage. Thus managers asked themselves: "Aren't there any people out there willing to perform dull work uncomplainingly even if they don't stay for long?"

Their answer was "yes, middle-aged housewives." From 1965 to 1974, the percentage of jobless women hoping to find work rose for every age group except those under twenty.[25] In 1974 an astonishing 53 percent of all nonworking women in their thirties claimed they wanted to find jobs. Most of these women, who had probably held full-time jobs earlier, were now married young mothers who possessed the "Three New Sacred Treasures," symbols of consumer affluence.[26] They hoped to move from public housing to their own condominiums or single-family homes, send their children to college, and occasionally take family trips. But they needed more money to pursue this middle-class lifestyle. In addition, they had more free time thanks to household appliances and a drop in the average family size to 3.5 members by 1975. Finally, the industrial structure no longer provided extensive opportunities for homemakers to work in family businesses or in self-employment.

These women in their thirties or older, however, accepted a gendered division of social responsibilities. They did not want to neglect their family for the sake of a job. Neither did their husbands, who returned home exhausted from workplaces that emphasized performance and merit, want them to do so. These women could handle jobs that called for work from 10 A.M. to about 4 P.M. and also do the housework. Leaving the house and making new friends was emotionally fulfilling. Without such an outlet, full-time homemakers in nuclear families were isolated socially and had to be unusually strong willed to stay healthy.

Thus the steady increase in homemakers who held part-time jobs represented a perfect fit between the capitalist logic of demand and the supply response of women. The 1979 *Public Opinion Survey on Women* conducted by Japan's Prime Minister's Office clearly demonstrates this supply-side response.[27] When asked how they felt about working, 40 to 50 percent of the women replied, "I will quit my job when I have children, but when they grow up I would like to work again." Ten to 20 percent responded that they planned to continue working even after they had children. And the percentage of those who wished to be employed as a part-time worker rose sharply, from 30 percent in 1968 to 45 percent in 1979. The percentage of those who wanted regular, full-day work remained barely changed: 11 percent in 1968 and 12 percent a decade later. These attitudes explain why the graph for women's employment by age dropped for women in their mid-twenties, and later rose, resulting in the shape of an "M."

Bolstering the belief that in Japan women had to adjust careers to fit their family obligations was a deeply rooted consciousness of a gender-based role division. In 1979, 29 percent of the women surveyed firmly agreed that "the husband works outside the family and the wife takes care of the household," and another 41 percent "tended to favor" this position. Later, the international push for equality between men and women had an effect in Japan, and women increasingly questioned the legitimacy of a gendered division of work roles. Thus, according to a repeat of this survey in 1990, opinions had shifted a good deal. Just 25 percent of women in 1990 agreed that "the husband works outside the family and the wife takes care of the household," and over 43 percent disagreed.[28] Still, 64 percent of women preferred the in-and-out work pattern: "I would like to work again when the children grow up."[29] I should also note that the proportion of women who said they would "continue working for a long time after finding a job" reached 14 percent, the same as the proportion who would choose to "become homemakers upon getting married or having children."

Recent Decades: 1975–1995

Four Workplaces

I now turn to recent patterns of women's work and age cohorts. Following the analysis in one 1980 study, one may classify women's jobs in seven broad occupational categories and in three age-types. The age-types are as follows: *young jobs,* in which workers under thirty account for over 40 percent of all employees but less than 30 percent are over age forty; *mixed jobs,* in which both workers under age thirty and those over forty exceed 30 percent of the total; and *middle-aged jobs,* in which less than 30 percent are under thirty years old and over 40 percent are over forty.[30] Listing the seven standard groups of occupation along one axis and further dividing these into the age-types, one can classify particular jobs as in Table 7.4. This table lists the categories containing at least 5 percent (about 590,000 people) of all female employees.

Even these stiffly worded categories, which follow the 1978 National Census, convey the salient characteristics of women's work. One can delve a little deeper into the nature of their work through information provided by women in interviews at four workplaces.[31]

Toshiba's Osaka Plant

On the conveyer line where electric refrigerators were assembled (the section preparing urethane to be attached to the body of the refrigerator),

TABLE 7.4

Women's Work and Age Cohorts, 1978

Occupational Group	Age-Type	Examples of Job	Percentage of All Female Employees (%)
Professional and technical jobs	young jobs	data-processing technicians, nurses, pharmacists, nursery school teachers	6.5
Clerical jobs	young jobs	general and accounting clerks, key punch operators, typists	33.5
Sales jobs	mixed-aged jobs	store sales clerks	8.8
Technical or skilled factory jobs, production jobs, simple, manual jobs	young jobs	assemblers of electric machinery and precision machines, textile workers, sewing machine workers, tailors, chemical plant workers	7.0
Technical or skilled factory jobs, production jobs, simple manual jobs	middle-aged jobs	food processing plant workers, building and road construction laborers, other construction laborers, packaging and wrapping workers, metal machine workers, rubber-leather production work	15.4
Service jobs	young jobs	advertising firm staff, beauticians, waitresses, receptionists	5.9
Service jobs	middle-aged jobs	receptionists at recreation centers, cooks, janitors, household service workers, dormitory mothers	7.3

Note: "Examples of Job" only includes jobs that employ at least 5,000 women.

Source: Sōrifu (Prime Minister's Office), *Kokusei chōsa* [National census] (1978 edition).

thirty of 120 workers in 1970 were women, but by 1983 only eight or nine of 115 workers were women. These women, all in their twenties, are restricted to the "light" tasks of bunching together lead lines or attaching seals, barrier tape, or energy-conserving aluminum tape. All operating of automatic machinery is done by male workers. Women are assigned to jobs in which there is no likelihood of getting soiled by oil, no loud noise or any danger, and in which no demanding physical work is needed. More-over, they are not allowed to work with machines or electricity. This has been a common practice in Japan for a long time, as seen in the fact that although women accounted for 28 percent of all workers in plants manu-facturing general purpose motors in one 1962 survey, women who oper-ated machines numbered only 2.2 percent of the total.[32] But at this partic-ular workplace, women as well as men worked in jobs requiring some physical strength in the past; they tightened vises and lowered products from hangers. In the mid-1990s, at this plant women's jobs have been given their own identity, and the women themselves reveal their sense of femi-ninity by saying, "We aren't good at working with machines and electricity" and "We lack physical strength." Thus, gender-based work assignments are not controversial. It appears that, from the 1960s through the 1990s, young women in blue-collar workplaces have both quantitatively and qualitatively retreated under protection.

In my 1983 interviews, I observed that these women accessorized their work clothes with handkerchiefs, wore their hair long (formerly, this was prohibited), and worked in what they considered "an appropriately femi-nine manner" until they married. Labor unions conducted seminars for women workers on how to fix their hair and beautify their appearance.

Fuji Bank Branch in Front of Osaka Station

Thirty of the eighty employees are women. Their jobs consist of working at simple teletype terminals, serving as tellers at bank windows, and other miscellaneous tasks. They are not to make any decisions. In the loan sec-tion, they calculate interest on the basis of data provided them and record customer deposits or withdrawals, but they do not go out on assignments to negotiate with customers. When responding to telephone queries they can only provide publicly posted data. Business questions or complaints must be transferred to the men in charge.

On the Capital Funds Team of Sales Department 2, responsible for deciding how to keep on hand only the minimum amount of necessary cash, a senior male employee makes all the decisions as the "chief." A vet-eran (high school graduate) female employee, with twenty-one years in this branch, is no less capable of making the necessary decisions, such as esti-mating the funds needed for the following day. In fact, when the chief is absent from work, she does this. But in the main her daily routine consists of counting up the cash, bundling it and delivering it to the tellers, work that easily can be performed by inexperienced employees.

In the late 1960s, this veteran female employee decided to devote her energies to union activities because she felt she was "becoming an idiot by performing only simple, routine work." Yet she hesitated to fight for decisionmaking responsibilities in her work for several reasons. In addition to experiencing gender discrimination in job training, when she was a teller she briefly lost her self-assurance when she failed to measure up to the stringent error-detecting system and was required to write "a statement of self-criticism." Further, as the only married woman at the branch office, she had no natural allies. She felt that although "feudalistic" characteristics had disappeared from the workplace, the importance of women's labor at the bank had, if anything, decreased. According to this Fuji Bank employee, occasionally young women workers reacted against the bank's practices by "pretending not to hear" the manager's directions or by responding in "sullen" fashion. But, in general, they remained indifferent to their work and to the union and quit their jobs as soon as they married.

Since the 1986 passage of the Equal Employment Opportunity Law and the revised Labor Standards Law, the situation of female bank labor in Japan has changed significantly. The banks have replaced 20 to 30 percent of their regular female employees with part-timers and temporary workers. Many of these women were regular employees who quit their jobs after a short period of employment; they were subsequently "rehired" through temporary employment agencies that were wholly owned subsidiaries of the banks.

Osaka Branch of a Major Trading Company

In the export section of this trading company's shipping department, the male "persons-in-charge" are assigned the major jobs of selecting shippers and negotiating over prices and costs with the shipping company and the port authorities. The job of female "assistants" is to deliver documents and undertake other miscellaneous tasks. Of course, as one interviewee noted, "The work of the person-in-charge of shipping can be done by anyone who has served as an assistant for a few years." As a result, some female office workers who were dissatisfied with merely performing simple tasks began on their own initiative to encroach on the men's jobs. In summer 1978, however, the company established new categories of "general work" and "office work." The former was a designation fixed for "persons-in-charge" and the latter for "assistants." Women workers were notified to restrict themselves primarily to office work. Even though it was possible for a woman to be assigned to the general work category if she had worked for over six years and passed an examination, the new classifications in essence served to prevent female workers from crossing the boundaries of a gender-based division of labor. Also, the substance of the orientation pro-gram for new employees was clearly differentiated by sex.

Large Supermarket: P Company, Q Shop

This market employs a mixed group of sixteen regular male employees, seven regular young female employees, twenty-two auxiliary employees (part-time homemakers, age thirty to fifty), and twenty-six part-time student workers. The most important changes in the workforce in the 1970s and 1980s were the decrease in the total number of workers and the replace-ment of regular women workers by auxiliary workers. Managers noted that the part-time homemakers "don't make the store more attractive" but do serve the store better as a workforce. Managers believe that hiring part-time women allows savings in wage costs and facilitates adjustments in the num-ber of employees as needed, and also that the part-timers do not shun work that gets their hands dirty, while their morale is higher than that of regular employees. Moreover, their knowledge as homemakers allows them to check for inappropriate pricing, and they provide the store valuable infor-mation about local events, such as those in the area's schools. The Labor Standards Law imposes few restrictions on their employment.

As a result, only a few full-time women employees remain at this large supermarket, working at the cash registers or on clerical tasks. At each sales unit (department), personnel consists of a male chief in charge of budget management, personnel assignments, and evaluations (he also fills in as a relief man); several newly hired young male employees; and part-timers or auxiliary employees who will undertake any job except carrying heavy goods. In the fresh fish department, for example, part-time work involves cooking, arranging the fish on plates, packaging, pricing, and displaying the fish on the counter. Part-time women's hourly wages in 1983 ranged from 400 to 700 yen (US $1.70 to $2.90 at 1983 exchange rate), depending on their performance evaluation and length of service. (They get a 10 yen per hour raise with each year on the job.) Whether these women worked out of absolute need to earn a living or a desire for an extra margin seemed to depend on the economic level of the neighborhood where the store was located.

The preponderance of homemakers among supermarket part-timers is typical; in the 1990s as well as the 1980s, homemakers made up 90 percent of part-time workers nationwide. Breaking this down by industry for 1990, 26 percent of all part-timers worked in manufacturing industries, 40 percent were employed in wholesale and retail sales industries, and 27 percent were in the service sector. By occupation categories, one finds that 24 per-cent did production work, 20 percent were engaged in service work, and 26 percent were in sales.[33] The presence of part-time homemakers in fac-tory work offset the decline in young single women willing to take these jobs. Table 7.5 presents 1980s data, but these figures usefully summarize a situation for part-time workers that remains unchanged in the 1990s. It is

TABLE 7.5

Employment Conditions of Part-Time Women Workers (all industries)

	1970 June	1976 June	1980 June	Full-Time Women Workers 1980
Number of years employed	2.0	2.9	3.3	6.1
Number of days worked per month	22	23	23	23
Scheduled hours worked per day	6	6	6	7.9
Hours actually worked per week	30.8	32.2	32.2	43.1
Pay per hour (yen)	161	399	492	646
Pay differential relative to full-time women workers (1.00 as base)	0.899	0.806	0.76	1.00
Annual bonus (1,000 yen)	16.0	57.4	72.8	364.8
Differential of bonus relative to full-time women workers	0.178	0.215	0.20	1.00
Average age (years old)	37.9	40.7	41.3	34.8
Number of workers (1,000s)	271	486	831	6,215

Source: Shinotzuka Eiko, *Nihon no joshi rōdō* [Female labor in Japan] (Tokyo: Tōyō Keizai Shinpōsha, 1982). Also, relevant volumes of Rōdō shō, ed., *Chingin kōzō kihon chōsa* [Basic survey of wage structure].

shocking to see that both hourly wages and bonuses of part-timers are dramatically lower than those of regular women workers, even though the working hours are in fact not very different.[34]

Accepting Diversification

Certain fundamental assumptions introduced previously explain the prevalence of these conditions for women in the workplace today. The responses to a survey conducted in fall 1980 on the management of women workers are of special interest in fleshing out these assumptions.[35] The survey deserves careful examination because of its bold framing, a quality not usually seen in government surveys. Some of the responses are listed in Table 7.6. I should add that the companies surveyed, for the most part, plan to increase their hiring of women workers, above all of high school graduates in their twenties.

The table reveals a complicated picture. Corporations employ women workers as temporary, cheap employees to be used in simple, auxiliary jobs, and they also follow a sexually tinged policy of seeking women's "charming" presence "to make the workplace bright." And yet, managers bemoan the women workers' lack of ambition in their work, though admitting this is the inevitable consequence of their own policies.

A similar corporate stance is evident in the list of job openings for women workers in the magazine *Torabayu* in the early 1980s. According to Shinotzuka Eiko's analysis of this listing, the many glamorous jobs with English names stipulate age as the primary qualification (70% of the jobs are for women under thirty), but only a handful of jobs specify education as a qualification. "Job-related qualifications" are not mentioned at all.[36] The contradictory needs of managers are neatly summed up by the two largest job categories listed in *Torabayu*. In the first place are ads for store salespeople and receptionists, positions in which a young woman's sex appeal plays a role; second come simple jobs as data-processing terminal operators, the substance of which differs little from the blue-collar tasks that these women wish to avoid. The very title of the magazine, the Japanese pronunciation for the French word *travaille*, conveys glamour and suggests that women's work is a sort of fashion choice.

Some additional survey results, shown in Table 7.7, further attest to the unchanging assumptions of labor management for women. The percentage of women in technical or skilled work and research or engineering jobs is low. The percentage in routine, single-skill work, clerical work, and storefront sales is high. The need for business firms to maintain a gender-based division of labor and gender-based routes of escape from routine jobs did not lessen over the years. There is no evidence that technological innovation has brought a decrease in the proportion of simple, routine work, broadly defined. With the advent of slowed economic growth in 1975, fewer high-level posts were available, so managers became even more

TABLE 7.6

Survey of Labor-Management Policy Toward Women (abstract)

Advantages in Hiring Women	Percentage of Agreement	Reason Why Young Women Workers are Low Key About Their Work	Percentage of Agreement
Makes the workplace bright	71.5	Women tend to regard their jobs as temporary	80.1
Have dexterity not available in men	53.0	Women tend to be childishly dependent	51.7
Labor cost is cheaper	50.9	Jobs with responsibility are not assigned to women	33.3
Length of service is shorter and provides for flexibility in number of workforce	45.8	Differences in physical strength in men and women	22.4
They are serious and conscientious	33.6	They are not educated and trained as much as men	9.5

Disadvantages in Hiring Women	Percentage of Agreement	Reason Why Pay Differentials Increase as They Get Older Though They May Have the Same Education and Job Assignment	Percentage of Agreement
Low aspiration to improve their skills	50.7	As company policy women tend to be used in auxiliary positions	63.3%
There are many restrictions by Labor Standards Law applicable to them	44.2	Many women tend to dislike jobs with responsibilities	38.2
They dislike being transferred or given different assignments	43.6	Performance record worsens after they get married	23.9
Interpersonal problems tend to occur frequently	35.8	There are more women than men whose points of personnel evaluation are poor	22.4
Tend not to remain in the workplace very long	32.7	Women tend not to want to take tests for promotions	9.1

Note: Of the companies responding to the survey, 186 were manufacturing firms, 94 were trading companies, and 40 were financial and service firms.

Source: Koyō shokugyō kenkyūjo (The Institute for Research on Employment and Jobs), Research on Women's Employment (Tokyo: Koyō shokugyō kenkyūjo, March 1982), pp. 11, 18, 20, 34.

TABLE 7.7
Gender-Based Job Differentiation

Job Type	Manufacturing Industries		Tertiary Industries	
	Men (%)	Women (%)	Men (%)	Women (%)
Routine work	16.1	49.2	3.1	15.2
Technical or skilled work	20.8	10.8	3.6	7.2
Clerical work	20.9	33.2	26.1	35.3
Research or engineering	12.2	0.4	10.9	6.7
External sales	29.5	3.1	32.9	2.2
Storefront sales	0.4	3.3	23.4	33.3
Total (%)	100.0	100.0	100.0	100.0
Total (actual number)	31,872	13,904	—	—

Source: Osaka Prefecture, *Osaka fu niokeru fujin rōdō no jitsujō* [Actual conditions of women workers in Osaka Prefecture] 1980; and Takenaka Emiko, ed., *Joshi rōdō ron* [On female labor] (Tokyo: Yūhikaku, 1983), p. 122.

determined to insure advancement opportunities for men by limiting women's chances to cross the boundary to higher positions.

To be sure, this firm managerial stance does not rule out the possibility of opening opportunities, within certain bounds, for women to develop their ability. Nor does it prevent efforts of a few ambitious women to succeed in the world where merit and ability are the reigning principles. At the present time, when competition among firms has intensified and workforces are being cut back at many companies, there are some increases in numbers of multiskilled female workers, their involvement in QC activities, and their assignment to group leadership positions, professional work, and lower-level management posts.

This move toward equality of opportunity based on merit and ability came about first in response to the tide of external pressures that swept into Japan beginning in 1975 in the form of calls by the United Nations and the International Labor Organization for the elimination of gender-based discrimination. But as long as there is not a significant increase in the number of women who "remain at the workplace" and demand the enrichment of the work assigned to them, Japanese corporate managers will be able to withstand such external pressures.

The business establishment can easily accept the following three types of workers: a small number of career women who do not depend on the protection of the Labor Standards Law but advance to higher positions by developing their ability, large numbers of young women who, while depending on the protective clauses of the law, dedicate their youthful years to the firm by performing simple, routine work conscientiously, and part-time homemakers/workers with no high-level ambitions, who engage in unglamorous work. In 1986, along with offering nominally equal job opportunities to men and women, businesses in Japan successfully relaxed the "general protection" clauses in the Labor Standards Law, except those for "protection of motherhood." These clauses included such protections as limitations on overtime work and prohibition of late-night work. Of course, such changes in the law did influence the three acceptable types of workers just noted, but they were targeted primarily at a fourth type: female employees with long job tenure, who would not accept discriminatory pay raises and were sensitive to their rights under the law. In the 1990s as well, these women continue to be likely to lead demands for institutional and collective equality in all areas, including work assignments. A 1979 survey of the Electric Workers' Union Federation indicated that women who are especially sensitive to workplace gender discrimination are well-educated, older, and married, with long years of service. The ongoing objective of political and financial elites is to disperse this group, pushing its members into one of the three acceptable categories.

Over the past twenty years, these trends and pressures have certainly produced diverse images of working women. For example, one woman was torn between the eminently "natural" temptation to leave her job because her husband had been transferred or because her ailing, aged parents needed care and her intense desire, nevertheless, to continue her work as a market researcher.[37] In another case, a group of female employees at the Oita Bank in southwest Japan confronted their personnel division chief about discriminatory promotions. One woman asked him, "When the office head and all the male employees are out of the office making sales calls, I am given authority to serve as acting head. I certify documents and supervise young women workers. . . . What must I do to qualify as a grade five employee?"[38] Then there were the female members of the Japan Travel Bureau labor union who determined to expand their jobs to include work as tour conductors, while keeping their hours within the limits set by the Labor Standards Law. There are also examples of women spurred on by relentless office automation to become experts in the use of personal computers, making themselves ever more indispensable. And it is no longer unusual to run across ambitious women moving into new fields: taking on overseas assignments, selling cars door-to-door, driving delivery vans, and more.

Alternately, there are women, such as one in the union at the head office of the Standard Vacuum Oil Company, who assert, "We must avoid the stupid behavior of seeking to assimilate into the vulgar circle of men who aspire only to join the company elite. Even if our work is simple we must stick it out. Let's stay in our jobs. We must not be sucked in by the company's policy of 'ability development' which will only divide us among ourselves. We must stifle the aspiration of women to rise up in the company hierarchy."[39]

The great majority of women, however, have probably rejected this tough-minded unionist's posture of fighting to "stay in our jobs." The results of a fascinating survey on career aspirations conducted by the Electrical Workers' Union Federation help show this. One sees a tremendous gap between men and women regarding future occupational goals. Men's aspirations are (1) "to gain managerial or supervisory positions" (23.1 percent), and (2) "to serve out their working days" (25.7 percent). The proportion of women who give these replies are merely 2.9 percent for (1) and 13.9 percent for (2). In sharp contrast, only an insignificant percentage (11.7%) of men choose option (3), "accept whatever transpires," but 27.8 percent of women choose this reply. As for option (4), "retire at an appropriate time," the percentages are 9.1 percent for men and 41.2 percent for women.[40]

These women in the electrical industry probably aspired to return to work when their children grew up, or else expected they would have to return to work. In a 1982 survey by the Prime Minister's Office, 49.5 percent of the women responded: "It is best to quit working while the children are small and go back to work when they reach a certain age."[41] And, as noted previously, 64 percent of women in the 1990s choose such an employment pattern. According to the 1982 *Basic Survey of Employment*

Structure the proportion of economically active homemakers reached 50.8 percent, an increase of 4.2 percent in just three years. According to the same survey, this proportion reached 53.7 percent ten years later, in 1992. Although these employed homemakers include self-employed and family workers (16.3%), the increase no doubt reflects the rise in part-time home-maker/workers who hold this attitude toward returning to work.[42] It is clear that this "in-and-out" working pattern remains the dominant one among homemakers. Perhaps this pattern will persist, however unsatisfactory it may be in terms of equality of the sexes.

How to Continue Working?

As stated previously, labor force participation of Japanese women, when charted by age, follows the shape of an "M." For about ten years from age twenty-five, the curve dips as women leave jobs due to marriage, childbirth and child rearing, and it rises as women in their thirties then return to the labor force. As this curve makes very clear, the modes of working and the consciousness of women workers are governed by the tightly interlocked phenomena of a gender-based division of labor throughout society, the pattern of contemporary family life, and the extent of cooperation that husbands of working couples are willing to provide. In the face of this reality, it is only common sense for a woman to opt for any one of the following patterns of labor. A woman can continue working; she can quit for a while and start again; or she can concentrate on being a homemaker after marriage. She can make her choice on the basis of necessity and possibility; and it should be acknowledged that any of these paths can be emotionally and intellectually satisfying.

Nonetheless, I cannot deny my preference for the choice to continue working. I feel this way because there are still many low-income families who must depend on the wife's earnings to cover basic living costs and because the firmest foundation for equality with a husband rests on a woman's demonstrated earning power. The problematic aspects of the full-time homemaker that I wish to emphasize, however, are first, the understandable fact that housework fails to offer the human fulfillment that work in the larger society does—the realization that "the fruits of my labor are being enjoyed by other people, by strangers." Second, if a homemaker seeks this fulfillment through noneconomic activities other than housework, the limitless demands of her husband and children are certain to shrink or eliminate the time and energy available for what they would view more as hobbies. That is, for a woman who remains in the household, the only connection to the larger society is indirect, mediated through husband and children. In order to break out of this indirect relationship through unpaid activities, she has to rely on the understanding of her husband. When the homemaker, deprived of her subjective choice and compelled to depend on this understanding, encounters a "company man" insensitive to her mature, heartfelt desires, the result is what has been called "the spiritual insecurity of the housewife." A 1983 headline in the *Asahi* newspaper shouted "Depressed Housewives in Their Early 40s."[43] And in America, Barbara Sinclair reported that "far fewer than expected of the working women and more than expected of the housewives, for example, had actually had a nervous breakdown. . . . Clearly being only a housewife is the problem. It literally makes many women sick."[44]

In *The Autumn of the Housewives*, the journalist Saito Shigeo presents a vivid account of the precarious psychological state of the wives of company men.[45] This "autumn" is mainly the product of the homemakers' own frustrations at having an excessively indirect relation with the larger society. Moreover, the extent of their frustration is defined by their status as wives of managers or of elite employees of major business firms.

Thus, at the opposite pole from the homemaker buried in her autumnal thoughts, stands the young wife in a farm family, introduced to us in the fine report of Saki Ryūzō.[46] At age thirty-one, this woman took her children and fled the northern Japan family farm, where her husband and mother-in-law insulted and exploited her. She found a job as a hostess at a downtown Tokyo cabaret that provided child care facilities for their employees, and she earned an enormous amount of money. This courageous, ordinary woman was thus able to realize a life for herself outside the oppressive customs of the patriarchal family system. At the same time, she admitted, "I make lots of money, but the work is indecent." The trials endured by both types of wives inhere in the present state of Japanese women.

Of course, a homemaker can avoid depression by returning to work without taking the bold steps of this hostess with children. When she does so, however, the job awaiting her is usually part-time. For a traditional commoner's family, this employment pattern in which a woman first fulfilled her vocation as the caretaker of the household was an eminently rational choice. It is also a healthy means of escape from the autumnal depression that still tends to afflict the wives of elite white-collar salary-men. But how remarkably mild is the reaction of women to the cunning ways of business firms and men. Despite discriminatory practices in pay, promotion, and allocation of work, their view of part-time work is usually favorable. The system safely evades criticism because participants agree that part-timers are nonregular employees, not entitled to the protections and benefits of regular workers.

Finally, I end this section by examining two issues that must be debated frankly if I am to argue in favor of "continuing to work."[47]

Problem One: Unions or Courts?

Generally speaking, the movement for gender equality in Japan's workplaces fights discrimination by relying on the Labor Standards Law and the 1986 Equal Employment Opportunity Law (EEOL) rather than on labor unions. People carry on this struggle by invoking the law and taking their cases to court. They choose this tactic of necessity. Especially since about 1965, labor unions dominated by men have usually accepted managerial practices that discriminate against women, so as to soften the impact of ability-based assessment and promotion policies upon career male employees. As a result, even as they recognize the limitations of their strategy, individuals or groups of women have seen no choice but to rely on the courts, independently of unions. And yet, I must reiterate that the workplace atmosphere will determine whether ordinary women even try to fight for rights already guaranteed them by law. Even if some activists are able to breach the barriers of managerial rights through judicial, administrative, or legislative means, their effect in actually overcoming discrimination in wages, promotion, and work assignments is indirect, at best. I have been told of numerous examples of women, sensitive to their rights, who won court battles but nonethelesss found it impossible to continue working because they were isolated in an unchanged workplace atmosphere.[48]

Thus the key to achieving equality, in my view, is neither the individual's consciousness of civil rights nor her legal knowledge; it is the atmosphere created in the workplace by most of the women there, or at least by a particular stratum. This atmosphere can only be created by industrial actions. As long as such activity is even remotely possible, women workers must adhere stubbornly to goals of coming together in union activities, of winning the right to act within the existing unions on behalf of women's rights, or perhaps in some situations forming a regional women's union along the lines of "Nine to Five."[49] One model is provided by the women office workers of Japan Bank and Trust, whose action against discriminatory promotions in the 1970s was introduced previously. They prevailed in a struggle focusing primarily on workplace activism, and only secondarily on building links to external organizations.

Problem Two: Special Protection Versus Equality

In debates over the EEOL, women activists have split over the relationship between "general protections for women" (going beyond protection of mothers) and equality. A bold reexamination of this issue is needed, with attention to designing a mode of working that will make it possible for women to continue in their jobs. Here are various possible positions linking the equality-versus-protection debate with various images of women's work.

First, if one takes for granted that women will be confined to routine work in a narrow work sphere, one can vehemently and justifiably demand special protection that restricts women to such jobs and can oppose any equality that sacrifices protection. Indeed, this is probably the gut-level position of large numbers of women in Japan. They desire equality with men in raises and job security, but out of a combination of feelings that they "don't want to undertake it" or "can't handle it," they take a passive position regarding access to so-called men's work, which entails stress and imposes heavy responsiblities. Some women dislike the idea of seeking advancement as part of the elite, and others worry that working "like a man" might ruin their happiness as a woman. In either case, they prefer to be protected and not required to engage in demanding work. This stance, by its very existence, implicitly criticizes the system of exalting efficiency and sorting fellow workers via merit and ability assessments. Women who take this position have possibly come to recognize the indispensable nature of routine labor and have come to be aware of the dignity and worth of those who do such work.

But reviewing postwar history, one sees that the right to be protected from difficult work has obstructed women who seek an equal partnership at work and has diminished the spiritual strength of working women. Even in factory or office work, women can be much more self-reliant and creative than at present. Men only appear to be more creative in their work than women because the latter are saddled with bothersome miscellaneous and auxiliary tasks that sap the energy required for important work.[50] An attitude that defiantly exalts "the freedom of the discriminated" (freed from the pressures endured by the company men) can only accept uncritically a workplace gender relationship embedded in the traditional combination of men's cunning and women's docility. Such a stance ultimately leads women to become disillusioned with the realities of work and to choose not to remain in the workplace. The idea that women should remain at work must be premised on an endeavor to expand their sphere of work and enrich the contents of their jobs.

Second, if the expansion of Japanese women's sphere of work is defined to be the opening up of opportunities for women to move into high-level professions and managerial posts in major institutions (as is the case with the American discourse on job equality),[51] then one must accept equality without special protection. Considering the rigorous selection process that an employee must undergo before reaching higher positions, special rules to protect women undeniably restrict their potential to advance. In fact, when the protective clauses of the Labor Standards Law were in force, before 1986, the only way for a woman to make full use of her competence in a front line professional or managerial position was to violate quietly the protective clauses of the law. Of course, removing protection did not automatically guarantee women equal opportunities to move upward but it at least removed one major reason for denying such opportunities. Indeed, many women wish to remove the legal shackles preventing career advancement and devote their full spirit to their work, including professionals such as newspaper reporters, "office ladies" who want to use their experience and move into decisionmaking positions, and divorced women or widows who desire greater income by taking on jobs defined as men's work.

But equality without protection runs the serious risk of harming women in the first position, discussed previously, who desire a different sort of equality—one with protection. I believe that women's current attitudes toward work have ensured that loosening protective legislation has not led immediately to practices such as revived late-night shifts, overtime on a par with men, or elimination of menstrual leaves; relatively few women seem to feel either the heavy economic hardship or the sense of responsiblity for a job that would lead them to put up with such conditions. In other words, the "freedom of the discriminated" is proving strong enough to prevent the revival of these practices, so far. Yet the removal of protective legislation at the very least is hastening the process of replacing full-time women employees with part-time workers. Protective legislation must be weakened or eliminated carefully and gradually, with consideration for the situation in particular industries or occupations.

Third, in Japan, the majority of activists and academics concerned with women's issues seek equality *and* protection. Unlike the first position, and in common with the second position, they seek an expanded work sphere for women; but they also argue that protection must be maintained. They reluctantly admit that protection does restrict women seeking expanded career opportunities. Refusing to recognize this would be to ignore the importance for career development of personnel evaluations that reward an employee's total commitment. But advocates of this position turn managerial logic on its head to argue that managerial expectations for men's work should be brought into line with expectations for women, thus eliminating women's disadvantages in the face of corporate performance norms.

Certainly this position is idealistic. Who are the agents, and what are the means, of a strategy to realize this logic? Does one work through the state (the law) or through labor unions (negotiations and contractual agreements)? In Japan, one should not place too much faith in the law. On one hand, it would be very difficult, for example, to regulate by law either the working pattern of Japanese salary-men (exemplified in their long overtime hours) or the intense workplace atmosphere that drives them to "workaholism." The actual conditions of daily work make it difficult for people to impose change from outside the production site.

On the other hand, to pursue reforms through union activities within financial or industrial enterprises is *theoretically* possible. But it seems *practically* impossible to persuade male union members, so committed to displaying their abilities and triumphing in the strictly selective competition to advance, to join in a struggle that absolutely requires cooperation between men and women workers. Quite simply, the problem is that men and women do not at present share the sort of common work experience that is a precondition for any joint struggle in the workplace.

I believe there is a fourth position free of the drawbacks of these three. This is a way to expand women's work sphere while rejecting the competition produced by a philosophy of equality of opportunity. This alternative is to change the nature of existing jobs. It entails, *first*, the participation of women in the wide range of work now undertaken by nonelite men, and *second,* the effort of these workers to extend their sphere of decisionmaking authority while remaining in such jobs.

This initiative is not an especially novel idea. For example, in factories young women do take on difficult jobs operating automatic machines, and in offices female "assistants" encroach on the job of the male "person-in-charge." At present there are virtually no jobs commonly performed by men that women cannot perform because of physiological reasons. In today's unnatural situation, workers simply accommodate themselves to the gender division of work modes; men do their jobs in a "manly" fashion, and women do theirs in a "feminine" fashion. Even if this unnatural situation is ended, men and women will be acutely and mutually aware of the opposite sex. But while possessing this awareness, they will enjoy working together on the same jobs at the same workplace.

The next step for such a collectivity of men and women working together is to win from management decisionmaking power over work methods and pace, job assignments, and workplace regulations. These powers will help make existing work interesting for employees and thus will make it easier for them to continue working, reducing the need to escape. Thinking back to the first three positions outlined above, if one roughly divides jobs into, first, upper-level jobs for a small number, and second, lower-level jobs for most workers (and if one accepts these numbers and categories as given), then to pursue equality of opportunity and even equality of results is simply to raise the question of who gets to hold upper-level jobs.

The fourth position differs. By putting it forward, one urges working women and men to enrich the nature of the work of lower-level jobs by encroaching upon the authority now reserved to the upper-level category. This can be called "equality in decisionmaking rights." Perhaps such equality cannot be extended without limit. Nonetheless, a move in this direction would enhance the dignity of the nonelite male and female workers in lower-level jobs and increase their ability to remain in the workplace. Moreover, if employees carry on the struggle in this way, something one might call a "logic of women workers" that does not exalt efficiency over all other values in the workplace could prevail, leading workers to challenge the control of management.

If this movement to enlarge the scope of lower-level jobs gains ground, women workers will be more actively engaged and challenged, but their jobs are also likely to become more stressful. Yet to forge an alliance with the significant numbers of men also trapped in lower-level jobs, any movement of women for greater autonomy and control at work must accept this challenge. And once the movement has advanced to this point, two external pressures will further support the drive to bring more auton-

omy to lower-level jobs. First, international movements against gender discrimination will support these efforts. Second, the slow economic growth
that has choked off prospects for promotion as the traditional male escape
route from lower-level jobs will lead these men to support the activism of
their female coworkers.

In the same spirit, the need for general protections that go beyond protection of motherhood should be decided with reference to women's ability to speak out on the character of work at the production site. To use the
force of the law to bring men's working conditions into line with those stip-
ulated by protective laws for women will be almost impossible. Accepting
this, I reluctantly favor gradual revision of protective regulations for
women, as a quid pro quo for instituting a system whereby men and
women engage in the same kind of work. Many women may be unhappy
with such a course; however, I do not see how people who remain protected and isolated from the ferocity of the workplace will in practical terms
retain any credibility as they campaign to change the Japanese salary-man's
workplace (world-renowned for its ferocity), to restrain the competition
and selection processes that prevail there, and to make it a kinder, gentler
place. That is, one could say, the reality of workplace political science.

In other words, the foundation for joint industrial action by men and
women to overcome their common hardships and share the joys and sor-
rows of work as equal partners is common hardship itself. One should not
forget that, in many nations, such joint struggles carried on by labor unions
have gained workers a degree of protection and well-being in the workplace, in practice, but without legal force, which is greater than the protections specified in Japan's legislation for women. Of course, protective
provisions could themselves be the result rather than the cause of gender-
based discrimination at work. Therefore, protective measures should certainly not be dropped before concrete proof exists that discrimination at the
workplace has ended. My main objective is to articulate a strategy for workplace activism through shared hardships and joint action, a strategy that will
ultimately minimize the tendency for men to view women as auxiliary
workers who need protection at the production site and who, therefore,
should find their vocation in housework.

Why focus on the idea of "shared hardships" with such a convoluted
discussion? I would like to explain by recalling some points made by
Morisaki Kazue in her book *Pitch Dark*, points that I often considered as I
wrote this chapter.[52]

Before and during World War II, women as well as men worked in
Japan's coal mines. Under premodern management, their lives were a daily
struggle against poverty and an extremely difficult working environment.
The inside of the mines was a place of cruel physical labor, hard for us to
imagine. Yet their labor had a profound impact on the formation of their
self-identities. In the postwar era, the new protective laws banned women

from working in the mines; men began to feel a sense of inferiority about working with women; and women were "rescued" from the dark underground world. It was at this point that the women themselves began to feel that their lives had become somewhat meaningless. They would say, "Now I'm down in the dumps, doing things like planting flowers. In the old days, I used to work."

When they were working on a par with men, their sexual relations were on a level of equality, too. They told Morisaki, "We didn't have to do what the men used to tell us"; and, "The mine was not a place where men could do what they wanted with women." Young women, too, "felt strong and upright," acted as freely as they wished, and spoke up forthrightly. In the eyes of former women miners, postwar women were concerned only about making themselves look pretty and considered themselves happy for not having to work; as one miner said, these former miners had become "worthless." The words of these women as they reflect back on their lives today sound beautiful and poignant: "When my husband goes out alone to work and comes home with a smug look on his face I feel a sense of sorrow well up in me. He's the only one who gets to work. . . . There is no meaning to a human being's life unless one works."

After recording these remarks, Morisaki wrote in her postscript: "These women mine workers do not consider housework that disappears into the 'household' framework as 'work.'. . . Their admittedly grim mine labor gave them [an equality with men that in turn produced real] pleasure, as they crushed underfoot the gendered morality that confined women within the family system."[53] The days when mine work can be regarded as a typical mode of labor in Japan are long past, and one must not forget the harsh dangers and thus celebrate this labor nostalgically. Nonetheless, today, when "work outside the home" is commonplace for women, one must reevaluate the former self-confidence and the current lament of these veteran women mine workers, both of which have been ignored as aberrations in the postwar discourse on women's liberation.

Reflections in 1995

In the previous section I occasionally referred to conditions obtained since the passage of the Equal Employment Opportunity Law of 1986. Here, I outline in greater detail the ways this law has changed, and has failed to change, the treatment of women working under the Japanese management system.

Japan's EEOL was certainly unambitious. It merely required that employers "make efforts" to eliminate gender discrimination in recruitment, hiring, job assignments, and promotions. It gives the state only weak powers of enforcement. The law reflects the will of employers, who wish to assign jobs unrestrained by any legal requirements. Still, at a minimum it violates the spirit of the EEOL to use gender as a criterion in determining an employee's career path. In this context, since the mid-1980s, labor managers have been applying various policies of merit-based assessments, formerly limited to men, to women as well. In general, the major change in Japanese-style management under the EEOL has been to admit some women to the world of meritocratic personnel administration.

Thus, an avenue has been opened by which women might escape from simple, repetitive labor, so long as they display abilities and enthusiasm "just like men." Since the law took effect, many companies have adopted a new tracking system in which career-oriented jobs are designated "managerial track positions," and supplementary positions with little prospect for advancement, previously designated explicitly as "women's jobs," now bear the label of "general positions."[54] In theory, women (as well as men) can now choose to be employed in either managerial track or general track positions. However, when a woman is so brave as to choose the former, managers sternly declare that they want women to develop their capabilities and that they aim to make full use of women's talents. But if women choose the managerial track, according to male managers, they must be independent and must be prepared to shoulder the same hard work as men do. Women must also cultivate a properly ambitious attitude toward life, enduring heavy work loads, long hours of overtime, and sudden job transfers to distant sites. With such austere appeals, one can easily read a managerial expectation that most women would rather settle for the general track, with its traditionally "women's" jobs.

Women workers adapt to this situation in one of two ways. A small number accept the meritocratic challenge. Most often they enter managerial jobs in areas in which female labor has always played a major role, such as the public sector, food processing, apparel and fashion industries, retail or wholesale consumer sales, and insurance industries. Some may enter newer lines or do work in which feminine sensibility and "charm" is seen to be an asset, such as the expanding service and information technology industries. Here, they develop long-term careers as specialists or managers, all the while resolutely bearing the strains of hard work, "functional flexibility," and the possibility of sexual harassment. And, of course, all of these women face huge difficulty enjoying both their chosen careers and normal family lives. The reason for this difficulty is clear enough: It is because of the existence of the male-centered working style of the company man and the remarkably persistent social consciousness that posits homemaking as the chief role for women. In such an environment, women who pursue working careers may end up deciding not to marry. Or, if they do marry, such women and their husbands may join the ranks of the DINKs—double-income, no kids. Thus one sees the following shocking results of a survey commissioned by the Ministry of Labor: 59 percent of female managers ranked section chief or higher were single; of the remainder who were married, only 36 percent had children.[55] All together, 74 percent of those surveyed had not raised children. Of course, my intent is not to criticize these women for choosing to remain single, get divorced, or refrain from having children. Nor would I deny that a woman's work may at times be of such interest as to consume every bit of her energies. But if virtually all career women must sacrifice a significant part of their personal and emotional fulfillment to perform their jobs effectively, one must conclude they have been forced to lead one-dimensional lives.

Most women in Japan, however, reject the dubious privilege of racing along the managerial track. They work in sales or office jobs, or as factory labor. As the male managerial elite hoped, they settle for jobs customarily defined as "women's work." A survey conducted in 1992 delineates this situation. Asked if they desired the kinds of jobs that men generally have, only 7 percent answered "definitely" or "if at all possible." About 65 percent replied they "wouldn't want to," and about 25 percent said that they were not sure.[56] Further, in a 1990 Labor Ministry survey, just 29 percent of women asserted they "wanted to advance" in their jobs, but nearly 70 percent said they did not. Thirty-eight percent of the women held no desire to advance because "responsibilities would get heavier," and 36 percent said they were "satisfied with their present jobs." Another 25 percent pointed out that "such work would be incompatible with running a household," and 17 percent feared their "working hours would increase."[57] These results clearly reflect the nonelitist attitudes of the majority of female operatives and office workers in Japan.

Most women, then, reject the invitation to advance through developing and displaying their abilities because Japanese-style management demands much more than the ability to achieve reasonable results at a job of certain dimensions. Additionally, the system demands an extreme degree of "functional flexibility" and the willingness to dedicate one's entire life to a company.[58] Faced with such demands, it seems that many women decide the status quo is perhaps all for the best: Those who become employees that sacrifice virtually their entire everyday lives to the company are almost all men; women are different, they can find fulfillment in their duties wherever these may be, in society at large, in the community, and even in the home. Women who hold such views ask, "If the only way to advance is by turning into a total company person, who needs a promotion?" They say that they want the freedom to raise their children, take part in volunteer activities, travel, or just have time to themselves. They understand how odious the system is that robs individuals of their time and energy, requiring sudden overtime or job relocation and demanding constant study to keep abreast of latest technologies and the sacrifice of free time for company-sponsored *kaizen* activity. Thus, when women in Japan look for a job as either operative or office worker, most "naturally" choose those classified as general positions over managerial track positions.

Even if one rejects the career track, however, other options exist besides simply resigning oneself to a "woman's job." Those who wish to preserve what one may call the "freedom of the discriminated" can today choose from a large number of part-time, nonregular positions. Many in fact do choose this path, and for reasons worth noting. When the EEOL went into effect, restrictions on women's working hours were relaxed, so many female office employees must now work longer hours than before. Also, so-called women's jobs have themselves become much more stressful due to the constant streamlining of workforces and the "just-in-time" rationalization of both production and information-processing jobs. Also, as the pay increases for men (and a few women) on the managerial track, the wage level of those on the general track has declined in relative terms. A veteran female worker in this track, especially a woman who is married, today finds herself earning less in comparison with her male coworkers than she did before. Full-time women workers with regular jobs on the general track find that these jobs offer far less security and stability than they once did. They unsurprisingly find the greater freedom of choice that part-time jobs offer in terms of working hours and workloads to be attractive. These jobs are also free of the heavy responsibilities of full-time positions.

Affirming the "freedom of the discriminated" is a healthy sentiment for a working person. But as long as working women in Japan take pride in this freedom, their work conditions will remain uncertain, and the lack of interest they take in their jobs will doom their experience of work to a merely bearable emptiness. For these nonregular employees, the more brilliantly the freedom of the discriminated shines, the darker the gloom of uncertainty and emptiness becomes. Left in this position, the majority of working women who live by the freedom of the discriminated meet the expectations of the Japanese-style system of management just as well as those few women who "work as hard as men," although in a different way. Those who wish to enjoy the freedom of the discriminated end up choosing the nonregular women's jobs that offer such freedom. Although corporate society relies mostly on men to form its organizational and functional nucleus, it sees in part-time female workers a trustworthy force of people who can carry out those simpler, but necessary, chores in the workplace, while at the same time remaining dutiful wives and mothers at home.

The corporate society of contemporary Japan evokes these two typical images of workers. At the center is the typically male employee who enjoys the prospect of life-long employment, but must cope with the rigors of functional flexibility and compete to show his dedication and drive by becoming a workaholic who neglects his family. On the periphery are the working women in nonregular positions, who take on most of the simple and supplemental work in the companies, while at the same time taking care of the home. These women provide the company with the flexibility to adjust the size of the workforce and the wage bill whenever economic conditions require a rationalization of personnel. The Japanese style of management operates smoothly thanks to the mutual dependence, understanding, and love of these two types of workers. Shall the corporate man and woman thus live happily ever after?

Notes to Chapter 7

1. In 1986, soon after the original (Japanese) version of this chapter was written, Japan's Equal Opportunity Employment Law was established. I have written in Japanese on the more recent shop floor situation, including the limited effectiveness of this law, in *Nihonteki keiei no meian* [Light and darkness of Japanese management] (Tokyo: Chikuma Shobō, 1989) and "Kigyō-shakai to rōdō" [Company society and labor], in Yasumaru Yoshio, et al., eds., *Nihon tsūshi zikan* [History of Japan], vol. 21 (Tokyo: Iwanami Shōten, 1995). Also, I have brought the story up to date at the end of this chapter.

2. Until roughly 1980, Japanese discussion of gender discrimination and how to end it focused exclusively on problems such as the prevalence of the traditional "man as breadwinner, woman as homemaker" division of labor; the position of homemakers; wage differences between the sexes; and the protection of motherhood. It did not touch on the issue of discrimination in regard to what positions were available to women or the content of these jobs. Many of the studies written on the subject during this time lack up-to-date description or analysis of what work was actually like for women in the workplace. One notable exception is Takenaka Emiko and Nishiguchi Toshiko, *Onna no shigoto, onna no shokuba* [Women's jobs, women's workplace] (Tokyo: San'ichi Shobō, 1962). I do not know whether the slow development of a realistic appreciation of gender discrimination in the workplace is unique to Japan. But it is certainly true, as I argued in Chapter 4, that the greatest deficiency of postwar democracy—the relative lack of concern for what labor should be like—constitutes one way in which Japan is different.

3. For a sensitive English-language ethnography of such workers see Jeannie Lo, *Office Ladies, Factory Women: Life and Work at a Japanese Company* (Armonk, N.Y.: M.E. Sharpe, 1990).

4. Sōrifu (Prime Minister's Office), *Kokusei chōsa* [National census], Tokyo, 1950. No precise data for the prewar years are available, but scattered statistics show a similar proportional breakdown.

5. Ōkōchi Kazuo and Sumiya Mikio, eds., *Nihon no rōdōsha kaikyū* [The Japanese working class] (Tokyo: Tōyō Keizai Shinpōsha, 1955).

6. On these goals see Morisawa Yōko, *Shinano no Onna* [Women of Shinano], vol. 2 (Tokyo: Mirai-sha, 1969), pp. 307–308.

7. Kamisaka Fuyuko, et al., *BG-gaku noto* [Business girl studies note] (Tokyo: San'ichi Shinsho, 1961), p. 110.

8. Research Institute for Bank Employees (RIBE), *Ginkō rōdō chōsa jihō* [Survey: Current report of bank labor], April 1980.

9. *Hiroba* [Forum] is a monthly journal edited by RIBE for the bank workers' struggles. For a study dating from the late 1950s of one such protest in Kyoto City Hall, about tea-pouring, see Susan Pharr, *Losing Face: Status Politics in Japan* (Berkeley: University of California Press, 1990), pp. 59–73.

10. On the lifestyle of prewar "factory girls," see, for example, Hosoi Wakizō, *Jokō aishi* [The sad history of women factory workers] (Tokyo: Iwanami-bunkō, [1925] 1954). "Orientation to natural desires" became a popular phrase in early postwar Japan. Essentially, it referred to the abandoning of the attitude of "self-restraint at all times" as described by Hosoi, in favor of a stance of trying to improve one's life by valuing one's natural desires. This kind of mind-set characterized the lifestyles of common people in early postwar Japan.

11. Itō Yasuko, "Sengo kaikaku to fujin kaihō," in *Josei-shi Sōgō Kenkyū-kai* [Women's History General Study Group], ed., *Nihon josei-shi* [History of Japanese women], vol. 5 (Tokyo: Tokyo University Press, l982), p. 306.

12. RIBE, *Ginkō rōdō chōsa jihō* [Survey: Current report of bank labor], February 1982.

13. Kamisaka Fuyuko, et al., eds., *BG-gaku nōto*, pp. 16–17, 209.

14. On forces supporting slogans of "peace and democracy" in this era, see John W. Dower, "Peace and Democracy in Two Systems," in Andrew Gordon, ed., *Postwar Japan as History* (Berkeley: University of California Press, 1993).

15. Higuchi Keiko, Nakajima Michiko, and Mukai Shōko, eds., *Shokuba—hataraki tsuzukeru anata ni* [Workplaces—To you who continue working at the workplace] (Tokyo: Chikuma Shobō, 1982), pp. 198–200.

16. Takenaka Emiko and Nishiguchi Toshiko, *Onna no shigoto, onna no shokuba* [Women's work, women's workplace] (Tokyo: San'ichi Shinsho, 1962), pp. 211–213.

17. For an excellent study of these legal cases, see Frank Upham, *Law and Social Change in Postwar Japan* (Cambridge: Harvard University Press, 1987), pp. 129–144.

18. Higuchi, et al., eds., *Shokuba*, pp. 49–51.

19. Rōdō shō (Ministry of Labor), *Joshi rōdō ryoku no dōkō* [Labor market trends of women workers], Tokyo, 1968.

20. Nakaoka Tetsurō, *Kōjō no tetsugaku* [Philosophy of the factory] (Tokyo: Heibonsha); *Rōdō genba no hanran* [Revolts on the shop floor] (Tokyo: Daiya-mondo-sha, 1974); Saitō Shigeo, *Waga naki ato ni kozui wa kitare!* [After me, the deluge!] (Tokyo: Gendai-shi Shuppankai, 1974); Kumazawa Makoto, *Rōdōsha kanri no kusa no ne* [The grassroots of workers' control] (Tokyo: Nihon Hyōronsha, 1976).

21. The following quotations are from this trading company's confidential document. I am unable to give a precise citation of this work.

22. Higuchi, et al., eds., *Shokuba*, pp. 93–96.

23. Labor Survey Center, *Rōdō chōsa jihō* [Current report of labor survey], August 1971.

24. Morisaki Kazue, *Tatakai to eros* [Struggle and Eros] (Tokyo: San'ichi Shobō, 1970), p. 88. In the 1950s and 1960s it was very common for groups of young women and men to form "circles" devoted to a hobby, such as music, writing, studying, or sports, all with an element of social activism and commitment to a new postwar democracy as part of the motivating spirit.

25. Sōrifu (Prime Minister's Office), *Shūgyō kōzō kihon chōsa* [The basic survey of employment structure], Tokyo, 1965 and 1974.

26. This is a play on the "three sacred treasures" of the imperial household. This term has referred to a shifting complement of modern consumer items since the 1950s. Around 1970 the treasures were "car, color TV, and air conditioner."

27. Sōrifu (Prime Minister's Office), *Fujin ni kansuru seron chōsa* [Public opinion survey on women], Tokyo, 1979.

28. Ibid., *Josei ni kansuru seron chōsa* [Public opinion survey on women], Tokyo, 1990.

29. Ibid., *Josei no shokugyō ni kansuru seron chōsa* [Public opinion survey on women's working], Tokyo: 1989.

30. This information is from the analyis by Ujihara Shōjirō, "Joshi Rōdō wa dono yō ni henkō sihta ka" [How has women's labor changed?], *Ekonomisuto*, April 20, 1980.

31. I compiled these accounts from interviews in 1983.

32. Rōdō shō (Ministry of Labor), *Rōdō seisansei tōkei chōsa hōkoku* [Report of the survey of labor productivity statistics], Tokyo, 1962.

33. Ibid., *Paatotaimu no jittai* [Conditions of part-timers], Tokyo, 1990 edition, pp. 8, 10.

34. Shinotzuka Eiko, *Nihon no joshi rōdō* [Female labor in Japan] (Tokyo: Tōyō keizai shinpōsha, 1982), p. 105.

35. The research is by Matsushima Shizuo and others, in *Koyō Shokugyō Kenkyūjo* [The Institution for Research on Employment and Jobs], ed., *Fujin koyō kenkyū* [Research on women's employment], March 1982.

36. Shinotzuka, *Nihon no joshi rōdō*, pp. 198–207.

37. Okifuji Noriko, *Onna ga shokuba o saru hi* [The day a woman leaves her job] (Tokyo: Shinchōsha, 1979).

38. RIBE, *Ginkō rōdō chōsa jihō* [Survey: Current report of bank labor], June 1977.

39. Higuchi, et al., eds., *Shokuba*, p. 57.

40. Inagami Takeshi, *Rōshi kankei no shakaigaku* [Sociology of industrial relations] (Tokyo: Tokyo University Press, 1981), p. 24.

41. Sōrifu (Prime Minister's Office), *Fujin ni kansuru seron chōsa* [Public opinion survey on women], Tokyo, 1982.

42. Rōdō shō (Ministry of Labor), ed., *Shōwa 57 nendo shūgyō kōzō kihon chōsa* [Basic survey of employment structure], Tokyo, 1982.

43. *Asahi Shimbun*, June 17, 1983.

44. Barbara Sinclair, *The Women's Movement: Political, Socioeconomic, and Psychological Issues* (New York: Harper & Row, 1979), p. 76.

45. Saitō Shigeo, *Tsuma-tachi no shishuki* [The autumn of the housewives] (Tokyo: Kyōdō Tsūshinsha, 1983).

46. Saki Ryūzō, *Nihon hyōmin monogatari* [The stories of drifting people in Japan] (Tokyo: Tokuma Shobo, 1977).

47. However, I will skip over two additional important issues facing women who continue their jobs: the longstanding problem of child care and the new issue of caring for the aged. Some studies that do address these problems include: Takenaka Emiko and Kuba Yoshiko, eds., *Rōdō-ryoku no josei-ka* [Feminization of labor force] (Tokyo: Yūhikaku, 1994); Yamanoi Kazunori, *Nihon no kōreisha fukushi* [The welfare for aged people in Japan] (Tokyo: Iwanami shoten, 1994).

48. This information comes to me from a female lawyer who has waged legal battles against gender discrimination in the workplace for many years.

49. Nine to Five is an organization of women office workers in Boston, Massachusetts.

50. Tanaka Mitsu, *Inochi no onna-tachi e* [To the women living vividly] (Tokyo: San'ichi Shobō, 1972), pp. 56, 302–303.

51. For example, Eli Ginsberg and Alice M. Yohalem, eds., *Corporate Lib: Women's Challenge to Management* (Baltimore: Johns Hopkins University Press, 1973).

52. Morisaki Kazue, *Makkura* [Pitch dark] (Tokyo: San'ichi Shobō, 1977). Morisaki, a superb documentary novelist and unique thinker, interviewed ten former mining women of the Chikuhō region about their work, life experiences, and consciousness in the prewar era and in the 1970s. She compiled her interviews into this book. Her research took place at the beginning of the 1960s. Although many researchers have overlooked this work, I think it is indispensable for the study of modern Japanese women's history and labor history.

53. Ibid., pp. 89–90, 122, 186, 217–219, 232–235.

54. These are my translations of the Japanese terms *sōgō shoku* and *ippan shoku*.

55. Josei shokugyō zaidan (Women's Occupational Foundation), *Joshi kanri shoku chōsa* [Survey of female supervisors and managers], Tokyo, 1990.

56. Nihon rōdō kenkyū kikō (Japan Institute of Labor) (Research Report No. 21), "Josei jūgyōin no kyariaa keisei ishiki to sapōto seido no jittai ni kan suru chōsa" [A survey of the career consciousness of women employees and the support system for women's careers], Tokyo, 1992.

57. Rōdō shō (Ministry of Labor), "Joshi koyō kanri kihon chōsa" [Basic survey of employment management of women], Tokyo, 1990.

58. On the special features of the meritocracy of Japanese-style management, see my *Hatarakimono-tachi naki egao* [Tearful smiles of devoted employees] (Tokyo: Yūhikaku, 1993).

8

Twenty Years of
a Bank Worker's Life

At 6:50 on the morning of January 7, 1978, a large truck owned by a self-employed businessman struck and killed a bank employee on his way to work. The victim was Kawabe Tomomi, age forty-seven. He had been working for Fuji Bank for twenty-three years, since graduating college, and he was a member of the bank's labor union until his death.

Over the course of his working life, what sort of commitments had Kawabe made to his job, his workplace, and his union activities? What did he study? What sort of controversies had he been involved in? How important was his family for him? Fortunately, Kawabe left behind a diary that fills sixteen college-ruled notebooks and helps answer these queries.[1] He kept this diary from 1965 to the day before his death. There are also recollections by Kawabe's friends, written and edited after his death. Using these as source material and augmenting them with various studies of the bank as a workplace, one can follow the life of this Japanese bank worker and the changes in his workplace. The inquiry offers a point of entry into the history of white-collar workers during Japan's extraordinary era of high-speed growth.

In the Union's Young Men and Women's Division

In 1955 Kawabe Tomomi graduated from the Faculty of Political Economy of Waseda University, one of Japan's premier private schools, and went to work for Fuji Bank. His college days had been a turbulent time. The "Bloody May Day" of 1952 saw police battle students protesting the signing of the U.S.-Japan Security Pact, under which American troops were semipermanently stationed in Japan. One week later, the related Waseda University Incident resulted in a violent clash between police and students on the Waseda campus.[2] Against this background, Kawabe undertook serious studies of Marxian economic theory and the history of Japanese capitalism. He joined a study group that examined political, intellectual, and cultural issues, and he helped publish the group's journal. In his hometown of Urawa, in Saitama Prefecture outside Tokyo, he and some friends started a Japanese literature reading club. Thus, Kawabe's lifelong interest in Marxism, literature, and literary theory started in his college years.

One might fairly claim that Kawabe began his intellectual life as a naive leftist who was developing a critical awareness of the age in which he lived and of the theories concerned with transforming society. But he was seriously attempting to come to terms with the relationship between such theories and his own sense of self, or subjectivity.[3] In this effort, Kawabe always kept a distance from the totalistic mode of thinking of the vanguard political parties, the Communist party in particular. At the same time, he had frequent ideological clashes with his father, a sober engineer who had endured the difficult years of postwar life hoping that his son would complete his education and obtain a stable job. In the end, Kawabe, like many college graduates of the 1950s, took a job with a major bank, both to make a living and to offer peace of mind to his aging parents. Yet he remained true to his beliefs, seeking to maintain a certain critical posture even as he took a job inside what he called "the fortress of monopoly capital."

In retrospect, it seems that during the first seven years of his career at Fuji Bank (1955–1962), Kawabe's critical posture did not cause him to feel much pressure or tension. But the character of bank work was changing as rapid technical innovations changed business offices in Japan dramatically beginning in the mid-1950s. These years saw the adoption of the punch card system (1954), the introduction of calculator registers hooked up to punch card machines in all offices (1959), and the installation of teletype networks linking separate bank offices.[4] These new instruments set the stage for the introduction of computers in 1960. At most banks, by 1963 the calculation of interest for ordinary savings accounts came to be centralized in a data processing center. This simplified office work, such as recording, calculating, compiling statistics and preparing reports, previously had been undertaken in bank branch offices. At the same time, a "teller-proof system," which separated accounting (using computer terminals) from the work of the tellers at the window, was instituted in 1960, and a "second phase standardization," which specified the overall daily workload to accord with the capacity of new machinery, was adopted in 1962.

Bank work was thus rationalized at a steady pace and became much more stratified as a result. It became more stimulating at the top and duller at the bottom. On one hand, the female bank employees were restricted to working as tellers or using computer terminals, and their work was increasingly routine. On the other hand, the male workers were gradually liberated from routine office work, and the proportion of their time spent on outside assignment increased. Further, the work pace for both men and women came to be determined by the policy of making the fullest possible use of computer capacity to manage bank capital efficiently. In sum, work in the bank was losing a certain human quality that had derived from skills gained via long experience and the cooperative quality of work.

But Kawabe's employer, the Fuji Bank, which prided itself on being number one in savings account assets, still maintained a family-like atmosphere. In the early 1960s, the imposition of stringent screening among the workers under a new technology regime does not yet seem to have arrived. The women workers' recollections of their workplace in those years are rosy. The bank sponsored trips and athletic events, and coworkers readily managed to plan hiking trips and birthday parties. There were "commuter line groups," informal social networks of employees taking a given train line to work. One of Kawabe's friends wrote of the workplace where Kawabe had served for his first three years: "At the Muromachi branch office, all those in managerial positions were good people. The young people were lively and the atmosphere was bright. . . . All of us in our group were enjoying the springtime of our lives."[5] An important point to note here is that the workplace, with its sense of community, which also included the managerial staff, was also the base for the young men and women's union activities.

Kawabe is remembered as an exceedingly sociable person by nature, who readily adapted to this work atmosphere. He soon became a central figure in several activities: a study group on finance organized by some young employees, the "chatter-box club" of the night-shift room, and the major annual debate at the union school. He attended discussion sessions organized by the bank's public relations magazine, and he also wrote articles in the union journal challenging the lifestyles of young workers and thus arousing the interest of some more senior activists. A voracious reader and a leftist intellectual, his writing was overwhelmed with footnotes, and its style was stiff. But with an amiable, easygoing personality, he was befriended by people. They gave him the affectionate nickname of "Abédon," and he emerged as the leader of the young men and women's group in the union.[6] At this point he was in no way isolated, either in the workplace or in the union.

In 1950s Japan, male white-collar workers who were college graduates with an intellectual bent often possessed both the inclination and a fair degree of freedom to criticize society. This was also a time when intelligent female high school graduates possessed a new democratic "postwar" consciousness that prompted some to challenge their discriminatory workplace status as "office flowers."

The atmosphere of the time made it possible for the male and female Fuji Bank employees to engage in a serious informal dialogue, the "chattering" of the night-shift group previously noted. The family style of social relations at Fuji Bank did not exert any pressure against such gab sessions. The activities of the youthful Kawabe are reflected in this diary notation: "I have many Tachiana's as companions (by this I mean ideal women who encourage me to live seriously but energetically)."[7]

To be sure, with the advantage of hindsight, one can easily see that the social consciousness of college-educated, white-collar male workers of the 1950s had not matured to the point at which they might link their political radicalism to a critique of their specific work situations. Likewise, the women who criticized their discriminatory treatment as "office flowers" did not question practices that restricted them to routine and simple tasks. Although these young men and women formed a coalition, they ignored issues of the hierarchy inherent in the work itself; their discussions centered on criticizing "premodern" features of society as a whole or supporting the left-wing parties on current political issues. In general, they gave little thought to questioning the particular quality of their working life as bank employees or pursuing labor union policies that might address that work.

A spirit of "class consciousness" and a spirit of "postwar democracy" had been sharply critical of the existing order since the late 1940s, the former centered in unions, the latter anchored in the student movement and the beliefs of pacifist intellectuals. But not until the 1970s did these two streams of thought in Japan begin to be elaborated into a systematic critique of work at the point of production or the hierarchical nature of careers. Previously, neither supporters of postwar democracy (as analyzed in Chapter 4) nor adherents of orthodox Marxism showed any concern for actual conditions at the point of production. Both ideologies suffered from a fixation with the idea that all of the laborer's problems could be solved if only the system upholding the present class structure was reformed. But toward the end of the 1960s, this understanding came under fire, mainly from young people concerned to oppose the "administered society" and from the New Left, whose adherents argued that worker alienation and hierarchies of power existed in any system.

Needless to say, Kawabe was conditioned by the concerns of the 1950s, so he initially offered no such critique. Nonetheless, because he was a young man interested in literature and concerned about the question of "selfhood" and the diversity of human beings, he seems to have been somewhat aware of the serious issue of stratification within the working class. For example, in 1958 he participated in a debate about middle-class workers published in a bulletin edited by the Research Institute for Bank Employees (RIBE), called *Hiroba* (Forum). This publication served as something of an organizers' journal, linking together activists employed at diverse financial institutions. In the bulletin Kawabe criticized the mainstream left-wing position that opposed categorizing white-collar employees as "middle-class" workers. He argued that, rather than focusing on general class consciousness, one should emphasize lifestyle consciousness in examining the specific problems of white-collar workers. He contended that union activities centered on the workplace could not be sustained unless the diverse nature and the different stages of the struggle at the production site were recognized and unless each person's selfhood was fostered during the course of the struggle.[8]

Fujimoto Yutaka, a former member of the Chiba Bank Union and Kawabe's ideological foe, recalled, "While we were considering everything simply in terms of historical materialism, waving the red flag and shouting out commands, Kawabe—a young man steeped in literature—seemed to have been undergoing an agonizing, deeper search for the mode of living proper for the salary-man."[9] At regional banks in these years, union activism was on the rise and strikes were frequent. But Kawabe was cautious in drawing conclusions about the so-called militance of bank employees based on such trends; it seems as if he understood that his own bank's union, controlled by middle-level male employees, was taking a turn in the wrong direction.

❖ ❖ ❖

Here, I examine in greater detail this "wrong direction." My main source of information is the Fuji Bank Employees' Union's official twenty-year history, published in 1975.[10]

In 1956 the Fuji Bank Employees' Union, together with unions of five other major banks, withdrew from the All-Japan Federation of Bank Employee Unions (*Zenginren*), a broadly based postwar federation of workers in financial institutions. Instead, the Fuji Union helped organize the Federation of City Bank Employee Unions (*Shiginren*), composed exclusively of employee unions of Japan's largest banks, the so-called city banks. The "three basic principles" adopted by the new Federation were: (1) vertical organization (the direct linkage of enterprise-based unions to the Federation); (2) the recognition of union self-governance (that is, the freedom of each enterprise union to withdraw from any joint Federation-led action); and (3) emphasis on economic struggles. The net result was to create a new federation that was relatively weak, vis-à-vis member unions, and that did not engage political issues, such as the U.S.-Japan military alliance. This split from the older federation was the banking industry's version of the *mindō* movement, in which anti-Communist factions (called *mindō* in Japanese) split off from existing union locals or federations in the name of democratization. In other industries, many such splits occurred in the late 1940s, and in some cases the new unions ended up becoming quite militant. But the belated *mindō* movement of bank unions did not move to the left even once. Instead, it tightly embraced the principles of meek in-company unionism. This stance reflects at least two characteristics of finance industry workplaces: First, full-time union positions rotate among male employees who regard these posts as part of their bank careers, and second, the true "rank-and-file employees" were women who worked only until they married.

Firmly controlled by these careerist men, until 1962 the Fuji Bank Employees' Union constantly criticized even the modest wage demands of the new Federation of City Bank Employee Unions as too uniform and rigid.[11] And although the Fuji Union did take one "political" stand, approving a resolution opposing a 1958 bill to revise the Police Duty Law, it remained neutral in the 1960 Mutual Security Pact controversy.* (One of Kawabe's friends responded to his union's refusal to join the *Anpo* [security treaty] struggle by stashing his necktie and employee identification card in his desk and marching with the antitreaty demonstrators from his university.) The most significant characteristic of this enterprise-based unionism, however, was less its refusal to join political battles than the gradual atrophy of union resistance to the bank's policy of rationalization.

In January 1960 the employees' union at Fuji Bank concluded a new labor agreement. The agreement banned union activities during working hours and strengthened bank authority in personnel matters. In addition, it restricted the working conditions about which the union had the right to negotiate to just sixteen items. Although the employees' union also sought and obtained a new right to file grievances concerning personnel decisions and added some new items (such as days off and vacations) as collective bargaining issues, its right to intervene in personnel decisions and in matters involving the character of work was unquestionably weakened. The "sacred domain" of the bank's managerial authority expanded, and the limitations thus imposed on the union's function later began to cast a dark shadow over daily life in Fuji Bank's offices.

Through the 1950s the employees' union had still been dealing thoughtfully with a number of serious issues. Although it did not bring the matter to the table for collective bargaining, it did, for example, raise an issue that worried employees: whether an annual "office skills tournament" would not in fact be linked to merit ratings that influenced raises and promotions. Its stance on excessive overtime work, an issue that constantly plagued the workers, also reflected a conscientious specificity. The union proposed that maximum monthly overtime be twenty-five hours for men and twelve hours for women. But beginning in about 1962, when teletype

---

*A revised Police Duty Law was introduced to the Diet in 1958 by the Kishi Cabinet in an effort to give greater investigative authority to the police. Unions, student groups, and peace activists all saw this revision as an effort to suppress their movements and vigorously opposed it. They succeeded in blocking its passage. The security treaty struggle (the *Anpo* struggle) of 1960 was a movement of these same groups in opposition to the renewal of the U.S.-Japan Security Treaty, which, they believed, forced Japan to cooperate with America's strategic military objectives in the Far East. It was the occasion of the largest political demonstrations in Japanese history, but these could not prevent the government from pushing the renewal through the Diet.

machines were introduced throughout the bank, the union failed to produce specific responses to the bank's policy of rationalization. Fuji Union's
role shrunk to the confidential gathering of data by a "rationalization committee" that submitted opinions to management. Part of the context for this
retreat was a more permissive administrative policy adopted by the Ministry
of Finance (MOF), which opened the gates to a rationalization race among
banks.

There are no materials that reveal Kawabe's inner thoughts during this
period, but it appears certain that, in about 1960, he began to question the
concept that "a good bank employee means a good union member," and
he aligned himself with the radical left wing that confronted his union's
course head-on. In this year Kawabe wrote a "statement on wages" in
which he criticized both the policy of separate wage negotiations at each
bank and the imminent management drive to introduce a new "job wage."
Kawabe advocated united wage bargaining, to be led by the Federation of
City Bank Employee Unions together with the Federation of Regional Bank
Employee Unions. He planned to organize an *informal* study group using
his policy statement as the text. From the perspective of the union leaders,
this "informal" activity amounted to the formation of a dissident faction,
and as a result, Kawabe was never offered the chance to serve a stint as a
full-time union officer, even though this position typically rotated to each
male bank employee at about the time in his career when he was developing a self-awareness as a future manager. Despite his increased experience and age, Kawabe's union consciousness, reflected in his "wage statement," remained that of a member of the union's "Young Men and Women's
Department." His isolation from his age cohort of male employees had
begun.

In spring 1963, after a typical series of postings at three branch offices
in Tokyo in his first eight years with the bank, Kawabe was transferred to
an Osaka branch office, located in front of the railroad station in Dojima
District. He had married the younger sister of his hometown friend three
and a half years earlier, and he was now age thirty-four. Contrary to custom, only his friends in the union, not the branch manager or the Tokyo
bank's employees, saw him and his wife off at the Tokyo Station when he
transferred to Osaka.

Kawabe's Ordeal in the Late 1960s

The turning point in Kawabe's story comes during the period from 1966 to
about 1970. In these years the workplace history of the Fuji Bank and the
personal history of Kawabe Tomomi begin to overlap. Before I present an
examination of Kawabe's own trials, I must sketch some new developments
in the bank's personnel management in the 1960s, and the labor union's
response, keeping in mind the changes in the union already noted.

In February 1966, without any advance warning, Fuji Bank introduced a new personnel system with the goal of implementing what the bank called a fair pay system, which would reflect the demonstrated ability of workers and their contributions to building the bank's business. The system would divide bank employees into eleven categories, and associate employees (security guards, messengers, cleaning staff) into two categories, on the basis of their assessed ability to carry out their jobs. These categories were designed to reflect a standard bank employee's *position* and *qualifications*. Specifically, ordinary employees were classified as clerks, from first to fourth class. The position of deputy branch manager, which in other companies was occupied by the equivalent of the section chief, was classified as assistant superintendent. The department chief was designated as vice superintendent or superintendent (all of the employees just mentioned were union members). The deputy division chief was designated as vice councilor, and the branch manager was councilor or senior councilor. Those holding positions above these officers were bank directors or executives.

According to my interviews, there were about fifty personnel evaluation criteria considered in deciding on promotions to higher grades and offices. These criteria were not made public. It appears, however, that it was tacitly understood within the bank that a male employee with average ability could rise to second-class clerk in two years, third-class clerk in seven years, and fourth-class clerk in ten years. But in general, and particularly for promotion to ranks beyond this, length of service was not a decisive criteria.

According to the Fuji Bank Employees' Union's "Twenty Year History," the union pointed out three problems with this new personnel system. These points and the bank's response were as follows:

1. During the time of change-over to the new system, won't there be sex discrimination in assigning ranks? Response: In practice the majority of the female workers will be classifed as second-class clerks, but we will give them opportunities to develop their ability, so they can receive positive evaluations. Also, it is undeniable that in reality there are social restrictions that affect women's jobs.
2. The criteria for personnel evaluation should be made public. Response: This is not possible. We expect to maintain a fair system by training the evaluators and by conducting individual interviews.
3. Is the bank not required to win the union's agreement in order to adopt this system? Response: This system rationalizes personnel management, a matter that traditionally has not been included among the items for negotiation. Moreover, this system does not directly change working conditions. We only agree "to negotiate with the union when changes in pay scale are introduced."[12]

The union leaders were satisfied with the bank's explanation. But just three months later, this wonderfully understanding union found itself faced with a management proposal, in accord with the spirit of this new personnel system, to introduce a new wage system based on job ability and qualifications. The bank proposed dividing the existing pay system, mainly based on seniority, into two components: *base pay* that would remunerate "improvements in the individual's ability" and *qualification pay* based on the ability of employees to perform their present jobs. The pay differentials among employees at a given qualification level would diminish, but differences between levels would increase. Once this system was adopted, pay raises would be granted in two separate categories, and in both instances the amount would depend upon personnel evaluations.

What could the union's leaders do about this proposal? They had already agreed that they were not to intervene in personnel affairs, and they were not in any case opposed to "meritocracy" in the treatment of workers. After a two month "long-term struggle" that involved meetings at all branch offices, protest telegrams, regional demonstrations, resolutions, individual petitions, but no strike, the employees merely succeeded in restoring to a slight degree the seniority factor in pay raises, winning a small across-the-board raise for fourth-class clerks and associate bank employees, and gaining an overall raise of 9.1 percent. Satisfied with these gains, the employees' union agreed to accept the new pay system.

These new personnel and wage systems, premised upon confidential, multilevel personnel evaluations, were the catalytic elements driving almost all male bank employees to compete fiercely with each other to demonstrate their competence. They also served to divide employees and melt their opposition to other workplace rationalization measures, which were being issued in swift succession. As with so many Japanese workers in this period of rapid economic growth, a relationship of mutual reinforcement emerged between employees willing to compete over merit and ability and the union's cooperative stance in accepting rationalization policy and giving up its voice in matters of production and personnel management.

Looking back at its nominal struggle over the new pay system, the union's "Twenty Year History" concludes, "If it is true that the new, more meritocratic system directly weakened the union organization. . . then we must ask ourselves 'what has been the purpose of our twenty-year history?'. . . We would like to believe that after a long, painful struggle the organization in fact became much stronger."[13] This is an oddly fascinating statement. In a sense, the union organization did emerge stronger from this struggle, but it did so only by silencing the voice and suppressing the activity of clear-eyed activists who continued to criticize the new competitive system.

Clearly, it was to achieve this type of strength that the union in 1967 changed its electoral system. Instead of allowing its members to choose union representatives in multibranch, regional elections, the union now permitted employees at each branch to choose one representative. This action made it easier for the bank's branch managers to interfere, however. Further, union regulations were changed to enlarge the authority of the central committee as a decisionmaking body.

Many male employees adapted to the new conditions and focused on getting ahead in the bank. Those who worried about the negative impact of competition and rationalization upon daily life in the workplace became a minority, and a division among employees inevitably followed. The bank officials feared above all that a dissenting minority might encourage and bring to the surface the latent antirationalization sentiment of the female office workers, who constituted about half of the employees and who were upholding the enterprise at its base. For this reason the bank's managers discriminated against the union's minority faction in granting raises and promotions, with the goal of making them look undistinguished even in the eyes of the women employees, thus isolating the men and breaking their spirits.

Fourth-class clerk Kawabe, now in his mid-thirties, with over ten years of service, clearly faced a critical decision as these policies unfolded. He was a competent loan officer, and his own philosophy had led him to respect the legitimacy of "various lifestyles." So at this stage, he probably could have decided to throw in his lot with the majority with little difficulty; but Kawabe unhesitatingly took his stand with those who were discriminated against. His diary allows an examination of this decision.

❖ ❖ ❖

For the rest of his life, Kawabe Tomomi was a loving husband and father at home and a conscientious employee at work. Additionally, he was both a determined workplace activist who opposed the mainstream union leadership and a diligent student who pursued an antiestablishment logic, an unwavering admirer of those who devoted themselves to resistance. Although his emphasis varied over time, Kawabe never neglected any of these multiple aspects of his persona. One imagines that he derived pride and delight from keeping this balance, but this endeavor also clearly produced contradictions and grave psychological strain.

In the late 1960s, the burdens of work, which in later years were to weigh heavily upon him, were still manageable. During the busy season, when accounts had to be closed and preparations for auditors had to be made, he often returned home late at night; and when section meetings were held to make decisions on loans, he often felt the pressure of competition among banks, which drove Kawabe and other bank employees ever more intensely. But at this point, there is no mention in his diary of being "busy" or "exhausted."

Under these favorable circumstances, Kawabe fondly observed every move of his eldest son, Kōichirō, born in February 1965. He enjoyed leisure activities with his family and regularly commemorated special family events with celebrations at home. At the same time, he set for himself the task of "advancing as a bank worker–revolutionary proletarian," immersing himself in Marxian writings and taking copious notes. His interest lay in "the relationship between alienation and exploitation." He was instructed and moved by reading numerous works on this theme.[14] Believing that as a member of the masses he would gain something (*etwas*) in developing his self-awareness, he became an ardent reader of the works of Yoshimoto Takaaki. He was also deeply interested in theories dealing with the struggle over wages, an urgent practical issue for him.

Kawabe had already taken a stand with the anti–Communist party New Left. From about the end of the 1950s, Japanese Marxists split into two camps: the Old Left, which comprised the Communist party and left wing of the Socialist party, and the New Left, which rejected Stalinism, criticized existing socialist systems, and led the attack on the revitalized structure of Japanese monopoly capital. The lines of this split were not so clearly drawn in regard to the problems of labor in the workplace, however. Against the Communist party, which advocated solving such problems through political struggle, the left wing of the Socialist party (linked to the Sōhyō Union, or the General Council of Trade Unions of Japan) and part of the New Left stressed the need for workplace struggle launched by labor unions. Despite his anti–Communist party stance, Kawabe took the unusual course (for an activist of his position) of studying the writings on wages of Takagi Tokuo, a Communist scholar, which he compared to Kishimoto Eitarō's "Theory of Horizontal [cross-company] Wage Rates." Kawabe was searching for arguments to criticize the practice of job-specific wages.

Fortified by these studies, Kawabe became a high-spirited member of a circle critical of his union's course. He had always joined in office recreational activities and mingled socially with the main body of branch employees, and this helped him bring together a group of over ten fellow bank workers who were critical of the new personnel system, the new ability- and qualification-based pay system, and the new bonus system that linked bonuses completely to the bank's ability to pay. Kawabe's plan was to organize a "good conscience faction," a united front encompassing the Communist party faction and the New Left activists. It appears that Kawabe's group cultivated allies among union officers in the branch local and among local representatives to the enterprise-wide union assembly, and he pushed the branch local to criticize those at the enterprise-level union headquarters. Moreover, Kawabe admired and was drawn to the youthful energy of the women bank employees in his circle, Takaya Reiko and Kanō Fumiko.[15] These ties were clearly a source of strength for Kawabe, and they helped enable him to ignore the pressure brought to bear on him by the bank's middle management, as the ideological leader of his circle.

In November 1966, Kawabe tried to organize a companywide activist group at Fuji Bank. The reforms implemented by the union's cooperative mainstream leadership had aimed to tighten its hold over the members. These reforms were beginning to have an impact, and antimainstream activists were being targeted for frequent transfers. Feeling threatened, they agreed to Kawabe's proposal, and in July 1967 the new Fuji Bank Activist Workers' Group published the first issue of a pamphlet, *Tōron no Hiroba* [*Forum for Debate*] designed as a vehicle for activists at different branches to exchange information and express their opinions. The *Forum for Debate* was mailed or hand-delivered to trusted fellow workers, and Kawabe was one of the main writers. Thus commenced the struggle against the union's leadership.

The articles in each issue of *Forum for Debate*, all written with pen names to protect their authors from retribution, paint a vivid picture of the struggle of the minority faction as it demanded more vigorous, less centralized union activity focused on the work site.[16] They also depict the swift, unilateral advances of the rationalization program that completely transformed the Fuji Bank workplace in the closing years of the 1960s, while the employees' union lapsed into complete silence on operations and personnel issues. With the *Forum for Debate* pamphlets as the main source, one can analyze the changes in the bank's work and management policies that were the target of opposition by Kawabe and his colleagues; one can see how the forceful implementation of these changes eroded the Kawabe faction's resistance.

Several new policies of the Ministry of Finance served as background. In 1964 the MOF adopted a policy to accelerate the restructuring of financial institutions; in 1967 it began implementing uniform accounting standards; and in the following year it finally granted financial institutions the freedom to relocate branch offices. In line with these government measures, bank managers responded to the requirements of manufacturing industries at this time of extremely rapid growth. They tried to streamline their businesses and accumulate large amounts of capital in their banks. As a result, competition among financial institutions became ever more intense. Because the MOF still tightly regulated interest rates for deposits and loans, interbank competition could only focus on reducing the number of office workers and increasing each bank's share of savings deposits.

A technological development overlapped with these political and economic changes. Until the mid-1960s, data processing at the major city banks was based on an off-line system, and from about 1967 through the early 1970s the major banks shifted to computerized on-line data management. Fuji introduced an on-line, real-time data processing system for regular savings in 1967 and for fixed-time deposits the following year. In 1969 seventy-seven of Fuji's key bank offices were linked to a centralized data processing center. Compared to the old off-line operation, the new system required that female computer-terminal operators and tellers undertake simple tasks more accurately and more swiftly, at the computer's pace, and male workers now had to rush about more frantically than ever as salesmen. The numerous policies of rationalization adopted in this changing policy and technology environment were linked intimately. They instilled in the employees the determination to compete with other banks and work in a manner suited to the on-line system.

At Fuji Bank, the first step in the rationalization process was a program to mobilize employees more completely to achieve company objectives. As early as 1966, the bank introduced what it called "total employee planning," in which *all* workers engaged in sales activity. This was part of a campaign to "make every office a new office." When the union raised what it called "questions" about this policy, bank managers stated that participation was not compulsory—"We definitely will not establish individual employee sales quotas for savings accounts."[17] But these promises were often broken. In a few branch offices where the union was strong, some employees refused to fill out "introduction cards" with the names of acquaintances who could be asked to open savings acounts, but in most branch offices all the employees were given these cards and were forced to make the rounds to solicit depositors. In fall 1967 Kawabe wrote in *Forum for Debate,*

(In my branch office). . . beginning with the current campaign to collect promises from customers that they will deposit a portion of their bonuses with the bank, a qualitative change occurred in the "total employee planning" campaign. It was escalated to the point where a virtually complete quota system prevailed. A significantly increased number of people were mobilized, and the "posting of results" fostered a bourgeois-like competition among employees.[18]

This mobilization of employees became increasingly intense in 1968 with the start of a three-year plan to strengthen the organization, epitomized by the Much More Sales (MMS) campaign. The chief goals of the three-year plan were: (1) achieving a target of one trillion yen in individual deposits and 5 trillion yen for total deposits; (2) implementing staffing limits at each office and reducing hours-per-task by 20 percent; (3) reducing material costs; and (4) firming up the head office structure. To reach the first goal, the head office handed down the numerical target for deposit solicitation to each branch office, and the branch's managers set each individual employee's numerical goal.

In January 1969, one unionist presented the following "workplace report" to *Forum for Debate*:

The "project staffs" have to prepare a chart indicating results for the customers assigned to each [male] employee and enumerate the reasons for the increase or decrease in the number of customers solicited. Each employee has to visit 20 prospective clients each day and has a quota of 30 contracts for Diners Club credit cards. The [female] tellers have to obtain one fixed-term deposit each day, distribute calendars and other items, practice phrases of greeting during the morning assembly, strive to prevent customers from closing accounts, etc. All employees are forced to undertake these activities "voluntarily."

The report continues:

No matter how hard I try to catch up, my work piles up day-by-day. . . . Young workers are brainwashed to put in overtime without recording their hours. The ideological attack (against me) continues relentlessly. The other three people assigned to the project, upon hearing these attacks, proceed to enslave themselves even more. . . . A dark pall hangs over the entire office, like smog.[19]

These measures were not accepted entirely without resistance. Also according to *Forum for Debate*, the female employees at the Ashikaga branch office criticized the branch manager's disregard of the dividing line between public and private affairs and his excessive intervention in the private life of the employees, and they eventually staged their own protest without the formal help of the union. They carried out movements to "ignore the branch manager" and to "refuse clerical preparatory tasks prior to audits."[20] The Ashikaga women succeeded in stopping several practices: requiring all employees to undertake sales visits; requiring competition to solicit deposits; awarding special individual commendations to high achievers; and violating the legal limit on women's work hours. Yet the union officers and the male bank employees for the most part either stood on the sidelines or else openly criticized this truly necessary struggle. It is no surprise that the more typical form of "resistance" by female employees was to resign voluntarily. Quit rates among women in fact rose dramatically in these years.

The second feature of late-1960s rationalization woven into the three-year plan at Fuji Bank was a Taylor-like system to cut the number of hours per task. The bank's goal was to reduce workforce size by increasing work intensity by about 20 percent. To this end, managers introduced norms for the volume of office work. The bank undertook job analyses and time studies and surveyed the progress of employee skill acquisition. For example, in the I Branch Office, the Job Development Section videotaped and analyzed the work pattern of all the sections in the bank. With a ratio of one investigating official for every three employees, the surveyors analyzed the work routine of each employee minute-by-minute. They even calculated time spent away from the desk, including time spent in the toilet and at lunch. Thus, managers who complained, "The accounting department currently has 1.6 excess workers; why can't you finish your job by five o'clock?" were now supported by scientific data of a sort.

The union reacted calmly. "This new system is simply a clearer way of setting staffing levels. As for work load norms, we must adjust for imbalances in the employees' efficiency in the branch offices, and in any case the tightening of work rules is not a bargaining issue under the current labor agreement. Similar measures have already been put into practice in other banks, so we cannot object."[21] Such was the union's reaction! Yet reports of a more demanding work pace during this period are countless. Moreover, the drive for more systematic data processing led to increasingly intense pressure for employees to achieve a "no miss" job performance.

A third piece of the rationalization program was greater pressure to curtail recorded overtime. In 1965, the bank inaugurated a campaign to "finish work by five thirty," and in 1967–1968 this aim was tightened to "finish by five." Needless to say, the bank's goal was to save money on overtime. Soon enough, strict implementation of "finish by five" became one criterion in assessing each branch office's performance. But the workload was increasing at the same time. One "natural" outcome was a more intense before-five work pace and a change in the workplace atmosphere. Naitō Mitsuko of the Dojima branch office later testified as follows in support of Yonekawa Kiyoko's (her real name) suit against an unjust transfer (discussed later): "Criticisms about 'misses' became common in various sections. . . . People would accuse each other, saying it is your group's fault that we haven't been able to finish by five thirty. The atmosphere became heavy and unpleasant as people began to snap at one other."[22]

For male bank workers, another natural outcome was new worry about personnel evaluations, leading to the "voluntary" underreporting of actual overtime. Katayama Tetsuya, Kawabe's colleague, recalled the late-1960s situation in a 1982 publication.[23] Katayama was an officer in his branch union. One day he was called to a manager's office and asked to carry over his overtime hours to the following month because his overtime report for the current month was higher than expected. Katayama refused this request, and he was punished with negative marks in the next round of personnel evaluations for bonuses and pay raises. This much he was willing to endure; what crushed him was the attitude of his coworkers. They had promised each other to report their *actual* overtime hours, but Katayama now discovered he was the only one who had kept the promise. Further, the younger workers at other branches saw that Katayama, the oldest unranked bank employee and the object of criticism by supervisors, had recorded his actual overtime hours. They did nothing to defend him; however, these junior workers felt secure in using him for cover. They took Katayama's hours as a safe ceiling and submitted reports for overtime up to the number of his hours.

Regarding this incident, Katayama wrote, "I could not help but be shocked at the attitude of my junior coworkers who made no apologies to me. . . and remained indifferent to my being set up alone as management's target."[24] This is a crucial point. The competition among the workers had created a situation that enabled the bank to cover up actual overtime hours and that caused the "loyal" bank employees to calmly let the union activist stand alone. Katayama's painful recollection is the most telling evidence of the workplace changes that occurred during this period. From this time on, it became the common practice of "successful" employees to *underreport* the actual time spent on a job when they submitted overtime sheets.

In the final dimension to the rationalization drive of these years, managers took forceful steps to suppress unofficial union activities and the recruiting of new members to the dissenters' circle. For example, beginning at about this time, supervisors began relentlessly to question Kawabe's friends about when and where they met him (especially female employees, who could not be kept in line with threats of delayed promotion because they enjoyed no such prospect in the first place). The supervisors checked workers closely to make certain they did not have close ties with any "outside organizations," meaning so-called circle movements with links to the Communist or Socialist party and to groups with "questionable" ideology, such as *Rōen* (Workers' Theater) and *Rōon* (Workers' Concerts).[25] Some branch offices even had employees followed or had private detectives compile surveys on their behavior. Workers were required to submit detailed reports about the purpose of their vacations and personal trips. Both male and female activists in the union who criticized the bank's labor policy or the union's course were given undesirable transfers. The most likely targets were married, veteran women employees, who could speak up with real authority at a particular workplace and whose family obligations made moving impossible. When faced with a compulsory transfer, they had no choice but to quit.

In June 1968, one such activist, Yonekawa Kiyoko, brought a case against her transfer to the Tokyo District Court. Yonekawa had been reassigned from bank headquarters in Tokyo to the Yokohama Bank, about two hours' commuting distance from her home. She contended that her transfer was an arbitrary exercise of management authority, an unfair labor practice, and a violation of a woman's right to work. She asked that the transfer be rescinded. Before taking her case to court, Yonekawa had appealed to the union for help, but the union leaders were unsympathetic, claiming they could not challenge the bank's legitimate personnel authority and that a two-hour one-way commute was not unreasonable. Kawabe reacted quickly. He sharply criticized the union's passive stand and wrote a forceful essay in the September 1968 issue of *Forum for Debate,* full of specific ideas on how to overcome the union's position.

Although it took seven years, Yonekawa won her case, the first of its kind involving a major bank. Fuji Bank agreed to reassign her to the Fukagawa Branch, located at a more reasonable commuting distance, and the court awarded her a 2 million yen settlement. Many courageous witnesses testified during the suit, revealing the true state of affairs at the bank, including the increased workload, the manipulation of transfers in order to target activists, and personnel policies to deny women employees their menstrual leave.[26] In addition, one rally to support Yonekawa drew 2,300 workers from numerous banks. This support clearly encouraged the union's minority faction, but for the Fuji Bank this significant legal challenge by Yonekawa was ironically a golden opportunity to flush out her supporters so as to discriminate against them. Ultimately, the long struggle appears to have made conditions for Kawabe's circle even more difficult.

❖ ❖ ❖

From the late 1960s into the 1970s, Kawabe Tomomi's intellectual journey turned decisively toward the New Left. While he continued his reading of the young Marx, and, faced with the need to put his ideas into practice, read intensively about "contemporary industrial rationalization" and the restructuring of Japan's financial system, Kawabe during this period was most deeply engaged by the All-Japan Student Federation's (*Zengakuren*) struggle at Haneda Airport to prevent Japan's Prime Minister Satō Eisaku from visiting Vietnam (October, 1967). Following this event, Kawabe became especially interested in the reasoning and actions of the student movement and the antiwar faction of the labor movement, as manifested in Japan's anti–Vietnam War movement, the attempt to prevent America's nuclear-powered aircraft carrier *Enterprise* from entering Japanese ports, the destruction of the Asian and Pacific Council (ASPAC), and the international antiwar day (October 21, 1966) established by Sōhyō (the trade union council). He also entertained high hopes for the student struggles at Tokyo University.

Beginning in June 1968, students in the Tokyo University chapter of *Zengakuren* had occupied the centrally located Yasuda Lecture Hall, and it appeared that entrance exams for the following academic year would have to be cancelled. From January 18 through January 19, 1969, 8,500 riot police stormed the hall and ousted the students in a violent pitched battle. Kawabe's diary for January 19, 1969, reads, "Yasuda Hall has fallen. . . . My heart is overwhelmed." After this episode Kawabe began to read the works of various prostudent scholars.[27]

The fervent support offered by this bank employee in his late thirties to the student movement's All-University Joint Struggle (*Zenkyōtō*) was undoubtedly greater than the students manning the barricades could have imagined. Kawabe came to internalize the introspective slogans of the student movement circa 1969. Reflecting on his own job as a loan officer, for example, he said, "[I must] reject any qualities within me that harm others." Observing his surroundings at the workplace, he told himself to "seek solidarity but do not fear being alone."

Moved by such concerns, in these years Kawabe avidly read over ten magazines and newspapers regularly, including the *Asahi Journal* (whose editorial policies he regarded highly) and other publications representing both Old and New Left and factional and nonfactional circles. According to his diary, he was most critical of the Japan Communist party and the Revolutionary Marxist Faction (Kaku maru), but he regarded most highly the Marxist Students' League Hard-Core Faction (Chū kaku), which advocated daring battles in the streets.[28] By the beginning of 1960, the New Left had fractured into an array of groups commonly referred to as the "five currents and thirteen factions." Most influential among these were the Chū kaku faction and the Kakumaru faction, and the rivalry between them grew extremely bitter. But in hindsight, the differences in the ideas each group subscribed to and the tactics each utilized are so insignificant that the issue does not merit exploration.

Yet, because Kawabe continued to consider himself a worker fighting at the production site, he slowly began to derive ideas from the notion of "unity" demanded by the Communist Workers' party and from the "basic stand" of the workplace Antiwar Faction, which focused on the labor process where the everyday life of bourgeois society is enacted. As Kawabe came to recognize the contradiction that "those who are exploited also become the inflictors of harm," a lesson he derived from the All-University Joint Struggle movement, he paradoxically buttressed his determination to focus his energies on the production site. Thus, beginning in autumn 1969, he became drawn to tactics such as workplace rebellion, acquisition of power on the shop floor, and formation of a workers' council. In order to put these tactics into practice he concluded that a workplace antiwar movement at Fuji Bank had to be started with people who shared his views.

But in Japan, this moment when the New Left student movement and the antiwar labor movement reached their peak coincided precisely with the brilliant success of managerial reforms at big business production sites.

Kawabe continued his intellectual odyssey in the face of the bank's thorough implementation of the operations and labor management policies discussed earlier. Or perhaps it is more accurate to say that precisely because of the bank's thoroughgoing control, Kawabe devised a dreamlike agenda so that he would not be crushed under the system. Taking a hard look at the situation at the workplace, one finds that from about the time the Yonekawa litigation started, the energy of the dissenting circle of unionists at the Dojima Branch to criticize the union headquarters had just about disappeared, and Kawabe was virtually isolated. For example, at the special union meeting to consider calling off the 1969 pay raise struggle, the only person who spoke out critically was Naitō Mitsuko, who testified at the Yonekawa trial, and Kawabe cast the sole negative vote.

There are many reasons for the decline of branch office union activities. First, there was the simple but important fact that the employees were overburdened with soliciting deposits and meeting work quotas, so activists were unable to attend official union meetings or informal get-togethers. Kawabe's normal work load—which included submitting reports, balancing accounts, as well as preparing for the various audits by the Ministry of Finance, the bank, and the branch office head—had become heavier than ever. On top of that, he had to undertake additional work to assess and improve the branch office's financial situation, and he was required to attend frequent meetings to discuss ways to achieve Fuji Bank's goals. Kawabe often worked until 10 P.M.

Moreover, in June 1968 the bank had introduced a certification examination, and Kawabe had to prepare for it by reading a series of texts on bookkeeping, civil and commercial law, inheritance and gift taxes, financial analysis, business dealings involving bank drafts and checks, and more. Following this, for several months he had to prepare answers for a correspondence course sponsored by the National Bankers' Association. Strictly speaking, these business studies were not compulsory. But one must keep in mind that it was in 1968 that the chief and deputy chief of the personnel section began to conduct annual individual interviews of employees. These interviews provided the personnel managers in charge of employee evaluations with their most significant material. Topics of discussion included evaluation of general performance (meeting work norms); ability (knowledge of the job, attainment of recognized credentials); and attitude and personality (for example, employees' opinions on the Yonekawa trial). Needless to say, one's score on the business certification exam and a certificate from the National Bankers' Association correspondence course figured importantly in the ability portion of this assessment, and probably the attitude portion as well.

If pressures of the work itself constituted a general obstacle to employee participation in union activities, then additionally, the bank's personnel policy of identifying and exploiting the weaknesses of specific individuals compelled Kawabe's comrades to drop out of the activist circle one by one. First, in June 1967, Takaya Reiko, who had been recruited to the dissenting circle by Kawabe and had been the object of his admiration, cut her ties to Kawabe's group. She had been active in opposing the reduction in the number of typists, but it appears that she decided (or perhaps she was told by supervisors) that if she continued to fight for this cause, the future career of her fiancé, employed in the same workplace, would suffer. In September of the following year she resigned her job. Kawabe was "forlorn."

Next, in August 1967, Takemura Seiichi, a member of Kawabe's circle and a union representative from the branch office, was forced to resign his job on suspicion of embezzlement of bank funds. The true story is still not clear, but it appears that Takemura indeed had made personal use of bank funds, although he later returned the money. (One report is that the embezzlement was uncovered when his wife informed on him.) Also, Takemura had arranged use of a bank car to have an electric fan delivered to Kanō Fumiko's mother in the hospital. He then took the car on a drive (a fact uncovered evidently because he was being followed). The bank used these misdeeds to force the resignation of this activist. For some time after this, managers were able to use Takemura's case as an object lesson for the employees.

The Takemura case involved Kawabe's other "Tatyana," Kanō Fumiko; she was punished for her role by having her bonuses reduced, and she was removed from her job as teller. With the encouragement of Kawabe and others, she recovered temporarily from the shock of these events, and she even decided to become a candidate for the union's branch office committee. But for some reason she abandoned her candidacy and concentrated on taking care of her sick mother. Fellow activists, such as Naitō Mitsuko, tried to encourage her, but she began to consider their friendship a nuisance, and she left the battlefront. In July 1969 she resigned from her job. Kawabe recorded in his diary, "My thanks for seven years of hard work." In October 1970 Kanō wrote a letter to Kawabe, who had been transferred to Tokyo. She included in the envelope a copy of the magazine *Seichō no Ie*. This publication of a powerful "new religion" started in 1929 signalled Kanō's turn from activism concerning labor and social problems to religion for solace.

Kawabe faced other problems as well. In the context of the Fuji Bank, his stance as an anti–Communist party leftist put him on the margins of the activists opposed to the union's mainstream. His position was stubbornly to support a united front of all activists in the bank, even though his diary shows that he had given up hope on the Communist party. From about the summer of 1969 Kawabe was forced to disagree openly with Communist party activists who were beginning to emphasize legal tactics, such as the Yonekawa trial, at the expense of organizing in the workplace. At the National Meeting of Activists convened that September, his report was criticized as "overestimating the enemy's power." This repudiation served as a secondary cause for the gradual decline and inactivity of the Fuji Bank Activist Workers' Group and its *Forum for Debate* and of another ad hoc group called the "Kansai Meeting of Activists."

Despite the continual flow of events that tended to isolate him, this veteran, middle-aged loan officer did not abandon his resistance at the workplace. He encouraged his fellow activists not to abandon the struggle. Transcending his political disagreement with the Communist party group, he fully supported those who fought the bank's stringent surveillance and its retribution toward the supporters of Yonekawa's court battle. He frequently joined conferences to discuss measures to deal with the bank's repressive policies. In 1969 Kawabe, together with Naitō, persisted in trying to get the branch's union local to take up Yonekawa's cause. In March 1970 he wrote a recommendation on behalf of Naitō's candidacy for the branch's union committee. When the union's election administrators attempted to remove from Naitō's statement of candidacy any reference to the Yonekawa case, Kawabe sharply criticized the union for violating the members' freedom of election. He thus challenged the "single-party regime" electoral system that prevailed in practice. Even as the bank was targeting supporters of the Yonekawa litigation, and despite his criticism of the Communist party, Kawabe did not hesitate to support Naitō fully, although Naitō had testified on behalf of Yonekawa at the public trial and was considered a Communist party supporter. In addition, at meetings of the branch's union, Kawabe pointed out the huge lag in pay increases given to dissenting union activists. Kawabe put all his strength into these kinds of stressful frontal attacks at the workplace.

By this time, however, Kawabe and his allies had been isolated to such an extent that the union easily ignored even their most legitimate criticisms. The ultimate cause of this turn of events was the successful rationalization of operations and labor management at Fuji Bank, begun in 1966 and made possible by the union's retreat from any attempt to regulate the work process or personnel management.

Male bank employees had committed themselves to competing to prove their adaptive ability and merit, thus following the route to company-defined success and advancement. Female workers had meekly submitted to the constraints of semiskilled labor, until quitting at marriage. Their routine labor was required by the on-line data processing system deployed by bank capital. At the same time, for this system not to demoralize the male or the female workers, managers had to unite employees in fervent support of the bank's objective: triumph in interbank competition. It was easy for managers to justify a few dirty tricks to suppress employees who refused to unite behind corporate goals that required alienation of and competition among workers.

Kubota Tomoko wrote in the January 1969 issue of *Forum for Debate*: "We are all fragmented in the workplace. Our solidarity in recent days is particularly weak. No matter what we do, most people do not join us. We have much that we would like to say. But there is no place to express our views. We don't know what to do. . . . This is because most people want to run away from the gloomy workplace as soon as possible."[29] It is important to note that many employees in Japan, not just the *Forum for Debate* dissidents, felt isolated at work. The new management system and changed working conditions had eliminated any margin for relaxation from workplace life.

In general, human relations among the bank employees were atomized, as can be seen in evidence presented by Okonogi Keigo, a psychiatrist in charge of mental health at the Fuji Bank health management center. He stated that an initial "drastic increase in the number of patients" occurred about 1967–1968, just the time when the rationalization program had increased the workload. He further noted that these were also years of frequent personnel transfers, when "human relations were shallower. . . and the workplace environment changed completely." A second surge in patients came in the years 1973–1974 when, in addition to a new round of transfers, the "image of the bank employee changed to that of salesman" and "many people could not adjust to this situation."[30] In sum, a world of labor in the workplace that managed to slightly distance itself from the logic of the enterprise had somehow survived from the 1950s to the mid-1960s; but in the face of rationalization, this world collapsed.

A Course Burdened with Contradictions

In September 1970, Kawabe Tomomi was transferred back to Tokyo after seven years in Osaka, and he began work at Fuji Bank's branch in Bakuro-chō. The following April he settled into a new home in suburban Ageo City, outside Tokyo. For thirty-nine-year-old Kawabe, both the pleasures and the worries of his life away from the bank increased. Soon after putting up his new home, he was dragged into a dispute with the builder over responsibility for repair costs due to damage from rain leakage. In addition, troubles among relatives continued for a year before his aged mother happily agreed to live with him. But his heaviest psychological burden was the genetic heart defect of his oldest daughter, Makiko, born in April 1969. As Kawabe noted in his diary, she was later diagnosed as suffering from "right heart defect accompanied by the four Fowler symptoms," or "dislocation of the large aorta." She had frequent colds, ran high fevers, and vomited, and her parents worried greatly. Kawabe's wife, Kazuko, became a member of the Society to Protect Children with Heart Disease.

Yet it appears that, beginning in these years, Kawabe truly enjoyed the time he could spend with his family. He wrote frequently in his diary about watching his children grow up, about conversations with his wife, and about the pleasure of having dinner or taking excursions with his family. Kawabe never failed to jot down his relief when a family member recovered from even the slightest ailment. In particular, he felt special concern and love for his fragile daughter, Makiko, and tears welled up in his eyes when she would call out something like "Look, there is a rainbow."

Beginning in the mid-1960s Kawabe's diary shows occasional entries stating "complete rest today." He worked in the family's garden and played catch with his son, Kōichirō. The plot of land that he purchased in 1968 came to 75 *tsubo* (1 *tsubo* equals 3.3 square meters), including a private path. One after another he planted trees, including hemp-palm, boxwood, plum, cherry, and peach, and he even planted grape vines. In 1973 he recorded for the first time "Our own grapes!" He enjoyed painting the house and watering the grounds. Beginning with volume nine of his diary, which starts on September 1972, Kawabe ended his practice of pasting photographs of innocent-looking young actresses on the covers of his note-books. His farewell to young comrades in Osaka at the end of the 1960s and his transfer back to Tokyo marked the end of his protracted youth. This self-styled "revolutionary proletarian" discovered life as an ordinary father and fully enjoyed a brief golden age as a homebody.

Kawabe allowed himself "to rest and relax completely" in these years, in part due to frequent health problems caused by fatigue. From about this time he experienced trouble with chronic high blood pressure. He caught frequent colds and often purchased "Pablon Gold," an over-the-counter cold medication. The cause of this fatigue and exhaustion was, of course, his continually increasing workload at the bank. As the 1970s progressed, in his diary entries he would increasingly record nothing but "busy" or "tired" for three days in succession. His notations indicated that his average overtime stint lasted until after 9 or 10 P.M. and that he frequently did not reach home until 11 P.M. The entries in which he took the trouble to empha-size that "I had a leisurely talk with my wife," or "I had supper at home for the first time in a long while," or, most notably, on December 31, 1971, "I finished work at seven. Got home at 8:40, [and] managed to catch the [tra-ditional New Year's Eve] TV show 'Red vs. White Songfest'" show us how rare such pleasures were.

During the recession that began in 1975, work in the Fuji Bank loan department grew busier than ever. This resulted, no doubt, both from pres-sure on all the branch offices not to let Sumitomo Bank surpass Fuji and from the bank's urgent need for aggressive lending in new fields to over come the capital glut caused by stagnant investment in industry. This situ-ation placed special pressure on the loan department. Out of exhaustion, Kawabe frequently lost his appetite as well as the "energy to read books." And yet, his diary entry for July 1 reveals that the pressure continued: "This month's quota of loan reports is already set at 19." To make matters worse, in the early 1970s National Railroad workers often went on strike, and Kawabe, who commuted by train from Ageo, had to stay over at a hotel near the bank on these occasions.

❖ ❖ ❖

The entries of the early 1970s were written on the eve of the second stage of technological innovation at Fuji Bank. A comprehensive on-line com-puter system was about to be introduced by which calculations involving savings accounts, automatic transfer of funds, and activity concerning checking and loans were processed in a fully integrated manner using indi-vidualized customer data. The bank's ability to facilitate computerized data processing by unilaterally imposing ever more intensive labor seems to have reached a limit. Fuji instead sought to inculcate in workers a will to strive "voluntarily" for objectives defined with greater numerical precision than ever. In spring 1969 Kawabe had published an essay in *Forum for Debate* pointing out that a business technique called management-by-objective was now the core bank policy to control its employees. In my opinion, the banking industry moved toward so-called voluntary goal-setting more rapidly than other industries for two reasons: the male bank employees' sales activity outside the office was not clearly defined, and the bank's ability to control every little detail was limited; yet the results of the employees' work could be measured directly in monetary terms. In effect, what emerged was a policy of forcing the employees to achieve a certain monetary quota. But this coercive policy was defined as "voluntary work" because it involved employee self-reporting of their activities and results.

Saitō Shigeo's investigative report, *After Me, the Deluge*, contains abundant examples of bank work under this new regime, in early 1974.[31] He described the job of teller as being as simple and dull as working on a conveyor belt. The teller's work pace was rigidly fixed by the capacity of the machines being used. As part of a "no mistakes campaign," a chart was posted listing the percentage of mistakes made by each individual. At a Mitsui Bank branch, each work group set deposit targets, and the result of each individual's success in soliciting deposits from clients was diagrammed for all to see on a chart, which boasted that the entire united body of employees had achieved "a perfect record for three consecutive quarters" in making the quota of new accounts.

At Fuji Bank, the entire bank's quota for soliciting depositors was divided into shares allocated to each branch office, where each deposit officer was required to set his own semiannual quota. The officer's supervisor then made some "adjustments" and assigned each person a quota for the period. The new quota was usually 10 to 20 percent greater than the actual results of the previous period. Once a month the branch prepared a summary account for which employees had to report their progress. Some branch offices divided all their personnel into small teams, cutting across departments, and had them compete to gain the greatest number of accounts. The results were then made public at the following day's morning assembly. Each team was to sing a "fight song" such as "selling with a one-two punch!" Of course, the bank took account of both an employee's gung-ho spirit and the actual results in individual performance evaluations. Saitō claimed that the cumulative effect of divergent ability performance ratings upon the annual salary of two university graduate employees with eighteen years seniority, one a high-flyer and the other still an unranked employee, could be as much as a two million yen differential. One of Saitō's informants as he prepared his book was Kawabe Tomomi, and one can say that Kawabe's exposé of the bank's practice was one of his most significant activities.

Throughout his career Kawabe worked as a loan officer. The setting of excessive quotas for new depositors did not affect the loan officers directly, as it did the deposit officers, but as a result of some particular banking practices it no doubt imposed a heavy indirect burden. First, unless the person or business firm that contracted for a loan took out the money in one lump sum, the balance of the authorized loan remained as a deposit account in the lending bank. Also, banks customarily required borrowers to maintain restricted-use "compensatory deposits" of a fixed amount as the condition for providing a loan. Such practices willy-nilly involved the loan department employees in the drive to increase deposits for the bank. Moreover, the bank frequently mobilized "all-employee sales drives" that included loan officers in soliciting depositors.

And yet, a curiosity remains about many aspects of Kawabe's work. How did he evaluate his primary job, that of loan officer? Apart from his clear unhappiness at the workload, what did he think of his job in the loan department, which placed him at the frontline of the bank's profit-making activities?

For example, did Kawabe Tomomi consider his job, one that required him to pass judgment after meticulously analyzing the business activities of the loan applicants, to be interesting? As the final decision concerning all loans was actually made by the head of the branch office, did Kawabe ever agonize over the fact that as an ordinary employee, he had very little decisionmaking power? Did he believe that his job left him any room for maneuvering to, in some measure, curb the logic of capital? For instance, did he ever think that he, as a worker on the frontlines, might be able to restrain, if only slightly, the actions of a bank that had a firm policy of loaning to corporations that enforced a stringent labor policy, or to restrain loans to big businesses that profited by causing environmental pollution or manipulating market prices? Kawabe's diary is completely silent on these questions. Especially in the 1970s, when he mentioned almost any business activity he simply recorded the epithet "Nonsense!"

Kawabe was a meticulous worker. Reportedly, his "draft proposals for loans were written on the basis of meticulous analyses of the companies that the bank dealt with," and they were therefore often used as "fine teaching materials" for younger, less-experienced employees.[32] What then did he mean when he called these activities "nonsense?" I wish I could have questioned Kawabe about this, but to shed light on these questions I have only his very brief comments at a panel discussion recorded in the five-hundredth issue of RIBE's *Forum* in early summer 1972.

The key point of this fascinating discussion, intended to explore the relationship between the way finance industry workers lived and the substance of their work, is the significance and limitations of the "specialist" role. One of Kawabe's fellow workers argued, "So long as we have qualifications worthy of a specialist, our right to a voice on business policy issues is likely to increase." This man claimed that if a worker in the loan department attempted to withhold loans to "merchants of death" or "businesses that pollute the environment"—and the bank was forced to accept this because that employee's ability as a worker could not "be dispensed with"—then that person's "power as an individual [can come] to life even in the capitalistic bank. Is this not the case?" Kawabe replied that in the future such efforts to be discriminating in selecting loan recipients should be "extremely important as a basic principle in our lives as white-collar workers."[33] But he pointed out that at that time a loan officer could not develop the capacity to make critical judgments concerning loans, could not that is, become a specialist in the first place without accepting the bank's business logic.

Regrettably, the exchange did not progress beyond this point, but it appears that Kawabe's strategy was to induce bank employees to indict unfair bank policies from within. When in June 1971 the women office workers of the Showa Electric Works (Shōwa Denkō) exposed their own company's responsiblity in the Niigata mercury poisoning case, Kawabe noted in his diary how deeply impressed he was.[34] Perhaps his comments during this 1972 *Forum* panel reflect the impact of this incident. But even so, the question remained as to how bank workers should conduct themselves in their daily routine on the job. "After all, I work because I must do so to eat. But the company that I work for has many problems. . . . Sensing these contradictions in my life I turn to literature, but I still plod along under these conflicting pressures without defecting from the cause."[35]

Three months later Kawabe was to learn how difficult it was for a single employee to expose his company when it became necessary to do so. In September 1972 Kawabe worked overtime for six days to prepare a prospectus for a certain trading company, in essence a plan to rescue its failing business. "To succeed, this prospectus requires the company to make good on a plan to fire 100 persons. And I wrote it. And probably they will be fired! I did not initiate an 'exposé.' Should I have done so? Was I right not to?"

Theorizing is always easier than practice. Keeping this in mind, perhaps one can say that, at this stage, those who were active in the bank industry's labor movement needed a theory of a transitional process that might bridge the deep gulf that existed between veteran bankers' enjoyment of a certain degree of power inherent in their work and the need to reclaim the social meaning of this work. The heart of this theory of a transition process must be a concrete analysis of the possibilities that exist for a group of unranked employees—who have accumulated considerable work ability through long experience—actually to encroach upon the decisionmaking authority that they cannot formally wield without managerial status. Without such a vision, it would be difficult to win over ordinary bank workers (who could only try to find meaning in their work by gaining some degree of status and power) to the idea of curbing the competition to "get ahead."

Moreover, the only way to win over the transitory female employees would have been for the women's liberation movement, just then emerging, to permeate the workplace. The movement's agenda had to be that of creating a new lifestyle that could allow office women to claim stable positions in the workplace and organically link these positions to a collective endeavor to expand women's decisionmaking power in their daily work. Finally, such a theory needed a strategy for changing labor unions into entities that could concern themselves with issues of work itself and the mutual relationships of male and female employees.

The discussion session recorded in the five-hundredth issue of the *Forum* did question the nature of bank employees' work. But as throughout the postwar era, well into the 1970s left-wing thinking tended to remain relatively indifferent to several critical issues: the stratification of work itself within the working class; the relationship between authority and meaningfulness in performing work; the effect of competition on human relations; and the expansion of the concerns of labor unions beyond bread-and-butter unionism. The persistence of this traditional left-wing perspective would appear to explain the fact that serious debates of tough-minded activists, like those of the *Forum* group, stopped short of such theoretical advances.

At such a moment, what was Kawabe trying to learn anew, or learn for the first time, as he still conscientiously soldiered along at his job without abandoning his confrontation with bank capital?

❖ ❖ ❖

Except for his days off, Kawabe could only eke out time for reading in the early morning, on his way to work, and late at night. This period never came to more than ninety minutes at a stretch. Thus he probably never finished reading the many books and articles frequently mentioned in his diary. However, the themes that interested him and the books that impressed him in the first half of the 1970s reveal his strenuous search for ideas that might sustain him as a critic of the existing system.

To begin with, he read about major current events such as the international currency crisis of the "Nixon shock," bank mergers, environmental pollution trials, the Sayama affair,* and the Solzhenitsyn affair. He con-

---

*In 1963, in the Sayama affair a *burakumin* youth was accused and convicted of the kidnap-murder of a high school girl. The *burakumin* were an outcaste class in early modern Japan. Liberated by law in the 1870s, the *burakumin* remain subject to widespread informal discrimination to this day. The Burakumin Liberation League claimed the young man was innocent but was charged and convicted because he was a *burakumin*. Eventually (1992), the trial result was overturned and he was declared innocent.

tinued reading New Left newspapers and magazines, but the New Left movement itself was plainly deteriorating, as revealed in incidents of internal violence, lynchings within the Japanese Red Army, terrorist killings in the Tel Aviv Airport, and a bombing of Mitsubishi Heavy Industries' corporate headquarters. These events deeply depressed Kawabe. This middle-aged man's unusual support of extremist factions finally came to an end with the Asamayama Villa affair, in which a radical Communist group holed up in a lodging at Mount Asamayama after engaging in internecine killings. After this incident, Kawabe gradually stopped reading factional literature and returned to the theoretical study of Marxism, and such works continued to be his favorite readings for the remainder of his life.[36]

During this period Kawabe also read the works and reviews of liberal or leftist Japanese literati and critics, past and present.[37] Futabatei Shimei and Nakano Shigeharu, in particular, had been Kawabe's favorite writers since his twenties. Kawabe, who had endured over ten years of bitter struggle with the capitalist institution of the bank, looked anew to these writers for guidance and encouragement after he entered his forties. A human being can only live in accordance with the reality imposed on him, he felt, but like Futabatei one had to continue moving forward, however awkwardly and clumsily. Also, his interest in Japan's modernization was rekindled by the best-selling works on historical fiction of Shiba Ryōtarō. Yet he showed primary concern not for the elder statesmen of Japan's modern revolution who were featured in Shiba's work but instead hoped to grasp an image of the masses in Japan's modern history. After 1973 he continually reread several academic works that sought to recreate the spiritual or cultural world of common Japanese people in the nineteenth and early twentieth century.[38] Kawabe was searching for keys to transform the consciousness of the Japanese masses. He also came across my writings in the first half of the 1970s.

At about the time of the discussion in the *Forum*, Kawabe was desperately seeking a foundation for his ideas concerning work at the production site, but he had no confidence in this possibility. Hence, he continued, in his words, "the clumsy march forward along a path woven of failures and revivals and filled with the twists and turns of reality." He returns home late after working overtime and drinks sake alone from a ricebowl. He is still bitter about the "humiliations" endured at the workplace. He reads the poems of Nakano Shigeharu, whom he admires immensely. Then his spirit is uplifted and he feels better and thinks he will continue his resistance steadily and conscientiously.

Also, every day during September 1972 he read my *Restoring Human Rights to Labor*.[39] He wrote in his diary, "This book arouses the lethargic worker, strengthens his body and toughens his backbone so that he will be able to brush aside the sparks from the flame." In this book I analyzed the alienation, discrimination, and managerial control that characterized the

Japanese workplace of the early 1970s and discussed the need and possiblity for labor unions to go beyond merely "bread-and-butter issues" to carry on their fight to change this shop floor situation of both existing capitalist and socialist systems. I also referred to the theory of a transition process, introduced here previously. I doubt that Kawabe, who was still a rather orthodox leftist, would have accepted my position fully, for it is not very loyal to a Marxian analytic tradition.

According to Kawabe's diary, however, because he believed that there was no guarantee that the humanistic qualities of labor could be recovered automatically, even if a political revolution were to take place, he saw in the thesis of this book (which held that under the existing order of things unionism must exercise its wisdom and power to better the daily routine of ordinary workers) a way to strengthen the backbone needed by workers. It may be conceited to think this was the case, but *Restoring Human Rights to Labor* probably enabled Kawabe to visualize to some degree the meaning of stubbornly persisting at the production site, which he had only abstractly perceived until then. It may also have suggested strategies for carrying on a struggle there.

In August 1973 Kawabe touched upon the theory of "civil war" presented in the Chūkaku faction's newspaper, *Zenshin* (Advance). He indicated doubts about the thesis presented there, which was that "a revolution in an administered society must take the form of 'a civil war,'"[40] and he recalled my theory about "construction step by step of a steady, solid movement with work as the starting point."[41] According to an entry in his diary in January 1974, "I reaffirmed my stand as a revolutionary romantic. . . . It is necessary to establish firmly work as the basic perspective—join the 'labor' union movement." As for the route to "join" the movement, he had not decided whether to follow "Mr. Kumazawa's line of labor unionism" or to organize a new group that had cut its ties with the "antimainstream faction" within the existing union organization. Then, in 1975, as an extension of this line of thinking, he began to think that a system of "workers' self-management" that struggles against control by technocrats was the true stance of socialism. Such was the position he had reached at this time.

❖ ❖ ❖

The final noteworthy aspects of Kawabe's life in the early 1970s concern his union activities at the Bakuro-chō branch office and his ties to his activist comrades. In contrast to his Osaka years, in this period the pressures of work, fatigue, and a shrinking circle of comrades did not allow Kawabe to carry on his union activities continually. Still, there are two incidents worth noting.

First, in January 1973, Fuji Bank set a thirty-hour-per-month limit on overtime and announced that branch offices whose actual working hours exceeded this would be eliminated from consideration for general awards. Specifically, this meant that each branch office at the beginning of each period had to prepare an "administration chart," noting overtime estimates for those with managerial positions, and for male clerks, female clerks, and general workers. The main office would evaluate the branch manager's performance by comparing actual (reported) hours to these initial estimates. This was an "overtime budget system," designed to enforce a "system of finishing by five." In addition to a tighter work pace between nine and five, one inevitable result would be increased pressure on employees to put in unreported "service overtime."

To fulfill his duties, Kawabe had no choice but to work overtime until 9 or 10 P.M., day after day. Toward the end of 1972, at a meeting of the branch union, he criticized union headquarter officials for their inaction in the face of this impending policy. Further, at a meeting of loan officers he argued heatedly with management staff who were trying to enforce the overtime restriction policy. But Kawabe was already a "known trouble-maker" who had been advised by the management staff to refrain from such union activities if he wanted to be promoted, and he was unable to find any fellow workers in the branch who would join this battle. Further, one can see his isolation in that, in contrast to his previous assignment at the Dojima Branch, he never served as master of ceremonies at Christmas parties or took part in recreational trips while he worked at the Bakuro-chō Branch. The situation for middle-aged activists in other branch offices was more or less the same; bank employees had no choice but to submerge their grievances. (The pressure of this overtime budget system still weighs heavily over daily workplace life at Fuji Bank even in the 1990s.)

Also in these years, Kawabe often attended meetings of activists in the Tokyo-Yokohama region, and at these gatherings his conflict with the Communist party circle deepened. First, in 1972 and 1973 he refused repeated invitations to join the Party. This may have been largely due to information he had gleaned from his studies, but his criticism of the Communist party focused not only on its political strategy and party line but also on its theory of workplace union activity. After these continued refusals, Kawabe rarely attended meetings led by the Communist party faction. But to the extent possible, he supported and cooperated with Party activists, such as Kawada Minoru, whom he knew from their days of "united front" activities in Osaka. He shared the activists' anger and vehement opposition to union and managerial suppression of workplace dissenters, and he was consistent from first to last in opposing any "Red purge."

Second, in June 1975, toward the end of an unusually prolonged spring wage offensive, Kawabe castigated the headquarter organizers who were working to bring negotiations to a close and called on them to take more vigorous initiative to revive the labor movement. The next month, the daily frustration of the bank workers in the Bakuro-chō Branch boiled over in response to the resolution of this wage dispute. At the Bakuro-chō Branch union's July meeting, the settlement proposed by the executive committee at union headquarters failed to pass, with just eighteen yes votes versus thirteen no votes and thirteen abstentions. The manager of the branch office was shocked by this unprecedented division in the union and managed to postpone the next union meeting until after the bank's summer evening party. Then he evidently set out to win over the abstainers. (Although it may seem surprising, the fact is that many of the largest banks in Japan hold purely formalistic elections to select new union officers who have actually been hand-picked by managers of the bank. With the control that branch managers thus exert over the union, they can also intervene in the planning of its events and activities.)

Kawabe continued his battle by writing an essay criticizing the union and its most recent wage struggle and by seeking to publish it in the union paper. This action, in effect, amounted to a "struggle to democratize the union newspaper," and Kawabe proposed creating a combat operations committee of activists, both Communist party and anti-Party factions. He submitted his essay on August 20, 1975, but the editorial section of the union headquarters delayed responding, and, on September 22, finally refused publication. In early October, Kawabe's last battle ended with a heated argument with the union officers. This was a week after the Yonekawa suit was settled out of court in a compromise favorable to the plaintiff. In his diary one finds only a pasted-in article from the Communist party paper, the *Red Flag*, and no comment on this victory.

On the day of his final argument with the union officials, Kawabe was accompanied by Watanabe Hitoshi from his workplace. Since early 1974, Kawabe, Watanabe, and several other bank employees had been meeting occasionally at a members-only club in Roppongi, opened by a former salary-man at a company with which they had done business. He had organized the club "to escape the life of a salary-man," and at this site Kawabe and others formed the "Club on the Margin" to "talk about poetry while drinking good liquor." Kawabe's friends recall that he seemed to enjoy getting together with his female and male coworkers of all different ages and talking about poems that he loved. Though this club was certainly somewhat different from the "chatter-box club" that he had participated in in the late 1950s in the night-shift room, for Kawabe it no doubt meant the rediscovery of an intimate circle of friends from work.

The people in the Club on the Margin were probably not militant activists, but several of them, including Watanabe, wrote touching recollections of Kawabe. For example, according to Shijima Kōichi, "Because Kawabe-san was an extreme purist in the pursuit of ideals based on his readings, at times he was feared by some people as a radical theorist, but on the other hand he was extremely sensitive and he looked after his junior colleagues in a very thoughtful fashion."[42] And a young woman office worker, Aoki Yumiko, wrote that when she happened to be reading a book, Kawabe would speak to her about the author, revealing that "he knew something about a host of issues"; and as a result, she said, "I fooled myself into believing that I was always reading important works." Recalling these thoughts upon hearing of Kawabe's death, she remembered deciding that she "must really do some serious reading from now on."[43]

With Kuwano Atsuko, a younger graduate of Kawabe's university as well as a member of the Club on the Margin, Kawabe had a delicate, emotional, but distant relationship. Kawabe, who was forty-three years old at the time, was delighted that there was a youthfulness in him that caused him to be "attracted" to her, but he no longer sought to draw Kuwano into the antimainstream movement in a passionate fashion, as he once had done with Takaya Reiko. It seems that Kuwano was a refreshing presence who encouraged the worn-out Kawabe from afar in the last years of his life.

Last Years

At the end of January 1976, Kawabe Tomomi was reassigned to the Kanda branch office as team leader of the loan department. He wrote in his diary, "This is also OK." Perhaps he was thinking of the need to keep an appropriate distance between Kuwano and himself. But this turned out to be a year in which the heavy demands of his job made him a workaholic.

Kawabe's family life was happy. In 1974 his daughter Makiko spent five weeks in a hospital undergoing physical examinations, but she entered the first grade despite her physical weakness, and she often wrote letters to her father, who would read them after he came home late at night. He found it relaxing to talk with his wife for about an hour before going to bed. During train strikes, his wife drove him to and from the office. And Kawabe was also able to continue his studies, though at a slower pace. During this period he enjoyed reading a wide range of fiction and nonfiction, and he gave particular attention to Tatehara Masaaki's novels because Tatehara was Kuwano's favorite writer.[44]

But the time he could spend with his family or reading was extremely limited. Every morning he left his house at 6:45 and did not usually return home until about 11:00 P.M. In this one year (1976), the entries in his diary in which he mentions being busy because of work and being exhausted increased greatly. There are over fifteen periods during which the only notations for three to five days in a row are "busy" or "tired." On the job, an additional assignment called "investigative duty" was introduced, and in September, five new client companies were added to his workload. Here are some of his diary entries during this period:

May 21: Work. Many unpleasant matters. June 17: I doggedly confront those who drive me on so cruelly. August 13: I am tired. I continued working by skipping lunch but I cannot digest the work that has piled up sky high. October 28: Busy. I don't feel well because of a cold. But I clenched my teeth and continued working. Returned home at 9 P.M. Felt relieved. I debated whether I should have some *sake* or not but decided against it.

These days continued, leaving him isolated at the workplace and separated from his friends in the Club on the Margin.

Inevitably, his health broke down. In February and November 1976, he felt heavy pressure on his chest. The diagnosis was a weak heart, and the doctor prescribed medication. The record of his high blood pressure was: January, 170/112; March, 171/111; June, 160/111; and in August it finally came down to 150/104. Following this episode, he was troubled with chronic "borderline high blood pressure." He often caught colds that dragged on, and his appetite was poor. After enduring an especially busy year-end period, he wrote on New Year's Eve, "I really worked hard this year." But on the second day of the New Year, 1977, he had a fever of 104 degrees and could not get out of bed. Kawabe had a kidney infection and was bedridden for three weeks.

❖ ❖ ❖

January 1977 saw publication of the six-hundredth issue of RIBE's *Forum*. Kawabe had been constantly involved with this endeavor since the late 1950s, the point at which he began to question the slogan of the official union journal: "A good bank employee is a good union member." Toward the end of 1976 he was asked to write an article for *Forum*, so despite his busy schedule he took up his pen for the first time after a long hiatus. His essay warmly thanked the *Forum* for having encouraged him to travel "the long path that led [him] to achieve the self-awareness that [he is] a worker. . . working at a production site called 'bank.'" Then he continued, "to sustain the life struggle to sublate [*aufheben*] this awesome reality is truly an exhausting task."[45] Kawabe used as a reference point a theory of an "encroaching" unionism that seeks "to take over management's 'sacred' prerogatives by extending union activity into control of work on the shop floor."

> I ardently desire to bring order out of the massive notes that I have kept during the past decade and longer, to profoundly apprehend at each decisive point the history of our union, which reached its thirtieth anniversary in 1976, and to consider what kind of organization it must never become, if it is to indeed be a labor union "of bank workers, by bank workers, and for bank workers." By investigating this problem, I hope to be able to clarify the type of organization it ought to be. Mr. Nakaoka Tetsurō states that "only the sharp tension between the desire to establish solid ties with labor and the thinking that denies that labor is also the starting point of alienation which will allow us to sustain a movement to liberate ourselves

from alienation." As one of those who was formerly called a member of the "self-reliance faction" [in a 1958 dispute Kawabe was labeled as such], I would like to assert that what Mr. Nakaoka said can be realized at the site of bank workers' [daily activity] only by the kind of investigative process I propose."[46]

Even though Kawabe was in his sickbed through most of January, and especially because he recently had not had time to carry on his studies, he was eager to continue his inquiry and build his conceptual framework. From about January 11, after his fourth round of kidney dialysis, Kawabe began to read and take notes like a man possessed. But this effort to "revive" himself was his last concerted effort to further his learning. At this time as he studied theories of labor unions, he reread my *Restoring Human Rights to Labor* and compared it with the the Japan Communist party line. He also investigated political discourse by examining Muto Ichiyo's essay in *Tembō* (Prospect) and comparing it with the writings in the *Chūkaku* faction's *Zenshin* (Advance). He also commented, "[I] found some new ideas stirring up inside myself." He was deeply moved by Watanabe Kyōji's *Death of the Nameless People*.[47] Thus inspired, he sought to discover in Japan's indigenous ideas a movement that might break through the conventional social framework.

In his entry of January 19 Kawabe divided his favorite writers into two groups, which he labeled the "indigenous faction" and the "enlightenment faction." By this latter term Kawabe meant those intellectuals who sought to enlighten the "backward" masses of Japan by preaching ideologies first conceived in the West, such as liberalism, socialism, and Marxism. These writers saw political action as the most important strategy of the reform movement. In contrast, the indigenous faction was dubious of the uncritical adoption of such foreign ideas, and sought instead to promote reform in harmony with the homegrown ideas of the masses. Although this faction did not possess a well-developed image of an ideal system, it stressed the importance of working for reforms through civil and industrial action. Kawabe wrote, "I have learned from both factions but I am now leaning *somewhat* toward the indigenous faction." However, if the "enlightenment" faction is also seen as being "centered on 'self-hood,'" then "the route to link up with the 'indigenous' faction must also be discovered through one's own efforts." He understood my writings to argue that examining the active labor of ordinary workers was such a route. In effect, this romantic revolutionary had come to recognize the limitations of a certain kind of "enlightenment" thinking and "political" leadership in bringing about the autonomous resistance and subjective transformation of the Japanese masses.

After his return to work, some of Kawabe's main intellectual concerns, besides his continuing interest in the early Marx, fell into the enlightenment category: the theory of encroaching unionism via workplace struggle, Takagi Tokuo's writings on "economic democracy," and Iwata Masayuki's discourse on "systems of self-management." But the line of thinking that most attracted him was found in the writings of those he described as the indigenous faction.[48] He kept in mind the thesis that the revolutionary's energy moves forward in a straight line (for Kawabe, "straight" meant "in a progressive, enlightened manner"). He was particularly struck by the writings of Watanabe and Oketani Hideaki, noting, "My heart was cleansed" by their works. During his last years, Kawabe heard the words of the indigenous faction as both quiet encouragement and also as requiem.

❖ ❖ ❖

At the end of May 1977, Kawabe was finally promoted to assistant superintendent and deputy branch manager. This would correspond to section chief (*kakari-chō*) in a typical Japanese company. As we might expect, he jotted "Nonsense!" in his diary.

For eleven years under the new personnel system Kawabe had remained an ordinary fourth-class clerk. Most college graduates of age forty-six had already achieved positions of branch manager or headquarters' department chief (*kachō*). The differences between their annual salaries and Kawabe's ranged from one million to four million yen ($3,370 to $13,470 at 1976 exchange rates). Of course, Kawabe's goal had not been promotion. He had repeatedly rejected the advice of his superiors who told him to end his antimainstream union activism if he wanted to be promoted. Beginning in fall 1973, he annually reported to management that he was unavailable for transfer out of the Tokyo area because of Makiko's poor health, an attitude that for male workers in most Japanese companies is a virtually fatal blow to one's promotion chances. But even taking these factors into account, the ten-year delay in his promotion, compared to the standard practice, is striking.

Nevertheless, it is not clear why management decided to promote such a troublesome employee as Kawabe at all, even ten years behind schedule. Since 1972, the Federation of Regional Bank Unions had been leading an increasingly energetic struggle against management discrimination toward union activists. Perhaps this battle was bearing fruit and forcing the major city banks to preempt a renewed challenge by lessening their negative treatment of union dissidents, such as Kawabe. At the same time, with the advent of the period of low economic growth following the wild inflation of 1974, the conduct of the big banks—for example, their steady operating profits, their cornering of real estate markets, their life-and-death grip over smaller businesses—was coming under increasing criticism. Under these changing circumstances, the banks apparently had set out to bring into their camp the indomitable minority faction members. In sum, in the Japanese political and economic context of the late 1970s, even an activist's promotion could not be delayed indefinitely.

Kawabe's promotion did not lighten his workload. On the contrary, his work increased, with new assignments to take charge of safe deposit boxes, attend executive meetings, and elicit more intense work from his subordinates. Thus, in the wake of his recovery, Kawabe was burdened with a continuing heavy workload and fatigue. Especially during the busy period of September and October 1977, he was unable to take a break even if he was sick with a cold. In his diary he records the following:

> September 24 (Sat.): Very busy! My cold is not better. Sore throat. Continue to study *Right-wing Intellectual Currents*. September 25 (Sun.): Makiko, school field day. In bed all day with a cold. September 26 (Mon.): Busy! Cold no better. No appetite. Tired! September 27 (Tue.): Busy. . . . Cold no better. Tired! September 28 (Wed.): Busy! And the cold. Tired! September 29 (Thurs.): Busy, appetite returning gradually. Because of Kazuko's kind-hearted cooking. I'm grateful! Start to study Watanabe Kyōji's *The Jinpūren and Its Times*.[49] September 30 (Fri.): End of the month. Busy! No appetite. Tired! October 1 (Sat): Beginning of the month. Busy. Work until 7:15 P.M.! (And today is Saturday!) October 2 (Sun): In bed all day with a cold. Read Kurotaki Masaaki's *Recent Debates on Historical Materialism—On Civil Society and Socialism* (in the *Tohoku University Economics Annual*, 1976). October 3 (Mon): Busy! Sore throat! Not recovered fully from cold. Makiko has a headache. Did not go to school. But she did not throw up! October 4 (Tue): Busy. (Preparing for audit.) Finished work at 9:15 P.M. Nonsense! October 5 (Wed): (Special day off). . . Study Kobayashi Yūko's discourse on Sata Ineko's "Shadows in the Woods" (in Vol. 4 of *Kurenai*). October 6 (Thurs): Busy! Finished work 9:30 P.M. Nonsense! October 7 (Fri): Kōichirō's field day. Makiko stays home from school with headache. Finished work at 9:45 P.M.

For ten days in mid-November Kawabe had to work overtime daily until after nine or ten at night to prepare for and receive the audit. Entries of "busy" continue day after day through the end of the month. In the second week of December he had to "run around" on outside visits to increase the amount of individual customer savings deposits. December 27–29 he was busy with year-end work. On December 31, a Saturday, he worked till 4 P.M. and returned home at 6 P.M. He then relaxed by watching with his family the year-end TV specials, "Red vs. White Songfest" and "Parting Year; Coming Year." He wrote in his diary, "Here is where I find rest and happiness."

On New Year's day 1978, Kawabe collected his thoughts and resolved "to advance forward as a revolutionary proletarian." He was truly overjoyed that Nakano Shigeharu won the Asahi Prize. He resolved to "transform this joyful feeling into the inner energy to carry on tenaciously." But at the conclusion of his thoughts for the New Year, he inserted a clichéd wish for good health and "peace and harmony in the family." On the day of the previous year's Festival of Dolls (March 3), he had written, "The warm comfort of the family eases the pain of my job. I am determined to defend this with all my might."

His wife Kazuko, a warm, gentle person, was now forty-three. Kōichirō was in his first year of middle school. He liked to play tennis and would neglect his homework. His father, who did not have time to check up on him, would scold him when he found out. With no prospect of surgery to cure her heart ailment, Makiko continued to have minor attacks. She did well at school and advanced to the second grade. And Kawabe's aging mother, who was skilled in making "*barazushi*" (rice mixed with sushi ingredients) and rice dumplings, depended on him for moral support.

But this father was not destined to observe another Dolls' Festival. The New Year's vacation was a time for his family to make a ritual visit to a shrine, to shovel snow, and to play cards and *hyakuninshū* (an ancient game of identifying *tanka* poetry). Kawabe also used this time to continue his study of the young Marx. Thus the New Year holiday came to an end. In the greeting card that Kawabe sent this year to his close friends he cited the words of Okada Kōichi: "with the spirit of carrying on the work assigned to me, one nameless person among the undistinguishable mass of people, adhering to the creed of anchoring myself in my own daily life—with this as a starting point I plan to challenge the realities of today."[50]

On January 4 Kawabe wrote: "work begins." On January 6: "New Year's Party for the ranked officers. At Isegen. Nonsense!" His diary ends here.

Epilogue

Throughout his adult life, Kawabe Tomomi carried the burden of several profound contradictions. With Marxism as his intellectual core, he lived his whole life as a student of ideas concerned with transforming the existing system, and he displayed an impressive interest in analyzing current political conditions. But he was also a "literary youth," continually seeking to sustain a complex, irresolute, and untidy individual lifestyle. Individuals possessed of these two characteristics often become cold ideologues or highbrow cynics. But Kawabe shared in the popular culture of his times without reserve. He truly loved watching on television the traditional baseball rivalry pitting his alma mater, Waseda, against Keio University, as well as watching high school baseball, the year-end "Red vs. White Songfest," and American musicals. He was often attracted to his beautiful, bright female office colleagues, but at the same time he always cared deeply, almost indulgently, for his family. With a critical perspective on the existing system, he harbored profound doubts about the social significance of his own work at the bank, but he never failed to do his job correctly and meticulously. And although he viewed his union as practically hopeless, he never abandoned what often seemed to be a futile effort to reform "our union."

He was a serious, practical loan officer, an antimainstream union activist at the workplace, a persistent student who would not give up studying radical political theory, and a family centered father. Both between and within all of these characteristics lurked numerous contradictions. If Kawabe could have discarded the conflicting elements and saved only the mutually reinforcing combinations, his mental torment would have eased enormously. The positive results from "putting things in order" in this way would have enabled him to succeed in a certain area, in the commonplace sense of this term—for example, as a bank officer, a union leader, or a free-lance scholar of Marxism. However, how many ordinary salary-men are able to cleverly and neatly rearrange the contradictory characteristics of their lives, the diverse tendencies of their thought, simply because they do not mesh with each other? One sees the unmistakable authenticity of this little-known person in his unwillingness to discard as unimportant the con-tradictory elements that the conjunction "however" is barely able to link together. In a survey of his life, this authenticity is what one finds most impressive about Kawabe. It enabled him to live while staring into the abyss, and to struggle for change while burdened by contradictions. Putting his authentic dilemma more specifically in terms of my particular concerns, is it possible to be an antiestablishment union activist while working as a conscientious loan officer of a major bank? For twenty years Kawabe searched for an answer to this question; in the words of his friend Ichikawa Motoo, "exhausting his nerves to the limit."[51]

Where did Kawabe get the inner fortitude to continue these strenuous activities? I do not know. But judging from his diary, I imagine Kawabe was a person who could respond to beautiful concepts and words. With his contradictory personal characteristics, his life is the very emblem of an ordi-nary worker's existence in Japan's current system, but what he possessed in extraordinary measure was a fresh, vital sensitivity. Kawabe was even able to use language as a propellant in his day-to-day endeavors, deploy-ing and moved by phrases such as: "desires of the proletarians as human beings," "the power of ideas to uplift," "staring at the abyss," "it is foolish to hope, yet we cannot afford to despair," and Miyamoto Yuriko's words, "beautiful, bright spring follows the harsh, severe winter; the cute, loveable bog rhubarb shoots were nurtured in the frost." Kawabe was a naive young man who at the age of eighteen took a year off from school because of neurosis. He successfully transformed this weakness into a tenacious sen-sitivity that provided him with practical inner strength. The tendency to be swayed by concepts and words ordinarily may not be an indispensible characteristic for a union activist; but the history of Kawabe's working life indicates that humanistic concepts rooted in stern intellectual discourse were important in enabling him to continue the clumsy daily struggle of a white-collar worker.

Kawabe's friends at the bank who lament his death must, in any case, survive their daily life in the workplace. Soon after his death many city banks introduced the comprehensive (second stage) on-line system. One assumption is that with the completion of this system the workload of the bank employees will become somewhat lighter. But according to employees doing this work, reporting in places where their freedom to speak up has been guaranteed, this assumption remains no more than a hope. Aside from a new sense of alienation and health hazards resulting from the installation of video display terminals, such campaigns as the "major strategy to start Fuji Bank's great leap forward" (1980) were launched one after another. These operations forced the workers to rush around even more than they had to under the old Much More Sales campaign. In a highly competitive industry, major banks remain stressful workplaces.

Violations of the Labor Standards Law concerning work hours and overtime are more numerous in the banking industry than in any other business. This is a world in which the workers are required to prepare and submit to their superiors "administrative charts on results of daily activity" and "charts of calls made to clients." In such reports, they must indicate efforts made to achieve their "personal goal" for the acquisition of deposits and loans, their actual accomplishments, and their "self-criticism." These are then placed directly into the worker's performance review file.[52]

An interesting report concerning overtime in a major bank claims that "when the department chief announces 'end of the work day,' the employees shout back 'end of work,' and continue working. (This of course is overtime without pay)." The department chief observes this and formally reports to the branch director, "Their work is finished. Now they are just talking privately among themselves." Then the two "grin at each other." This surreal charade occurs daily.[53] As a result, even if employees put in over eighty hours of monthly overtime, they are only paid for twenty or thirty hours of overtime per month, in accord with the projected budget. Unpaid overtime comes to fifty hours per person, saving the bank about 100,000 yen (about US$455 at 1981 exchange rates). Also, many employees are induced to participate in hawkish "model QC" activities, in which they devise ways to make themselves work even harder. Some targets set by these workers are as follows:

1. Customer account section: Cover the entire commercial district and make thirty calls a day. Of these, five are new clients. Each employee is to gain five new depositors per month.
2. Loan section: Speed up business dealings on securities and mortages. Shorten time spent with customers.

3. Tellers: Shorten the waiting time of customers at the windows. Increase sale of cash cards. Each employee is to solicit fixed deposits of 20 million yen per month.[54]

In the early 1950s, 1,700 young bank workers attending the Fuji Bank Employee Union's Tokyo-Yokohama regional school linked arms and sang the "Internationale." That this experience was part of a culture that reached into the hearts of the bank employees is doubtful, but even so, Kawabe's colleague Katayama Tetsuya has said he has not forgotten the principle that he learned there: "Workers do not betray their fellow workers." Yet today, Katayama himself "glumly keeps his mouth shut" when his ideas are rejected coldly by young union officials who ask him, "Is there really any value in opposing the logic of the enterprise?"[55] But I would call out generally to bank workers in contemporary Japan: Can an organization that is totally unable to struggle against the daily workplace life described in this chapter be called a labor union? There is no alternative but to continue working, like Kawabe, to establish a true union, starting at the point where his trail so suddenly ended.

Even in the middle of the 1990s, to be sure, the policies of Japan's city bank employees union, the aspirations of male bank workers to get ahead, and the desire of most women bank workers to flee from their jobs after about seven years of service, form a vicious circle. But this circle is not likely to operate smoothly forever. The significance of the union for the bank workers is likely to change due to two trends: First, there is the combined effect of slow economic growth and the increasing number of both university graduate entrants and veteran workers. Second, there is the gradual increase in the number of women interested in advancing their careers. Both these tendencies are narrowing the prospects for male employees to get ahead. For this reason, it is necessary to talk of transforming, into a place where there is more self-control and greater personal space, the jobs workers are destined to hold and the workplace they are destined to inhabit. For this reason, it is necessary to endeavor stubbornly to squash the union line that sees work and personnel management as the sacred domains of managerial jurisdiction. Perhaps those who respond to such talk and such endeavors will increase in number. By conceiving such hope, the present minority faction will be able to nurture more than enough willpower to endure its current state of isolation.

Notes to Chapter 8

1. Kawabe Tomomi, "Diary" (1965–1978), 16 vols. Kawabe's diary remains in the possession of his wife, Kawabe Kazuko, who kindly shared it with me. All of Kawabe's quotes are from this source unless otherwise noted.

2. On May 8, 1952, Waseda University students captured a policeman who had entered the campus seeking to arrest a suspect from the Bloody May Day con-

frontation and forced him to write a letter of apology. Early the next morning, five hundred police entered the campus and attacked a group of about five hundred students engaged in a sit-in, arresting twenty-six of them and injuring many others. For details, see *Shiryō: Sengo gakusei undō*, vol. 3, Tokyo, 1969.

3. For more on the concept of, and debate over, subjectivity and the self (*shutaisei*) see Victor Koschmann, *The Subject of Action in the Era of Democratic Revolution in Japan, 1945-52* (Chicago: University of Chicago Press, 1996).

4. For more on technological innovations see, for example, Watanabe Shun, *Gendai ginkō kigyō no rōdō to kanri* [Labor and management in contemporary banks] (Tokyo: Chikuma Shobō, 1984).

5. Kawabe's friends, "Kaisō: Kawabe Tomimi—utsukushii hana sakaseru tame ni" [Recollections of Kawabe Tomomi: To make beautiful flowers bloom]. N.p., 1979, p. 104.

6. "Abé-don" is a take-off on the nickname "Saigo-don," given to Saigo Takamori, a popular hero of the Meiji Restoration.

7. Kawabe's reference is to Tatyana, the heroine in Pushkin's *Eugene Onegin*.

8. Ginkō rōdō kenkyūkai (Research Institute for Bank Employees [RIBE]), ed., *Hiroba* [Forum], no. 167 (June 1, 1958), pp. 18–19.

9. Kawabe's friends, "Kaisō—Kawabe Tomomi," p. 104.

10. Fuji Ginkō Jugyoin Kumiai (Fuji Bank Employees' Union), "Nijūnen shi" [Twenty-year history], Tokyo, 1975.

11. In 1962 the wage struggles at other industrial unions began to bear some fruit.

12. Fuji Ginkō Kumiai, "Nijūnen shi," pp. 296–299.

13. Ibid., p. 308.

14. In particular, he noted reading books by Kakehashi Akihide, Fujimoto Shinji, Sugihara Shiro, Hosomi Hide, and Kobayashi Yaroku, among others.

15. Pseudonyms will be used for all bank employees mentioned in this chapter, except Kawabe and Yonekawa Kiyoko.

16. After his death, Kawabe's friends told me what his pen name had been.

17. This quotation, and several in the next few paragraphs, are taken from the unpaginated, mimeographed pamphlets of the Fuji Ginkō Rōdōsha Yūshi Kai (Fuji Bank Activist Workers' Group), titled *Tōron no hiroba* [Forum for debate] (hereafter: Fuji Workers' Group, ed., *Tōron no hiroba*). These pamphlets were published between July 1967 and winter 1969. They capture in concrete detail the workplace conditions at Fuji Bank during that period. Unfortunately, many editions of the pamphlet have been lost, and no complete set exists at present.

18. Ibid., October 1967.

19. Ibid., January 1969.

20. Ibid.

21. Ibid.

22. "Yonekawa Kiyoko-san futō haiten hantai saiban tōsō no kiroku" [The record of Kiyoko Yonekawa's legal struggle against unfair transfer] (unpublished pamphlet), 1969, p. 22.

23. Katayama Tetsuya, "Yoki rōdōsha wa yoki Ginkōin ka" [Can good workers be good bank employees?], in RIBE, ed., *Ginkō rōdō chōsa jihō* [Survey: Current report of bank labor], no. 400, July 1982, pp. 35–37.

24. Ibid., p. 36.

25. These workers' organizations consisted of workplace-based groups of theater or music lovers who enjoyed plays or music sponsored by the national organization. The leaders were mainly Communist party or Socialist party members and supporters who also hoped to cultivate a progressive consciousness of "peace and democracy" through these social clubs. At their peak in the late 1950s and early 1960s, these organizations each had several hundred thousand members nationwide.

26. Japan is one of the few countries to offer women workers the right to paid days off each month for menstrual leave, a legacy of early postwar labor reforms and wartime ideologies concerned with protecting the femininity and fertility of women drafted to work in factories.

27. Some of the prostudent scholars are Yamamoto Yoshitaka (leader of the Tokyo University movement), Takizawa Katsumi, and Orihara Hiroshi.

28. For a useful, short discussion of these factions in the context of the movement to oppose construction of the Narita Airport, see David Apter and Nagayo Sawa, *Against the State: Politics and Social Protest in Japan* (Cambridge: Harvard University Press, 1984), pp. 143–150.

29. Fuji Workers' Group, *Tōron no hiroba*, January 1969.

30. Asahi Shimbun, Features Division, *Kaisha-ningen no karute* [Diagnosis of the company man] (Tokyo: Asahi Shimbunsha, 1979), pp. 197–198.

31. Saitō Shigeo, *Wa ga naki ato ni kōzui wa kitare* [After me, the deluge] (Tokyo: Gendaishi Shuppankai, 1974), pp. 282–299.

32. Kawabe's friends, "Kaisō—Kawabe Tomomi," p. 91.

33. RIBE, ed., *Hiroba* [Forum], no. 500 (June 1, 1972).

34. Also known as the Niigata Minamata case, a repeat of the original Minamata mercury poisoning since the 1950s. For a detailed discussion of the Minamata cases, see Frank Upham, *Law and Social Change in Postwar Japan* (Cambridge: Harvard University Press, 1987), chap. 2.

35. RIBE, ed., *Hiroba* [Forum], no. 500.

36. For example, Kawabe read works such as that of Fujimoto Shinji, *Kakumei no benshō hō* [Dialectics of revolution]; Hiromatsu Wataru, *Seinen Marukusu-ron* [The young Marx]; and Mochizuki Kiyoshi, *Marukusu rekishi-riron no kenkyū* [Study of Marxian historical theory]. Kawabe also had a high opinion of the "Commentaries on Marx" in the journal *Gendai no riron* [Contemporary theory].

37. Some of these critics are Futabatei Shimei, Ishikawa Takuboku, Kitamura Tōkoku, Miyamoto Yuriko, Nakano Shigeharu, and Yoshimoto Takaaki.

38. The works that Kawabe reread include Matsuzawa Hiroaki, *Nihon shakaishugi no shisō* [Japanese socialist thought]; Irokawa Daikichi, *Meiji seishin-shi* [The spiritual history of the Meiji era]; and a number of Yanagida Kunio's writings.

39. Kumazawa Makoto, *Rōdō no Naka no Fukken* [Restoring human rights to labor] (Tokyo: San'ichi Shobō, 1972).

40. Chukaku-ha (Marxist Students' League Hard-Core Faction), *Zenshin* [Advance], August 1973.

41. Kumazawa, *Rōdō no naka no fukken*, p. 316.

42. Kawabe's friends, "Kaisō—Kawabe Tomomi," p. 91.

43. Ibid., pp. 92–93.

44. His reading included works previously noted: Hiromatsu, *Seinen Marukusu-ron*; Mochizuki, *Marukusu rekishi-riron no kenkyū*; Takeuchi Yoshiro,

Kadai to shite no bunka kakumei [Cultural revolution as our theme]; Hirano Ken, *Bungaku undō no nagare no naka kara* [From the current of literary movements]; Gamō Yoshirō's writings on Mori Ōgai; and others.

45. RIBE, ed., *Hiroba* [Forum], no. 600 (January 1 and 15 [combined issue]), pp. 18–19.

46. Ibid.

47. Watanabe offered a critical history of modern and contemporary problems in Japanese thought that rejected the progressive view of history and attempted to rewrite modern Japanese history with a greater concern for the "little people," whom the violence of nature and society had erased from the record and condemned to obscurity. Watabe Kyōji, *Chisaki mono no shi* [Death of the nameless people] (Tokyo: Asahi Shobō, 1975).

48. For Kawanabe, the indigenous faction included especially Watanabe Kyōji, Matsumoto Kenichi's works, Takimura Ryūichi's study of Kita Ikki, and Oketani Hideaki's discourses on writers.

49. The *Jinpūren* (Divine Wind League) was a group of dissident samurai who opposed the modernizing program of early Meiji (1870s).

50. Okada Kōichi, *Bungaku no kanōsei e no tenbō* [A view of the possibilities of literature] (Tokyo: Original Publishing Center, 1977), p. 177.

51. Kawabe's friends, "Kaisō—Kawabe Tomomi," p. 108.

52. This information is from *Asahi Shimbun Keizai-bu* (Economics Division), *Ginkō* [Banks] (Tokyo: Asahi Shimbunsha, 1976), pp. 178–185, 194–195. The situation is the same in the 1990s.

53. Hotta Junpei, "Kōryō to shita ningen-fuzai no shokuba no naka de" [In a dessicated workplace without people], in RIBE, ed., *Ginko rōdō chōsa jihō* [Survey: Current report of bank labor] (November 1978), p. 38.

54. Koiso Akio, "Toshi-ginkō ni okeru QC sākuru katsudo ni tsuite no ichi-kōsatsu" [A Study of QC circle activities in city banks], in RIBE, ed., Ibid., August 1981, pp. 15–20.

55. Katayama, "Yoki rōdōsha wa yoki ginkōin ka," in RIBE, ed., Ibid., July 1982, p. 37.

9

Working Like Mad
to Stay in Place

Reflections on
Japanese Salary-men Today

The insightful critic of contemporary Japanese culture, Tsurumi Shunsuke, published his *History of Postwar Popular Culture* in 1984. This work is full of arresting and instructive observations, but toward the end Tsurumi launches into a discussion of "the social thought of Japan's ordinary citizens" that leaves me unpersuaded. According to Tsurumi, ordinary Japanese ridicule "gung-ho company men" or "children driven to study obsessively by their neurotic 'education mamas.'" That is, they view as comical the lifestyles of all who "put out stupendous effort to achieve high status." For Tsurumi, their attitudes reflect a "strong belief that leading an average lifestyle and livelihood is sufficient."[1]

Frankly, I believe that prevailing opinions among contemporary Japanese citizens, especially among salary-men from the mid-1970s through the 1990s, are in no way as complacent or detached as Tsurumi suggests. The salary-man of today, regarded by so many Japanese as the very emblem of the contemporary citizen, believes that to sustain an ordinary, middle-class lifestyle he has no choice but to "work like mad." And because few people can sustain such a pace with a negative self-image, even those salary-men who initially approach their demanding jobs with reluctance and skepticism eventually come to regard their commitment and pace of work as a normal, even a desireable, state of affairs.

❖ ❖ ❖

Several aspects of life in Japan lead me to this view of middle-class folk-ways. One is the inexorable dynamic of escalation in which the standards for an average life as imagined by ordinary people are always rising. People can never feel that "this is enough." Although a situation in which desires are constantly being processed into needs is in no way restricted to Japan, it is indeed a defining feature of contemporary Japanese society.

What, precisely, is the substance of an average standard of living in this time, in our Japan? That an average family in the mid-1990s possesses televisions, quartz watches, and cameras goes without saying. These are not only objects of average desire, they are also items most people can realistically expect to acquire at affordable prices. These are now "democratic goods" that can be enjoyed equally by all who achieve a basic level of household income. But if one raises one's sights a bit, the average lifestyle does not necessarily include the ability to send children to college, own a house, or join a golf club.

A kind of social scarcity limits the supply of homes in good neighborhoods, of expensive leisure activities, and of high education credentials that guarantee high-status jobs. For the masses to possess these is difficult. But nowhere in postwar Japan does one find strong support for the idea that families of ordinary salary-men should abandon the struggle to possess these things. The ruling classes certainly dare not express such a view. Conventional wisdom encourages people to seek these goals. As a result, the substance of an average lifestyle continually expands, and people frantically chase after scarce social resources as if they had a right to possess them. But because of this frenzied pursuit, an item of reasonable quality at a given price is bid out of reach; one finds only poor quality at that price and must pay an enormous price for decent quality goods. For example, a house that cost 20 million yen in the 1970s now costs 60 million (US$550,000 at 1996 exchange rates). A college entrance exam that a young girl or boy could previously pass by studying standard high school textbooks is now completely impossible unless a student starts to prepare in elementary school with special texts taught in an after-hours "cram school." Such are the special hardships of citizens in a land in which 90 percent of the people consider themselves members of the "mainstream class."

As many people have pointed out, one defining feature of the postwar democracy chosen by the Japanese people is the absence of clear-cut distinctions in the lifestyles of different social classes. Certainly this is a progressive choice. But this choice also compels masses of people to continue the quest for an average life bloated with scarce social resources, lest they feel inadequate, and it drives them to chase higher incomes to acquire these goods. Thus, no matter how affluent the society as a whole becomes, all must work ceaselessly to maximize their disposable incomes. Together with this general social pressure, changes in the atmosphere within large corporations since the mid-1970s have made the salary-men feel that they have no margin to relax in the workplace.

❖ ❖ ❖

From the mid-1970s onward, scarce social goods became increasingly necessary components of an average lifestyle, yet Japanese salary-men found it increasingly difficult to earn incomes to sustain such a way of life. Stated simply, the underlying cause of their difficulty was the more stringent screening of workers carried out in an era of "streamlined" management. The corporation directed sharper scrutiny at the entire workforce, in contrast to the 1960s when it granted relatively steady raises even to employees not on the fast track. In those days of less intense mobilization, one even observed tendencies toward diverse and laid-back lifestyles in the world of the salary-man, especially among younger workers. But since the late 1970s, working like mad has once more become the unchallenged norm. As one aspect of this reversal, total annual working hours per person (including overtime) declined slowly but steadily from 1960 to 1975 and then began to increase. By 1987 these hours stood at over 2,100 per year, far above the average for advanced industrial nations. Since then, a combination of international as well as domestic pressures has finally forced a reassesment of this state of affairs, and as of 1993 total annual hours, at least as reflected in official statistics, have fallen to about 1,920 per person. However, one must also remember the practice of so-called service overtime, which adds an extra 350 working hours a year to the life of the typical Japanese worker.

An important aspect of this more intense scrutiny is the practice of merit ratings or personnel evaluations. According to a survey conducted in 1979 by the Japan Recruit Center, 93 percent of the companies surveyed implemented some form of personnel rating. The evaluations were put to multiple uses; companies used them in setting raises (92% of those surveyed), determining bonuses (88%), and granting promotions (88%). At a general level, the ratings focused on the following factors: individual "performance" (in 92% of the companies surveyed), "ability to carry out the job" (80%), and the employee's "attitude and character" (76%). More specifically, managers typically recorded judgments on the following matters in the personnel evaluation files of employees: individual sales totals; willingness to engage in unreported overtime; frequency of reporting to work early, willingness to accept transfers, readiness to adapt to new technology, mental and physical toughness, willingness to join both official and unofficial company activities, and, occasionally, degree of support for the cooperative union leaders and their faction.[2]

Employees are thus scrutinized in depth, placed in competition with each other, and judged once again by the outcome of the competition. In this fashion, the company sets the employee's raises, bonuses, and promotions, makes job and workplace assignments, and ultimately determines the worker's ability to remain in a familiar worksite and feel comfortable and welcome there. The cumulative impact of this screening and sorting is substantial; by the time male employees reach their forties, the differences in promotions, pay raises, and bonuses among members of an entering cohort amount to annual pay differentials of one to three million yen (US$9,000 to $27,000). This is the very decade when the average life of the male employee imposes the greatest economic obligations. Often without too much sympathy, his family expects him to earn enough to cover the increasing costs of housing, education, and child rearing, pay for a mortgage, a family car, cram school tuition, family travel, and brand name clothing that the children desire. Faced with these obligations to pay for what everyone around him judges an average standard of living, a man "chooses" to endure whatever the company asks of him.

In this spirit of endurance, employees are not only screened and sorted rigorously in terms of "ability and will to work." They are expected to remain silent in the face of restriction or violation of their constitutional rights as citizens. Even Christians must join group outings to Shinto shrines to pray for employee safety, and workers are in fact unable to refuse overtime because of personal business. And in so-called workplace discussions, they cannot freely speak out to criticize the union's cooperative stance toward the company. Of course, in all these matters, a person of independent spirit has the institutional or legal right to refuse the company's demands. But the personal cost is well understood by all parties. The rating of one's "attitude and character" will suffer, and this in turn will affect income and future prospects with the firm. If someone sensitive to matters such as the constitutional rights of citizens were to criticize other workers for selling out their freedoms of belief and expression, the majority of coworkers would be likely to mutter "it can't be helped," and a minority would be certain to attack the critic, saying, "What does the constitution have to do with the shop floor, anyway?"

In this situation, one sees the harsh reality of the trade-off between two aspects of postwar democracy. Salary-men believe that to enjoy one social aspect of "democracy" as it has come to be defined in Japan—an average life in which most workers can possess certain scarce goods—they must surrender the rights and freedoms of democracy while at work, even though they spend more than half of their waking hours at their jobs. Only a minority of salary-men are able to avoid making this bargain with the devil. These are the fortunate few, either professionals or employees in large corporations, who are protected by strong democratic unions.

One extraordinary example that sheds light on this trade-off in social discourse and practice was offered in a recent documentary on the national broadcasting network (NHK). The program examined a company that made hidden listening devices. The company's spokesperson claimed these devices were only rarely used for inappropriate purposes such as investigating a wife's love affair or checking on the study habits of children. Most were used for "legitimate" purposes, he said. For example, he explained, companies used them to help in their personnel management: to discover the true feelings of employees, managers placed the devices in the company cafeteria or the union office.³ In this truly odd conception of "legitimate" use, we gain telling insight into the state of democratic consciousness among contemporary Japanese salary-men.

These remarks on "average" lifestyles and democracy have been made with the fairly well-off male employees of major companies, and their families, in mind. It goes without saying that the chance for employees of smaller companies to achieve an average lifestyle is not as great. And yet, the desire to pursue such a lifestyle is intense among these people as well. As a result, employees in such settings are likely to face even greater stress and less time for relaxation. The wives of small-company salary-men usually work full-time, and the husbands work frequent overtime, as well as night-shifts and holidays. A high proportion of those turning to loan sharks are small-company workers in their forties who for some reason find these opportunities for extra income closed off.

❖ ❖ ❖

To maintain an average lifestyle is to live with the pressure of earning more and more money. In the workplace, salary-men are separated in harsh fashion into those on the fast track and those who fall short, the so-called window-seat tribe.⁴ Thus, a mainstream lifestyle is sustained only by accepting the severe pressures of life at work. Intellectuals of refinement may laugh at those who work like mad to stay in place, but for the mass of people in Japan, there is no room for joking, no space to achieve a critical distance from the intensity of working life. This is my sole point in this brief concluding chapter.

Some critics of the contemporary scene disagree with me. They make the confident claims that jobs that allow independent decisionmaking are more numerous than ever in Japan, that young people today have more diverse career choices, that a desire to pursue a nonstereotypical life consistent with one's present income is widespread and growing stronger, and that "a gentler individualism" is on the rise.⁵ If one accepts this perspective, one arrives at a completely different conclusion. But can one really discern these trends as the dominant ones? The shift in the industrial structure toward knowledge- and information-intensive activities does not guarantee more diversity in the desires of citizens or more jobs offering freedom in decisionmaking.

We must ask some basic questions once again. Is there no other mode of living for the masses of people in Japan? Is it really necessary for ordinary people to struggle so desperately to own their own homes, rather than demand a sufficient supply of public housing? Must young people so feverishly cram for exams for the top schools with no sense of the kind of work they ultimately wish to do? Is it appropriate and necessary to undertake more huge construction projects of leisure facilities, which only raise the cost of enjoying the "natural" environment?

While people address these social issues in the public sphere, they must also challenge the status quo in their workplaces. Labor unions need to critique systems of screening and competition at work, and their corollary, the tacit acceptance of the suppression of human rights. These systems should not be regarded as the inviolable domain of managerial prerogative. Both in society at large and in the workplace, as consumers and as producers, people must take a hard-headed look at the substance of Japan's postwar democracy and the common sense of the people that supports it. Of course, in response to these prescriptive statements, Tsurumi Shunsuke would probably repeat his claim that "the mentality that delights in scolding the masses is not very democratic."[6] Perhaps he is correct. But as reformist political parties and labor unions make decisions about which goals to pursue and which to abandon, it is equally irresponsible or condescending merely to cater to the reigning consciousness of the people.

Notes to Chapter 9

1. Tsurumi Shunsuke, *Sengo Nihon no taishū bunka-shi* [A History of mass culture in postwar Japan] (Tokyo: Iwanami Shoten, 1984) pp. 189–190.

2. The survey of December 1979 conducted by the Japan Recruit Center investigated 486 companies. It is reproduced in the 1982 edition of Nihon rōmu kenkyū kai, ed., *Rōmu nenkan* [Labor management almanac], p. 239.

3. Nippon hōsō kyōkai (Japan Broadcasting Association [NHK]), *Ruporutaaji Nippon: Tochō* [Reporting Japan: Wiretapping], broadcast on April 28, 1983.

4. "Window-seat tribe" (*mado-giwa zoku*) refers to the fact that Japanese managers give mediocre white-collar male employees with no prospect for promotion window-side desks on the margins of the office, and little work of substance, in the hope of "encouraging" them to resign.

5. See, for example, Yamazaki Masakazu, *Yawarakai kojinshugi no tanjō* [The birth of a softer individualism] (Tokyo: Chūōkōron-sha, 1984).

6. Tsurumi Shunsuke, "Hidaka Rokurō to no taidan: Ima minshushugi no ne o saguru" [Discussion with Hidaka Rokurō: In search of the roots of contemporary democracy], *Sekai*, August 1983, pp. 40, 43.

About the Book
and Authors

In this groundbreaking volume, one of Japan's most insightful contemporary labor analysts assesses the "light and shadow" of Japanese-style management, explaining why Japanese employees have stood apart from workers in other industrialized countries. Kumazawa brings to life the intense combination of competition and community within Japanese workplaces. He highlights dilemmas facing Japanese labor on the shop floor and in the labor movement. His discussion ranges from the role of women to issues of quality control and self-management. Highly critical of the hierarchical and undemocratic nature of Japanese industry, he offers a sympathetic view from the inside of the difficulties of surviving in the workplaces of contemporary Japan.

Kumazawa Makoto is professor of economics at Kōnan University. **Andrew Gordon** is professor of history at Harvard University. **Mikiso Hane** is professor of history at Knox College.

Index